9th Workshop on Asian Translation (WAT2022)

Gyeongju, South Korea
17 October 2022

ISBN: 978-1-7138-9153-6

Printed from e-media with permission by:

Curran Associates, Inc.
57 Morehouse Lane
Red Hook, NY 12571

Association for Computational Linguistics
209 N. Eighth Street
Stroudsburg, Pennsylvania 18360

Phone: 1-570-476-8006
Fax: 1-570-476-0860

acl@aclweb.org

Additional copies of this publication are available from:

Curran Associates, Inc.
57 Morehouse Lane
Red Hook, NY 12571 USA
Phone: 845-758-0400
Fax: 845-758-2633
Email: curran@proceedings.com
Web: www.proceedings.com

COLING

International Conference on Computational Linguistics

Proceedings of the Conference and Workshops

COLING

Volume 29 (2022), No. 15

Proceedings of the 9th Workshop on Asian Translation (WAT2022)

The 29th International Conference on Computational Linguistics

October 17, 2022
Gyeongju, Republic of Korea

ISSN 2951-2093

Preface

Many Asian countries are rapidly growing these days and the importance of communicating and exchanging the information with these countries has intensified. To satisfy the demand for communication among these countries, machine translation technology is essential.

Machine translation technology has rapidly evolved recently and it is seeing practical use especially between European languages. However, the translation quality of Asian languages is not that high compared to that of European languages, and machine translation technology for these languages has not reached a stage of proliferation yet. This is not only due to the lack of the language resources for Asian languages but also due to the lack of techniques to correctly transfer the meaning of sentences from/to Asian languages. Consequently, a place for gathering and sharing the resources and knowledge about Asian language translation is necessary to enhance machine translation research for Asian languages.

The Conference on Machine Translation (WMT), the world's largest machine translation workshop, mainly targets on European language. The International Workshop on Spoken Language Translation (IWSLT) has spoken language translation tasks for some Asian languages using TED talk data, but there is no task for written language. The Workshop on Asian Translation (WAT) is an open machine translation evaluation campaign focusing on Asian languages. WAT gathers and shares the resources and knowledge of Asian language translation to understand the problems to be solved for the practical use of machine translation technologies among all Asian countries. WAT is unique in that it is an "open innovation platform": the test data is fixed and open, so participants can repeat evaluations on the same data and confirm changes in translation accuracy over time. WAT has no deadline for the automatic translation quality evaluation (continuous evaluation), so participants can submit translation results at any time.

Following the success of the previous WAT workshops (WAT2014 – WAT2021), WAT2022 will bring together machine translation researchers and users to try, evaluate, share and discuss brand-new ideas about machine translation. For the 9th WAT, we included several new translation tasks including Structured Document Translation Task, Video Guided Ambiguous Subtitling Task, Khmer Speech Translation Task, Two new translation tasks to the Restricted Translation task, Parallel Corpus Filtering Task, Bengali Visual Genome Task, 5 new languages to the Multilingual Indic Machine Translation Task and 1 new language to the Wikinews and Software Documentation Translation Task. We had 8 teams participate in the shared tasks. About 300 translation results were submitted to the automatic evaluation server, and selected submissions were manually evaluated. In addition to the shared tasks, WAT2022 also features research papers on topics related to machine translation, especially for Asian languages. The program committee accepted 4 research papers.

We are grateful to "SunFlare Co., Ltd." and "Asia-Pacific Association for Machine Translation (AAMT)" for partially sponsoring the workshop. We would like to thank all the authors who submitted papers. We express our deepest gratitude to the committee members for their timely reviews. We also thank the COLING2022 organizers for their help with administrative matters.

WAT 2022 Organizers

Organizing Committee:

Toshiaki Nakazawa, The University of Tokyo, Japan

Isao Goto, Japan Broadcasting Corporation (NHK), Japan

Hideya Mino, Japan Broadcasting Corporation (NHK), Japan

Chenchen Ding, National Institute of Information and Communications Technology (NICT), Japan

Raj Dabre, National Institute of Information and Communications Technology (NICT), Japan

Anoop Kunchukuttan, Microsoft AI and Research, India

Shohei Higashiyama, National Institute of Information and Communications Technology (NICT), Japan

Hiroshi Manabe, National Institute of Information and Communications Technology (NICT), Japan

Shantipriya Parida, Silo AI, Finland

Ondřej Bojar, Charles University, Czech Republic

Chenhui Chu, Kyoto University, Japan

Akiko Eriguchi, Microsoft, USA

Kaori Abe, Tohoku University, Japan

Yusuke Oda, LegalForce, Japan

Makoto Morishita, NTT, Japan

Katsuhito Sudoh, Nara Institute of Science and Technology (NAIST), Japan

Sadao Kurohashi, Kyoto University, Japan

Pushpak Bhattacharyya, Indian Institute of Technology Patna (IITP), India

Program Committee:

Chenhui Chu, Kyoto University, Japan

Sangjee Dondrub, Qinghai Normal University, China

Chao-Hong Liu, ADAPT Centre, Dublin City University, Ireland

Valentin Malykh, Huawei Noah's Ark Lab / Kazan Federal University, Russian Federation

Takashi Ninomiya, Ehime University, Japan

Katsuhito Sudoh, Nara Institute of Science and Technology (NAIST), Japan

Masao Utiyama, NICT, Japan

Xinyi Wang, Carnegie Mellon University, United States

Jiajun Zhang, Chinese Academy of Sciences, China

Technical Collaborators:

Luis Fernando D'Haro, Universidad Politécnica de Madrid, Spain

Rafael E. Banchs, Nanyang Technological University, Singapore

Haizhou Li, National University of Singapore, Singapore

Chen Zhang, National University of Singapore, Singapore

Invited talk: Machine translation of Turkic languages: Current approaches and Open challenges

Duygu Ataman

New York University

Abstract

Recent advances in neural machine translation have pushed the quality of machine translation systems to the point where they are becoming widely adopted to build competitive systems. However, there is still a large number of languages that are yet to reap the benefits of neural machine translation. In this context, we present a review of the neural machine translation technology and the results from a large-scale case study of the practical application of neural machine translation in the Turkic language family in order to realize the applicability of prominent architectures and learning methods, data sets as well as evaluation metrics in languages with different characteristics and under high-resource to extremely low-resource scenarios, in addition to identified limitations and promising directions for research to contribute to the extension of the applicability of translation technology in more languages and domains.

Table of Contents

Workshop Program

October 17, 2022 [UTC+9]

9:00–9:05 Welcome

Overview of the 9th Workshop on Asian Translation
Toshiaki Nakazawa, Hideya Mino, Isao Goto, Raj Dabre, Shohei Higashiyama, Shantipriya Parida, Anoop Kunchukuttan, Makoto Morishita, Ondřej Bojar, Chenhui Chu, Akiko Eriguchi, Kaori Abe, Yusuke Oda and Sadao Kurohashi

9:05–9:50 Invited Talk

Machine translation of Turkic languages: Current approaches and Open challenges
Duygu Ataman

9:50–10:30 Research Paper I

Comparing BERT-based Reward Functions for Deep Reinforcement Learning in Machine Translation
Yuki Nakatani, Tomoyuki Kajiwara and Takashi Ninomiya

Improving Jejueo-Korean Translation With Cross-Lingual Pretraining Using Japanese and Korean
Francis Zheng, Edison Marrese-Taylor and Yutaka Matsuo

10:30–11:00 Break

Investigation of Multilingual Neural Machine Translation for Indian Languages
Sahinur Rahman Laskar, Riyanka Manna, Partha Pakray and Sivaji Bandyopadhyay

15:20–16:00 Break

16:00–16:40 Research Paper II

Does partial pretranslation can improve low ressourced-languages pairs?
raoul blin

Multimodal Neural Machine Translation with Search Engine Based Image Retrieval
ZhenHao Tang, XiaoBing Zhang, Zi Long and XiangHua Fu

16:40–17:50 Shared Task III

Task Descriptions and Results: Multimodal
Shantipriya Parida

Silo NLP's Participation at WAT2022
Shantipriya Parida, Subhadarshi Panda, Stig-Arne Grönroos, Mark Granroth-Wilding and Mika Koistinen

PICT@WAT 2022: Neural Machine Translation Systems for Indic Languages
Anupam Patil, Isha Joshi and Dipali Kadam

English to Bengali Multimodal Neural Machine Translation using Transliteration-based Phrase Pairs Augmentation
Sahinur Rahman Laskar, Pankaj Dadure, Riyanka Manna, Partha Pakray and Sivaji Bandyopadhyay

Investigation of English to Hindi Multimodal Neural Machine Translation using Transliteration-based Phrase Pairs Augmentation
Sahinur Rahman Laskar, Rahul Singh, Md Faizal Karim, Riyanka Manna, Partha Pakray and Sivaji Bandyopadhyay

October 17, 2022 [UTC+9] (continued)

17:50–17:55 Closing

Overview of the 9th Workshop on Asian Translation

Toshiaki Nakazawa
The University of Tokyo
nakazawa@nlab.ci.i.u-tokyo.ac.jp

Hideya Mino and **Isao Goto**
NHK
{mino.h-gq, goto.i-es}@nhk.or.jp

Raj Dabre and **Shohei Higashiyama**
National Institute of
Information and Communications Technology
{raj.dabre, shohei.higashiyama}@nict.go.jp

Shantipriya Parida
Silo AI
shantipriya.parida@silo.ai

Anoop Kunchukuttan
Microsoft AI and Research
anoop.kunchukuttan@microsoft.com

Makoto Morishita
NTT Communication Science Laboratories
makoto.morishita.gr@hco.ntt.co.jp

Ondřej Bojar
Charles University, MFF, ÚFAL
bojar@ufal.mff.cuni.cz

Chenhui Chu
Kyoto University
chu@i.kyoto-u.ac.jp

Akiko Eriguchi
Microsoft
akikoe@microsoft.com

Kaori Abe
Tohoku University
abe-k@tohoku.ac.jp

Yusuke Oda
Inspired Cognition, Tohoku University
odashi@inspiredco.ai

Sadao Kurohashi
Kyoto University
kuro@i.kyoto-u.ac.jp

Abstract

This paper presents the results of the shared tasks from the 9th workshop on Asian translation (WAT2022). For the WAT2022, 8 teams submitted their translation results for the human evaluation. We also accepted 4 research papers. About 300 translation results were submitted to the automatic evaluation server, and selected submissions were manually evaluated.

1 Introduction

The Workshop on Asian Translation (WAT) is an open evaluation campaign focusing on Asian languages. Following the success of the previous workshops WAT2014-WAT2021 (Nakazawa et al., 2021c), WAT2022 brings together machine translation researchers and users to try, evaluate, share and discuss brand-new ideas for machine translation. We have been working toward practical use of machine translation among all Asian countries.

For the 9th WAT, we included the following new tasks/languages:

- Structured Document Translation Task: English ↔ Japanese, Chinese and Korean translation.
- Video Guided Ambiguous Subtitling Task: Japanese → English video guided translation for ambiguous subtitles.
- Khmer Speech Translation Task: Low-resource Khmer → English/French speech translation.
- Two new translation tasks to the Restricted Translation task: Chinese ↔ Japanese.
- Parallel Corpus Filtering: Japanese ↔ English parallel corpus filtering.
- Bengali Visual Genome Task: English → Bengali multi-modal translation has been added, similar to the recurring Hindi and Malayalam multi-modal translation tasks.
- 5 new languages to the Multilingual Indic Machine Translation Task (MultiIndicMT): Assamese, Sindhi, Sinhala, Nepali and Urdu.
- 1 new language to the Wikinews and Software Documentation Translation Task (NICT-SAP): Vietnamese.

All the tasks are explained in Section 2.

WAT is a unique workshop on Asian language translation with the following characteristics:

Proceedings of the 9th Workshop on Asian Translation, pages 1–36
October 17, 2022.

- Open innovation platform
  Due to the fixed and open test data, we can repeatedly evaluate translation systems on the same dataset over years. WAT receives submissions at any time; i.e., there is no submission deadline of translation results w.r.t automatic evaluation of translation quality.

- Domain and language pairs
  WAT is the world's first workshop that targets scientific paper domain, and Chinese↔Japanese and Korean↔Japanese language pairs.

- Evaluation method
  Evaluation is done both automatically and manually. Firstly, all submitted translation results are automatically evaluated using three metrics: BLEU, RIBES and AMFM. Among them, selected translation results are assessed by two kinds of human evaluation: pairwise evaluation and JPO adequacy evaluation.

2 Tasks

2.1 ASPEC+ParaNatCom Task

Traditional ASPEC translation tasks are sentence-level and the translation quality of them seem to be saturated. We think it's high time to move on to document-level evaluation. For the first year, we use ParaNatCom[1] (Parallel English-Japanese abstract corpus made from Nature Communications articles) for the development and test sets of the Document-level Scientific Paper Translation subtask. We cannot provide document-level training corpus, but you can use ASPEC and any other extra resources.

2.2 Document-level Business Scene Dialogue Translation

There are a lot of ready-to-use parallel corpora for training machine translation systems, however, most of them are in written languages such as web crawl, news-commentary, patents, scientific papers and so on. Even though some of the parallel corpora are in spoken language, they are mostly spoken by only one person (TED talks) or contain a lot of noise (OpenSubtitle). Most of other MT evaluation campaigns adopt the written language, monologue or noisy dialogue parallel corpora for their translation tasks. Traditional ASPEC translation tasks are sentence-level and the translation quality of them seem to be saturated. To move to a highly topical setting of translation of dialogues evaluated at the level of documents, WAT uses BSD Corpus[2] (The Business Scene Dialogue corpus) for the dataset including training, development and test data for the first time this year. Participants of this task must get a copy of BSD corpus by themselves.

Lang	Train	Dev	DevTest	Test-2022
zh-ja	1,000,000	2,000	2,000	10,204
ko-ja	1,000,000	2,000	2,000	7,230
en-ja	1,000,000	2,000	2,000	10,668

Lang	Test-N1	Test-N2	Test-N3	Test-N4
zh-ja	2,000	3,000	204	5,000
ko-ja	2,000	–	230	5,000
en-ja	2,000	3,000	668	5,000

Table 1: Statistics for JPC

2.3 JPC Task

JPO Patent Corpus (JPC) for the patent tasks was constructed by the Japan Patent Office (JPO) in collaboration with NICT. The corpus consists of Chinese-Japanese, Korean-Japanese, and English-Japanese parallel sentences of patent descriptions. Most sentences were extracted from documents with one of four International Patent Classification (IPC) sections: chemistry, electricity, mechanical engineering, and physics. As shown in Table 1, each parallel corpus consists of training, development, development-test, and three or four test datasets, including two test datasets introduced at WAT2022: test-2022 and test-N4. The test datasets have the following characteristics:

- test-2022: the union of the following three sets;

- test-N1: patent documents from patent families published between 2011 and 2013;

- test-N2: patent documents from patent families published between 2016 and 2017;

- test-N3: patent documents published between 2016 and 2017 with manually translated target sentences; and

- test-N4: patent documents from patent families published between 2019 and 2020.

[1]http://www2.nict.go.jp/astrec-att/member/mutiyama/paranatcom/

[2]https://github.com/tsuruoka-lab/BSD

Training		0.2 M sentence pairs
Test set I	Test	2,000 sentence pairs
	DevTest	2,000 sentence pairs
	Dev	2,000 sentence pairs
Test set II	Test-2	1,912 sentence pairs
	Dev-2	497 sentence pairs
	Context for Test-2	567 article pairs
	Context for Dev-2	135 article pairs

Table 2: Statistics for JIJI Corpus

2.4 Newswire (JIJI) Task

The Japanese $\leftrightarrow$ English newswire task uses JIJI Corpus which was constructed by Jiji Press Ltd. in collaboration with NICT and NHK. The corpus consists of news text that comes from Jiji Press news of various categories including politics, economy, nation, business, markets, sports and so on. The corpus is partitioned into training, development, development-test and test data, which consists of Japanese-English sentence pairs. In addition to the test set (test set I) that has been provided from WAT 2017, a test set (test set II) with document-level context has also been provided from WAT 2020. These test sets are as follows.

Test set I : A pair of test and reference sentences. The references were automatically extracted from English newswire sentences and not manually checked. There are no context data.

Test set II : A pair of test and reference sentences and context data that are articles including test sentences. The references were automatically extracted from English newswire sentences and manually selected. Therefore, the quality of the references of test set II is better than that of test set I.

The statistics of JIJI Corpus are shown in Table 2.

The definition of data use is shown in Table 3.

Participants submit the translation results of one or more of the test data.

The sentence pairs in each data are identified in the same manner as that for ASPEC using the method from (Utiyama and Isahara, 2007).

2.5 ALT and UCSY Corpus

The parallel data for Myanmar-English translation tasks at WAT2021 consists of two corpora, the ALT corpus and UCSY corpus.

- The ALT corpus is one part from the Asian Language Treebank (ALT) project (Riza et al., 2016), consisting of twenty thousand Myanmar-English parallel sentences from news articles.

- The UCSY corpus (Yi Mon Shwe Sin and Khin Mar Soe, 2018) is constructed by the NLP Lab, University of Computer Studies, Yangon (UCSY), Myanmar. The corpus consists of 200 thousand Myanmar-English parallel sentences collected from different domains, including news articles and textbooks.

The ALT corpus has been manually segmented into words (Ding et al., 2018, 2019), and the UCSY corpus is unsegmented. A script to tokenize the Myanmar data into writing units is released with the data. The automatic evaluation of Myanmar translation results is based on the tokenized writing units, regardless to the segmented words in the ALT data. However, participants can make a use of the segmentation in ALT data in their own manner.

The detailed composition of training, development, and test data of the Myanmar-English translation tasks are listed in Table 4. Notice that both of the corpora have been modified from the data used in WAT2018.

2.6 NICT-SAP Task

In WAT2021, we decided to continue the WAT2020 task for joint multi-domain multilingual neural machine translation involving 4 low-resource Asian languages: Thai (Th), Hindi (Hi), Malay (Ms), Indonesian (Id). English (En) is the source or the target language for the translation directions being evaluated. The purpose of this task was to test the feasibility of multi-domain multilingual solutions for extremely low-resource language pairs and domains. Naturally the solutions could be one-to-many, many-to-one or many-to-many NMT models. The domains in question are Wikinews and IT (specifically, Software Documentation). The total number of evaluation directions are 16 (8 for each domain). There is very little clean and publicly available data for these domains and language pairs and thus we encouraged participants to not only utilize the small Asian Language Treebank (ALT) parallel corpora (Thu et al., 2016) but also the parallel corpora from OPUS[3], other WAT tasks (past and

[3]http://opus.nlpl.eu/

Task	Use		Content
Japanese to English	Training		Training, DevTest, Dev, Dev-2, context for Dev2
	Test set I	To be translated	Test in Japanese
		Reference	Test in English
	Test set II	Test-2	Test-2 in Japanese
		Context	Context in Japanese for Test-2
		Reference	Test-2 in English
English to Japanese	Training		Training, DevTest, Dev, Dev-2, context for Dev2
	Test set I	To be translated	Test in English
		Reference	Test in Japanese
	Test set II	To be translated	Test-2 in English
		Context in English for Test-2	Context in English for Test-2
		Reference	Test-2 in Japanese

Table 3: Definition of data use in the Japanese ↔ English newswire task

Corpus	Train	Dev	Test
ALT	18,088	1,000	1,018
UCSY	204,539	–	–
All	222,627	1,000	1,018

Table 4: Statistics for the data used in Myanmar-English translation tasks

		Language Pair			
Split	**Domain**	**Hi**	**Id**	**Ms**	**Th**
Train	**ALT**	18,088			
	IT	254,242	158,472	506,739	74,497
Dev	**ALT**	1,000			
	IT	2,016	2,023	2,050	2,049
Test	**ALT**	1,018			
	IT	2,073	2,037	2,050	2,050

Table 5: The NICT-SAP task corpora splits. The corpora belong to two domains: wikinews (ALT) and software documentation (IT). The Wikinews corpora are N-way parallel.

present) and WMT[4]. The ALT dataset contains 18,088, 1,000 and 1,018 training, development and testing sentences. As for corpora for the IT domain we only provided evaluation (dev and test sets) corpora[5] (Buschbeck and Exel, 2020) and encouraged participants to consider GNOME, UBUNTU and KDE corpora from OPUS. We also encouraged the use of monolingual corpora expecting that it would be for pre-trained NMT models such as BART/MBART (Lewis et al., 2020; Liu et al., 2020). In Table 5 we give statistics of the aforementioned corpora which we used for the organizer's baselines. Note that the evaluation corpora for both domains are created from documents and thus contain document level meta-data. Participants were encouraged to use document level approaches. Note that we do not exhaustively list[6] all available corpora here and participants were not restricted from using any corpora as long as they are freely available.

2.7 Structured Document Translation Task

For the first time we introduce a structured document translation task for English ↔ Japanese, Chinese and Korean translation. The goal is to translate sentences with XML annotations in them. The key challenge is to accurately transfer the XML annotations from the marked source language words/phrases to their translations in the target language. The evaluation dataset for this task was created by SAP and is an extension of the software documentation dataset, which is used for the NICT-SAP task. It consists of 2,011 and 2,002 segments in the development and test sets respectively. Note that the dataset also comes with its XML stripped equivalent and can be used to evaluate English ↔ Japanese, Chinese and Korean translation for the software documentation domain. Given that there is no training data available for this task, it becomes more challenging.

2.8 Indic Multilingual Task (MultiIndicMT)

Owing to the increasing interest in Indian language translation and the success of the multilingual Indian languages tasks in 2018 (Nakazawa et al., 2018), 2020 (Nakazawa et al., 2020) and 2021 (Nakazawa et al., 2021b), we decided to enlarge the scope of the 2021 task by adding 5 new languages to the MultiIndicMT task, namely, Assamese (As), Urdu (Ur), Sindhi (Si), Sinhala (Sd) and Nepali (Ne). In addition to the original 10 Indic languages, alongside English (En), namely, Hindi (Hi), Marathi (Mr), Kannada (Kn), Tamil

[4]http://www.statmt.org/wmt20/

[5]Software Domain Evaluation Splits

[6]http://lotus.kuee.kyoto-u.ac.jp/WAT/NICT-SAP-Task

(Ta), Telugu (Te), Gujarati (Gu), Malayalam (Ml), Bengali (Bn), Oriya (Or) and Punjabi (Pa), we have a total of 15 Indic languages being evaluated this year. We used the FLORES-101 dataset's[7] dev and devtest sets for development and testing both containing roughly 1000 sentences each per language. FLORES-101 is N-way parallel which ensures Indic to Indic translation evaluation although we did not consider it this year.

The objective of this task, like the Indic languages tasks in 2018, 2020, and 2021, is to evaluate the performance of multilingual NMT models for English to Indic and Indic to English translation. The desired solution could be one-to-many, many-to-one or many-to-many NMT models. In general, we encouraged participants to focus on multilingual NMT (Dabre et al., 2020) solutions. For training, we encouraged the use of the Samanantar corpus (Ramesh et al., 2022) which covers 11 of the 15 Indic languages. For other languages, we asked users to use the corpora from Opus, specifically the Paracrawl datasets[8] for Nepali and Sinhala. We also listed additional sources of monolingual corpora for participants to use.

2.9 English→Hindi Multi-Modal Task

This task is running successfully in WAT since 2019 and attracted many teams working on multimodal machine translation and image captioning in Indian languages (Nakazawa et al., 2019, 2020, 2021a).

For English→Hindi multi-modal translation task, we asked the participants to use Hindi Visual Genome 1.1 corpus (HVG, Parida et al., 2019a,b).[9]

The statistics of HVG 1.1 are given in Table 6. One "item" in HVG consists of an image with a rectangular region highlighting a part of the image, the original English caption of this region and the Hindi reference translation. Depending on the track (see 2.9.1 below), some of these item components are available as the source and some serve as the reference or play the role of a competing candidate solution.

2.9.1 English→Hindi Multi-Modal Task Tracks

1. Text-Only Translation (labeled "TEXT" in WAT official tables): The participants are asked to translate short English captions (text) into Hindi. No visual information can be used. On the other hand, additional text resources are permitted (but they need to be specified in the corresponding system description paper).

2. Hindi Captioning (labeled "HI"): The participants are asked to generate captions in Hindi for the given rectangular region in an input image.

3. Multi-Modal Translation (labeled "MM"): Given an image, a rectangular region in it and an English caption for the rectangular region, the participants are asked to translate the English text into Hindi. Both textual and visual information can be used.

		Tokens	
Dataset	Items	English	Hindi
Training Set	28,930	143,164	145,448
D-Test	998	4,922	4,978
E-Test (EV)	1,595	7,853	7,852
C-Test (CH)	1,400	8,186	8,639

Table 6: Statistics of Hindi Visual Genome 1.1 used for the English→Hindi Multi-Modal translation task. One item consists of a source English sentence, target Hindi sentence, and a rectangular region within an image. The total number of English and Hindi tokens in the dataset also listed. The abbreviations EV and CH are used in the official task names in WAT scoring tables.

The English→Hindi multi-modal task includes three tracks as illustrated in Figure 1.

2.10 English→Malayalam Multi-Modal Task

This task was introduced in WAT2021 using the first multi-modal machine translation dataset in *Malayalam* language. For English→Malayalam multi-modal translation task we asked the participants to use the Malayalam Visual Genome corpus (MVG for short Parida and Bojar, 2021).[10]

The statistics of MVG are given in Table 7. As in Hindi Visual Genome (see Section 2.9), one "item" in MVG consists of an image with a rectangular region highlighting a part of the image, the original English caption of this region and the Malayalam reference translation as shown in Figure 2. Depending on the track (see 2.10.1 below), some of these item components are available as the source and some serve as the reference or play the role of a competing candidate solution.

[7] https://github.com/facebookresearch/flores

[8] https://opus.nlpl.eu/ParaCrawl.php

[9] https://lindat.mff.cuni.cz/repository/xmlui/handle/11234/1-3267

[10] https://lindat.mff.cuni.cz/repository/xmlui/handle/11234/1-3533

	Text-Only MT	Hindi Captioning	Multi-Modal MT
Image	–		
Source Text	The woman is waiting to cross the street	–	A blue wall beside tennis court
System Output	महिला सड़क पार करने का इंतजार कर रही है	सड़क पर कार	टेनिस कोर्ट के बगल में एक नीली दीवार
Gloss	Woman waiting to cross the street	Car on the road	a blue wall next to the tennis court
Reference Solution	एक महिला सड़क पार करने के लिए इं-तजार कर रही है	सड़क के किनारे खड़ी कारें	टेनिस कोर्ट के बगल में एक नीली दीवार
Gloss	the woman is waiting to cross the street	Cars parked along the side of the road	A blue wall beside the tennis court

Figure 1: An illustration of the three tracks of WAT 2022 English→Hindi Multi-Modal Task.

English Text: Two elephants standing in the water.

Malayalam Text: വെള്ളത്തിൽ നിൽക്കുന്ന രണ്ട് ആനകൾ

Figure 2: Sample item from Malayalam Visual Genome (MVG), Image with specific region and its description.

		Tokens	
Dataset	Items	English	Malayalam
Training Set	28,930	143,112	107,126
D-Test	998	4,922	3,619
E-Test (EV)	1,595	7,853	6,689
C-Test (CH)	1,400	8,186	6,044

Table 7: Statistics of Malayalam Visual Genome used for the English→Malayalam Multi-Modal translation task. One item consists of a source English sentence, target Hindi sentence, and a rectangular region within an image. The total number of English and Malayalam tokens in the dataset also listed. The abbreviations EV and CH are used in the official task names in WAT scoring tables.

2.10.1 English→Malayalam Multi-Modal Task Tracks

1. Text-Only Translation (labeled "TEXT" in WAT official tables): The participants are asked to translate short English captions (text) into Malayalam. No visual information can be used. On the other hand, additional text resources are permitted (but they need to be specified in the corresponding system description paper).

2. Malayalam Captioning (labeled "ML"): The participants are asked to generate captions in Malayalam for the given rectangular region in an input image.

3. Multi-Modal Translation (labeled "MM"): Given an image, a rectangular region in it and an English caption for the rectangular region, the participants are asked to translate the English text into Malayalam. Both textual and visual information can be used.

2.11 English→Bengali Multi-Modal Task

This new task, introduced in WAT2022, uses a multimodal machine translation dataset in *Bengali* language. The task mimics the structure of English→Hindi (Section 2.9) and English→Malayalam (Section 2.10) multi-modal tasks. For English→Bengali multi-modal translation task we asked the participants to use the Bengali Visual Genome corpus (BVG for short, Sen et al., 2022).[11]

The statistics of BVG are given in Table 8. One "item" in BVG again consists of an image with a rectangular region highlighting a part of the image, the original English caption of this region and the

[11]https://lindat.mff.cuni.cz/repository/xmlui/handle/11234/1-3722

English Text: The sharp bird talon.

Bengali Text: ধারালো পাখি টাল

Figure 3: Sample item from Bengali Visual Genome (BVG), Image with specific region and its description.

Bengali reference translation as shown in Figure 3. Depending on the track (see Section 2.11.1 below), some of these item components are available as the source and some serve as the reference or play the role of a competing candidate solution.

2.11.1 English→Bengali Multi-Modal Task Tracks

1. Text-Only Translation (labeled "TEXT" in WAT official tables): The participants are asked to translate short English captions (text) into Bengali. No visual information can be used. On the other hand, additional text resources are permitted (but they need to be specified in the corresponding system description paper).

2. Bengali Captioning (labeled "BN"): The participants are asked to generate captions in Bengali for the given rectangular region in an input image.

3. Multi-Modal Translation (labeled "MM"): Given an image, a rectangular region in it and an English caption for the rectangular region, the participants are asked to translate the English text into Bengali. Both textual and visual information can be used.

2.12 Ambiguous MS COCO Japanese↔English Multimodal Task

This is the 2nd year that we have organized this task. We provide the Japanese–English Ambiguous MS COCO dataset (Merritt et al., 2020) for validation and testing, which contains ambiguous verbs that may require visual information in images for disambiguation. The validation and testing sets contain 230 and 231 Japanese–English sentence pairs, respectively. The Japanese sentences are translated from the English sentences in the original Ambiguous MS COCO dataset.[12]

		Tokens	
Dataset	Items	English	Bengali
Training Set	28,930	143,115	113,978
D-Test	998	4,922	3,936
E-Test (EV)	1,595	7,853	6,408
C-Test (CH)	1,400	8,186	6,657

Table 8: Statistics of Bengali Visual Genome used for the English→Bengali Multi-Modal translation task. One item consists of a source English sentence, target Bengali sentence, and a rectangular region within an image. The total number of English and Bengali tokens in the dataset also listed. The abbreviations EV and CH are used in the official task names in WAT scoring tables.

Participants can use the constrained and unconstrained training data to train their multimodal machine translation system. In the constrained setting, only the Flickr30kEntities Japanese (F30kEnt-Jp) dataset[13] can be used as training data. In the unconstrained setting, the MS COCO English data[14] and STAIR Japanese image captions[15] can be used as additional training data.

We prepare a baseline using the double attention on image region method following (Zhao et al., 2020) for both Japanese→English and English→Japanese directions.

2.13 Japanese→English Video Guided MT Task for Ambiguous Subtitles

This is a new Japanese→English multimodal task. We provide VISA (Li et al., 2022), an ambiguous subtitles dataset, including 35, 880, 2, 000, and 2, 000 samples for training, validation, and testing, respectively. The dataset contains parallel subtitles in which the Japanese source subtitles are ambiguous and may require visual information in corresponding video clips for disambiguation. Furthermore, according to the cause of ambiguity, the dataset is divided into Polysemy and Omission.

Participants can use the constrained and unconstrained training data to train their multimodal machine translation system. In the constrained setting,

[12] http://www.statmt.org/wmt17/multimodal-task.html

[13] https://github.com/nlab-mpg/Flickr30kEnt-JP

[14] https://cocodataset.org/#captions-2015

[15] https://stair-lab-cit.github.io/STAIR-captions-web/

only the VISA dataset[16] can be used as training data. In the unconstrained setting, pre-trained models, additional data from other sources can be used as additional training sources.

We prepare a baseline using the spatial hierarchical attention network following (Gu et al., 2021) with both motion and spatial features.

2.14 Low-Resource Khmer→English/French Speech Translation Task

This is the first time that WAT has hosted a speech translation task. The purpose of this task is to identify effective techniques for speech translation of Khmer into English and French. We expect that the low-resource nature of Khmer will pose a reasonable challenge. To this end, we have curated a dataset from the ECCC corpus (Soky et al., 2021), which is an international court dataset consisting of text and speech in Khmer, English, and French. The dataset used for WAT 2022 contains $11,563$, 624, and 626 utterances for training, validation, and testing, respectively. This dataset has a wide range of speakers: witnesses, defendants, judges, clerks or officers, co-prosecutors, experts, defense counsels, civil parties, and interpreters.

Participants can use the constrained and unconstrained training data to train their speech machine translation system. In the constrained setting, only the provided ECCC dataset[17] can be used as training data. Additionally, participants may use pretrained models such as BART, mBART, mT5, and wav2vec 2.0 as applicable. In the unconstrained setting, additional data from other sources can also be used.

We prepare a baseline using the transformer-based model presented in (Soky et al., 2021) for both Khmer→English and Khmer→French directions.

2.15 Restricted Translation Task

The Restricted Translation task was first introduced in WAT2021 (Nakazawa et al., 2021c). In this task, participants are required to submit a system that translates source texts under given constraints about the target vocabulary. At inference time, vocabulary constraints are provided as a list of target words and phrases, consisting of scientific technical terms in the target language. The system outputs must contain all these target words. We introduced English↔Japanese tasks in the previous campaign, and we also added Chinese↔Japanese tasks this year. We employ the ASPEC corpus for all the translation tasks and allow participants to use any other external data sources.

Restricted Vocabulary List Creation We built a new vocabulary constraints for the Chinese↔Japanese tasks by extracting phrase pairs from the evaluation data (“*dev/devtest/test*”) by the following steps: (1) extracting term candidates for each language, and (2) making the alignments between the extracted terms in both languages to make phrase-level translation pairs. More concretely, we automatically extracted the term candidates from the ASPEC corpus using `termextractor`[18]. We then obtained term lists for each sentence pair in the ASPEC corpus according to the extracted term candidates. To this end, we asked one Japanese-Chinese bilingual speaker to make alignments between the term lists for each sentence pair, and obtained the phrase pair lists. We conducted the source-based direct assessment (Cettolo et al., 2017; Federmann, 2018) on the dictionaries created by the process above. We employed another two bilingual annotators to give translation scores ranging $[0, 100]$ for Chinese→Japanese and Japanese→Chinese directions respectively. We then filtered out the translation pairs with average scores less than 50. Thus, we publicized the restricted vocabulary lists for each language direction, along with the corresponding source-side terms and annotation scores[19]. Table 9 reports the statistics of the vocabulary constraints in the evaluation data for English↔Japanese and Chinese↔Japanese tasks.

Evaluation Metrics We evaluate submitted systems with two distinct metrics: (1) BLEU score as a conventional translation accuracy and (2) a consistency score: the ratio of the number of sentences satisfying exact match of given constraints over the whole test corpus. For the “exact match” evaluation, we conduct the following process. In English, we simply lowercase hypotheses and constraints, then judge character-level sequence match-

[16]https://github.com/ku-nlp/VISA

[17]`https://github.com/ksoky/ECCC_DATASET`

[18]We used `termex_janome.py` and `termex_nlpir.py` for Japanese and Chinese texts, respectively. `http://gensen.dl.itc.u-tokyo.ac.jp/pytermextract/`

[19]All scores are publicly available at the task page: `https://sites.google.com/view/restricted-translation-task/2022`.

	En-Ja (# phrase, # char)	Ja-En (# phrase, # word)	Zh-Ja (# phrase, # char)	Ja-Zh (# phrase, # char)
Dev.	(2.8, 16.4)	(2.8, 6.6)	(1.2, 4.7)	(1.2, 3.8)
Devtest	(3.2, 18.2)	(3.2, 7.3)	(1.5, 5.5)	(1.5, 4.5)
Test	(3.3, 18.1)	(3.2, 7.4)	(1.4, 5.2)	(1.4, 4.2)

Table 9: Statistics of the restricted vocabulary in the evaluation data. We report average number of phrases and characters/words per source sentence.

ing (including whitespaces) for each constraint. In Chinese and Japanese, we judge character-level sequence matching (including whitespaces) for each constraint without any preprocessing. For the final ranking, we also calculate the combined score of both: calculating BLEU with only the exactly matched sentences. We note that, in this scenario, the brevity score in BLEU does not carry its usual meaning, but the n-gram scores will maintain their consistency.

2.16 Parallel Corpus Filtering Task

Machine translation systems are trained from usually large corpora obtained from noisy data sources. Noisy examples in the training corpora are known as the main cause of reducing the translation accuracy of the resulting models (Khayrallah and Koehn, 2018), and this problem can be mitigated by corpus filtering (Koehn et al., 2020), which removes problematic examples from the training corpus, so that the model is eventually trained by cleaner dataset than the data source.

The motivation for this task is inspired by the Parallel Corpus Filtering Tasks held in 2018, 2019, and 2020 Workshop on Machine Translation (Koehn et al., 2020), in which the participants are asked to filter the web crawled corpora, train the NMT model on the cleaner subsets, and evaluate its quality on a multi-domain test set. Unlike the tasks in the WMT, the Parallel Corpus Filtering Task in this workshop focuses on both filtering and domain adaptation.

Specifically, this task lets the participants train machine translation models under the following restrictions:

- The model architecture is fixed. The training program is provided as a fixed Docker image by the organizer, and participants can only run a specific training command to build their own model. The same image is used in the final evaluation.

Dataset	# sentences
JParaCrawl v3.0	25.7M
ASPEC Train	3M
ASPEC Dev	1.8K
ASPEC Devtest	1.8K
ASPEC Test	1.8K

Table 10: Number of sentence pairs in the corpora used in the parallel corpus filtering task.

- Training corpus is fixed. The whole corpus is provided by the organizer, and participants are requested to find a subset of the corpus that is more effective in achieving higher translation accuracy on the given model architecture.

- The test set is from a single domain (scientific paper domain) and its in-domain data is provided.

We adopted the Transformer model as the shared architecture for this task.[20]

We asked the participants to select a subset from JParaCrawl (Morishita et al., 2020), the noisy English-Japanese web-crawled parallel corpus, based on its cleanliness and domain-similarity. The baseline model is obtained by training the model on the whole set of this dataset. We also provide the in-domain clean English-Japanese corpus, the ASPEC (Nakazawa et al., 2016) dataset except for the 'test' sub-set, which is used in the evaluation.

We trained the model with the submitted data for both English-Japanese and English-Japanese. We evaluated the submission on both BLEU score (Papineni et al., 2002) and JPO adequacy as described in Section 6.1 on the ASPEC test set.

The corpus statistics are summarized in Table 10.

Team ID	Organization	Country
TMU	Tokyo Metropolitan University	Japan
NICT-5	NICT	Japan
sakura	Rakuten Institute of Technology Singapore, Rakuten Asia.	Singapore
CNLP-NITS-PP	NIT Silchar	India
NITR	NIT Rourkela	India
HwTscSU	Huawei Translation Services Center, 2012 Lab, Huawei co. LTD; School of Computer Science and Technology, Soochow University	China
SILO_NLP	Silo AI	Finland
nlp_novices	SCTR's Pune Institute of Computer Technology	India

Table 11: List of participants who submitted translations for the human evaluation in WAT2022

	ASPEC		NICT-SAP				Parallel
	Restricted		Unstructured		Structured		Corpus
Team ID	En-Ja	Ja-En	En-Ms (IT)	Ms-En (IT)	En-Ja/Ko/Zh	Ja/Ko/Zh-En	Filtering
TMU	✓	✓					
NICT-5					✓	✓	
sakura							✓
HwTscSU			✓	✓			

	Multimodal			Indic										
	En-X (TX)			En-X					X-En					
Team ID	Hi	Ml	Bn	As	Bn	Sd	Si	Ur	Ne	As	Bn	Sd	Si	Ur
CNLP-NITS-PP	✓		✓	✓	✓					✓	✓			
NITR				✓		✓	✓	✓	✓	✓		✓	✓	✓
SILO_NLP	✓	✓	✓											
nlp_novices	✓	✓	✓											

Table 12: Submissions for each task by each team.

3 Participants

Table 11 shows the participants in WAT2022. The table lists 8 organizations from various countries, including Japan, China, India, Singapore and Finland.

300 translation results by 8 teams were submitted for automatic evaluation. Table 12 summarizes the participation of teams across WAT2022 tasks and indicates which tasks included manual evaluation.

4 Baseline Systems

Human evaluations of most of WAT tasks were conducted as pairwise comparisons between the translation results for a specific baseline system and translation results for each participant's system. That is, the specific baseline system served as the standard for human evaluation. At WAT 2022, we adopted some of neural machine translation (NMT) as baseline systems. The details of the NMT baseline systems are described in this section.

The NMT baseline systems consisted of publicly available software, and the procedures for building the systems and for translating using the systems were published on the WAT web page. We also have SMT baseline systems for the tasks that started at WAT 2017 or before 2017. SMT baseline systems are described in the WAT 2017 overview paper (Nakazawa et al., 2017). The commercial RBMT systems and the online translation systems were operated by the organizers. We note that these RBMT companies and online translation companies did not submit their systems. Because our objective is not to compare commercial RBMT systems or online translation systems from companies that did not themselves participate, the system IDs of these systems are anonymous in this paper.

4.1 Tokenization

We used the following tools for tokenization.

4.1.1 For ASPEC, JPC, JIJI, and ALT+UCSY

- Juman version 7.0[21] for Japanese segmentation.

[20]The Dockerfile for constructing the training pipeline can be obtained from https://github.com/MorinoseiMorizo/wat2022-filtering

[21]http://nlp.ist.i.kyoto-u.ac.jp/EN/index.php?JUMAN

- Stanford Word Segmenter version 2014-01-04[22] (Chinese Penn Treebank (CTB) model) for Chinese segmentation.
- The Moses toolkit for English and Indonesian tokenization.
- Mecab-ko[23] for Korean segmentation.
- Indic NLP Library[24] (Kunchukuttan, 2020) for Indic language segmentation.
- The tools included in the ALT corpus for Myanmar and Khmer segmentation.
- subword-nmt[25] for all languages.

When we built BPE-codes, we merged source and target sentences and we used 100,000 for -s option. We used 10 for vocabulary-threshold when subword-nmt applied BPE.

4.1.2 For Indic and NICT-SAP Tasks

- For the Indic task we did not perform any explicit tokenization of the raw data.

- For the NICT-SAP task we only character segmented the Thai corpora as it was the only language for which character level BLEU was to be computed. Other languages corpora were not preprocessed in any way.

- Any subword segmentation or tokenization was handled by the internal mechanisms of tensor2tensor.

4.1.3 For Structured Document Translation Task

- No tokenization was explicitly performed.

4.1.4 For English→Hindi, English→Malayalam, and English→Bengali Multi-Modal Tasks

- Hindi Visual Genome 1.1, Malayalam Visual Genome, and Bengali Visual Genome come untokenized and we did not use or recommend any specific external tokenizer.

- The standard OpenNMT-py sub-word segmentation was used for pre/post-processing for the baseline system and each participant used what they wanted.

4.1.5 For English↔Japanese Multi-Modal Tasks

- For English sentences, we applied lowercase, punctuation normalization, and the Moses tokenizer.

- For Japanese sentences, we used KyTea for word segmentation.

4.2 Baseline NMT Methods

We used the NMT models for all tasks. Unless mentioned otherwise we use the Transformer model (Vaswani et al., 2017). We used OpenNMT (Klein et al., 2017) (RNN-model) for ASPEC, JPC, JIJI, and ALT tasks, tensor2tensor[26] for the NICT-SAP task, HuggingFace transformers[27] for the Structured Document Translation task and OpenNMT-py[28] for other tasks.

4.2.1 NMT with Attention (OpenNMT)

For ASPEC, JPC, JIJI, and ALT tasks, we used OpenNMT (Klein et al., 2017) as the implementation of the baseline NMT systems of NMT with attention (System ID: NMT). We used the following OpenNMT configuration.

- encoder_type = brnn
- brnn_merge = concat
- src_seq_length = 150
- tgt_seq_length = 150
- src_vocab_size = 100000
- tgt_vocab_size = 100000
- src_words_min_frequency = 1
- tgt_words_min_frequency = 1

The default values were used for the other system parameters.

We used the following data for training the NMT baseline systems of NMT with attention.

- All of the training data mentioned in Section 2 were used for training except for the ASPEC Japanese–English task. For the ASPEC Japanese–English task, we only used train-1.txt, which consists of one million parallel sentence pairs with high similarity scores.
- All of the development data for each task was used for validation.

[22] http://nlp.stanford.edu/software/segmenter.shtml
[23] https://bitbucket.org/eunjeon/mecab-ko/
[24] https://github.com/anoopkunchukuttan/indic_nlp_library
[25] https://github.com/rsennrich/subword-nmt
[26] https://github.com/tensorflow/tensor2tensor
[27] https://github.com/huggingface/transformers
[28] https://github.com/OpenNMT/OpenNMT-py

4.2.2 Transformer (Tensor2Tensor)

For the News Commentary task, we used tensor2tensor's[29] implementation of the Transformer (Vaswani et al., 2017) and used default hyperparameter settings corresponding to the "base" model for all baseline models. The baseline for the News Commentary task is a multilingual model as described in Imankulova et al. (2019) which is trained using only the in-domain parallel corpora. We use the token trick proposed by Johnson et al. (2017) to train the multilingual model.

For the NICT-SAP task, we used tensor2tensor to train many-to-one and one-to-many models where the latter were trained with the aforementioned token trick. We trained models for all languages except Vietnamese. We used default hyperparameter settings corresponding to the "big" model. Since the NICT-SAP task involves two domains for evaluation (Wikinews and IT) we used a modification of the token trick technique for domain adaptation to distinguish between corpora for different domains. In our case we used tokens such as $2alt$ and $2it$ to indicate whether the sentences belonged to the Wikinews or IT domain, respectively. For both tasks we used 32,000 separate sub-word vocabularies. We trained our models on 1 GPU till convergence on the development set BLEU scores, averaged the last 10 checkpoints (separated by 1000 batches) and performed decoding with a beam of size 4 and a length penalty of 0.6.

4.2.3 Transformer (HuggingFace)

For the Structured Document Translation task, we used the official mbart-50 model fine-tuned[30] for machine translation to directly translate the test sets. We used the HuggingFace transformers implementation to decode sentences using a beam of size 4 and length penalty of 1.0. The tokenization was handled by the mbart-50 tokenizer. Surprisingly, this naive approach actually yielded good results.

4.2.4 Transformer (OpenNMT-py)

For the English→Hindi, English→Malayalam, and English→Bengali Multimodal tasks we used the Transformer model (Vaswani et al., 2018) as implemented in OpenNMT-py (Klein et al., 2017) and used the "base" model with default parameters for the multi-modal task baseline. We have generated the vocabulary of 32k sub-word types jointly for both the source and target languages. The vocabulary is shared between the encoder and decoder.

5 Automatic Evaluation

5.1 Procedure for Calculating Automatic Evaluation Score

We evaluated translation results by three metrics: BLEU (Papineni et al., 2002), RIBES (Isozaki et al., 2010) and AMFM (Banchs et al., 2015a). BLEU scores were calculated using SacreBLEU (Post, 2018). RIBES scores were calculated using `RIBES.py` version 1.02.4.[31] AMFM scores were calculated using scripts created by the technical collaborators listed in the WAT2022 web page.[32] Note that AMFM scores were not produced for all tasks. For the Structured Document Translation task, we used only the XML-BLEU metric (Hashimoto et al., 2019), which takes into account the accuracy of XML annotation transfer. All scores for each task were calculated using the corresponding reference translations.

Except for XML-BLEU, which uses this implementation for evaluation, the following preprocessing is done prior to computing scores. Before the calculation of the automatic evaluation scores, the translation results were tokenized or segmented with tokenization/segmentation tools for each language. For Japanese segmentation, we used three different tools: Juman version 7.0 (Kurohashi et al., 1994), KyTea 0.4.6 (Neubig et al., 2011) with full SVM model[33] and MeCab 0.996 (Kudo, 2005) with IPA dictionary 2.7.0.[34] For Chinese segmentation, we used two different tools: KyTea 0.4.6 with full SVM Model in MSR model and Stanford Word Segmenter (Tseng, 2005) version 2014-06-16 with Chinese Penn Treebank (CTB) and Peking University (PKU) model.[35] For Korean segmentation, we used mecab-ko.[36] For Myanmar and Khmer segmentations, we used `myseg.py`[37] and

[29] https://github.com/tensorflow/tensor2tensor

[30] https://huggingface.co/facebook/mbart-large-50-many-to-many-mmt

[31] http://www.kecl.ntt.co.jp/icl/lirg/ribes/index.html

[32] lotus.kuee.kyoto-u.ac.jp/WAT/WAT2022/

[33] http://www.phontron.com/kytea/model.html

[34] http://code.google.com/p/mecab/downloads/detail?name=mecab-ipadic-2.7.0-20070801.tar.gz

[35] http://nlp.stanford.edu/software/segmenter.shtml

[36] https://bitbucket.org/eunjeon/mecab-ko/

[37] http://lotus.kuee.kyoto-u.ac.jp/WAT/

Figure 4: The interface for translation results submission

kmseg.py.[38] For English, French and Russian tokenizations, we used tokenizer.perl[39] in the Moses toolkit. For Indonesian, Malay, and Vietnamese tokenizations, we used tokenizer.perl actually sticking to the English tokenization settings. For Thai tokenization, we segmented the text at each individual character. For Assamese, Bengali, Gujarati, Hindi, Kannada, Malayalam, Marathi, Nepali, Odia, Punjabi, Sindhi, Sinhala, Tamil, Telugu, and Urdu tokenizations, we used Indic NLP Library[40] (Kunchukuttan, 2020). The de-

my-en-data/wat2020.my-en.zip

[38]http://lotus.kuee.kyoto-u.ac.jp/WAT/km-en-data/km-en.zip

[39]https://github.com/moses-smt/mosesdecoder/tree/RELEASE-2.1.1/scripts/tokenizer/tokenizer.perl

[40]https://github.com/anoopkunchukuttan/indic_nlp_library

tailed procedures for the automatic evaluation are shown on the WAT evaluation web page.[41]

5.2 Automatic Evaluation System

The automatic evaluation system receives translation results by participants and automatically gives evaluation scores to the uploaded results. As shown in Figure 4, the system requires participants to provide the following information for each submission:

- Human Evaluation: whether or not they submit the results for human evaluation;
- Publish the results of the evaluation: whether or not they permit to publish automatic evaluation scores on the WAT2022 web page;
- Task: the task you submit the results for;
- Used Other Resources: whether or not they used additional resources; and
- Method: the type of the method including SMT, RBMT, SMT and RBMT, EBMT, NMT and Other.

Evaluation scores of translation results that participants permit to be published are disclosed via the WAT2022 evaluation web page. Participants can also submit the results for human evaluation using the same web interface.

This automatic evaluation system will remain available even after WAT2022. Anybody can register an account for the system by the procedures described in the application site.[42]

5.3 A Note on AMFM Scores

Unlike previous years we do not compute AMFM scores on all tasks due to low participation this year. For readers interested in AMFM and recent advances, we refer readers to the following literature: Zhang et al. (2021b,a); D'Haro et al. (2019); Banchs et al. (2015b).

6 Human Evaluation

In WAT2022, we conducted *JPO adequacy evaluation* (Section 6.1).

[41]http://lotus.kuee.kyoto-u.ac.jp/WAT/evaluation/index.html

[42]http://lotus.kuee.kyoto-u.ac.jp/WAT/WAT2022/application/index.html

5	All important information is transmitted correctly. (100%)
4	Almost all important information is transmitted correctly. (80%–)
3	More than half of important information is transmitted correctly. (50%–)
2	Some of important information is transmitted correctly. (20%–)
1	Almost all important information is NOT transmitted correctly. (–20%)

Table 13: The JPO adequacy criterion

6.1 JPO Adequacy Evaluation

We conducted JPO adequacy evaluation for the top two or three participants' systems of pairwise evaluation for each subtask.[43] The evaluation was carried out by translation experts based on the JPO adequacy evaluation criterion, which is originally defined by JPO to assess the quality of translated patent documents.

6.1.1 Sentence Selection and Evaluation

For the JPO adequacy evaluation, the 200 test sentences were randomly selected from the test sentences.

For each test sentence, input source sentence, translation by participants' system, and reference translation were shown to the annotators. To guarantee the quality of the evaluation, each sentence was evaluated by two annotators. Note that the selected sentences are basically the same as those used in the previous workshop.

6.1.2 Evaluation Criterion

Table 13 shows the JPO adequacy criterion from 5 to 1. The evaluation is performed subjectively. "Important information" represents the technical factors and their relationships. The degree of importance of each element is also considered in evaluating. The percentages in each grade are rough indications for the transmission degree of the source sentence meanings. For Structured Document Translation, we instructed the evaluators to consider the XML structure accuracy between the source, the translation and the reference. The detailed criterion is described in the JPO document (in Japanese).[44]

[43]The number of systems varies depending on the subtasks.

[44]http://www.jpo.go.jp/shiryou/toushin/chousa/tokkyohonyaku_hyouka.htm

7 Evaluation Results

In this section, the evaluation results for WAT2022 are reported from several perspectives. Some of the results for both automatic and human evaluations are also accessible at the WAT2022 website.[45]

7.1 Official Evaluation Results

Figures 5 and 6 show those of ASPEC-RT subtasks, Figures 7, 8, 9, 10, 11, 12, 13, 14, 15, 16 and 17 show those of Indic Multilingual subtasks, Figures 18, 19 and 20 show those of Multimodal subtasks, Figures 21 and 22 show those of Parallel Corpus Filtering subtasks, and Figures 23, 24, 25, 26, 27, 28, 29 and 30 show those of NICT-SAP subtasks. Each figure contains the JPO adequacy evaluation result and evaluation summary of top systems. The detailed automatic evaluation results are shown in Appendix A.

8 Findings

8.1 NICT-SAP Task

This year we only had 1 submission from team "HwTscSU" who outperformed all previous years submissions. They claim to have fine-tuned on the devlopment set, which has a high degree of similarity to the test set. This action ended up giving large improvements in translation quality over non fine-tuned baselines. The human evaluation showed that around 80% of translations had a score of 4 or 5 indicating the high translation quality.

8.2 Structured Document Translation Task

We only had 1 submission this year from team "NICT-5" who used similar ideas as our organizer baseline where they used the M2M-100 model for directly translating test sets. They also used the detag-and-project approach where they translated the sentences without XML and then inserted the XML content using word alignment. They got better scores in 3 out of 6 directions, but were not too far behind in others. The human evaluation showed that over 60% of the translations were scored 4 or 5 for English to Japanese/Korean/Chinese whereas this number increased to 80% for the reverse direction.

[45] `http://lotus.kuee.kyoto-u.ac.jp/WAT/evaluation/`

8.3 Indic Multilingual Task

In contrast to WAT 2021, this year we had two teams who participated in the task, namely, "NITR" and "CNLP-NITS-PP ". They did not submit results for all pairs. Human evaluation was done only for Nepali to English translation, where the human ratings were mostly low. Due to poor and inconsistent participation, it is difficult to make any further observations.

8.4 English→Hindi Multi-Modal Task

This year three teams participated in the different sub-tasks (TEXT, MM) of the English→Hindi Multi-Modal task. The WAT2022 automatic evaluation scores for the participating teams are shown in Tables 43 to 46. The team "nlp_novices" obtained the highest BLEU score for the text-only translation (TEXT) for both the evaluation (E-Test) and challenge (C-Test) test set. The best performance is obtained by fine-tuned *Transformer* using OPUS Corpus as an additional resource. For the multimodal sub-task (MM), we received two submissions from the teams "CNLP-NITS-PP", and "Silo_NLP", respectively. The team "Silo_NLP" obtained the highest BLEU score for the multimodal translation (MM) for the evaluation (E-Test) by extracting object tags from images and using fine-tuned *mBART*. They used Flickr8 as an additional resource. The team "CNLP-NITS-PP" obtained the highest BLEU score for the challenge (C-Test) test set following transliteration-based phrase pairs augmentation and visual features in training using BRNN encoder and doubly-attentive-rnn decoder.

Human evaluation was done for the challenge test set text-only translation (TEXT) as shown in Figure 19. We observe that both BLEU and RIBES can correctly predict the quality of translation as measured by the manually annotated Adequacy. "nlp_novices" is the best submission with almost 35% of sentences reaching the highest rank of "Almost all information is transmitted correctly", see the JPO adequacy scale in Table 13 which was used in the evaluation.

8.5 English→Malayalam Multi-Modal Task

This year two teams "Silo_NLP", and "nlp_novices" participated in the different sub-tasks (TEXT, MM) of the English→ Malayalam Multi-Modal task. The WAT2022 automatic evaluation scores are shown in the Table 47, 48,

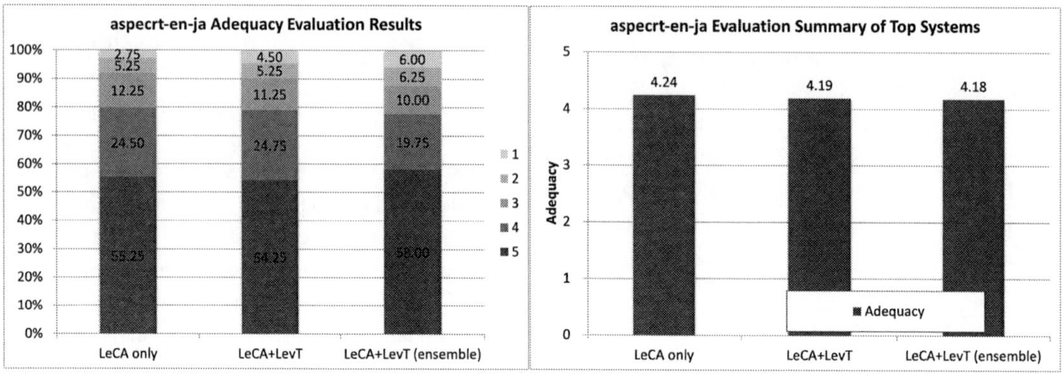

Figure 5: Official evaluation results of aspecrt-en-ja.

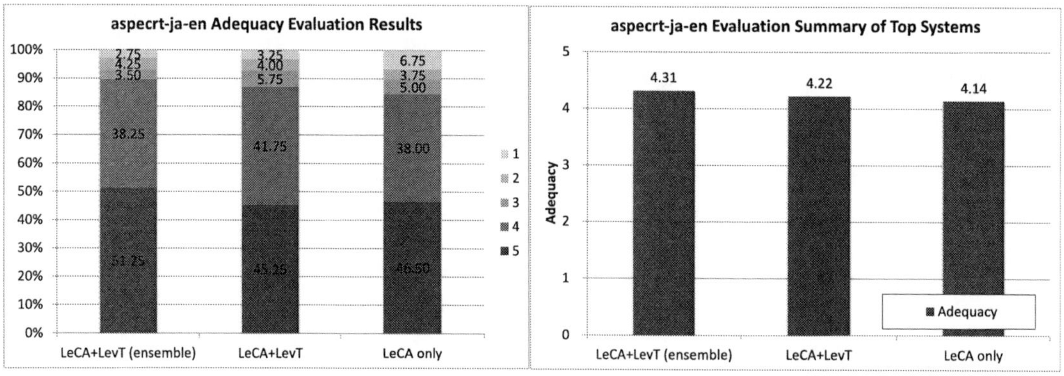

Figure 6: Official evaluation results of aspecrt-ja-en.

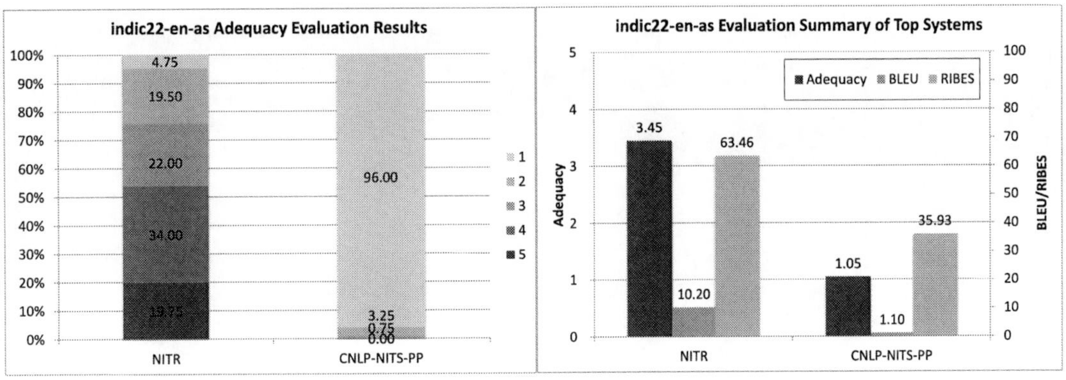

Figure 7: Official evaluation results of indic22-en-as.

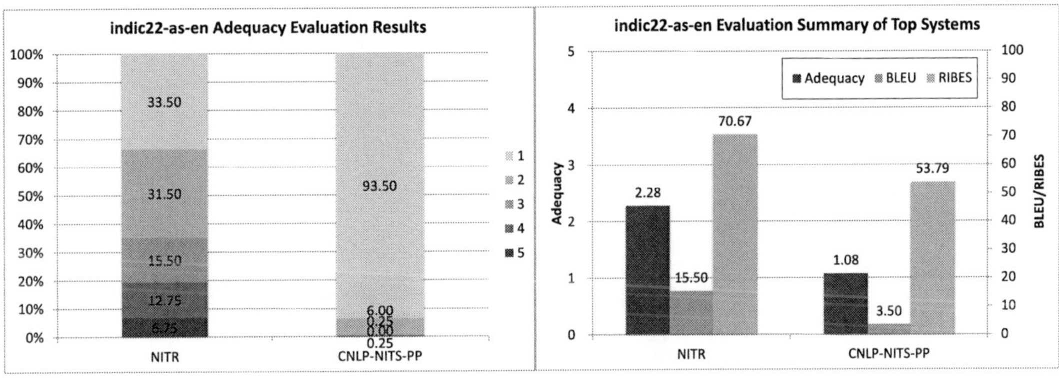

Figure 8: Official evaluation results of indic22-as-en.

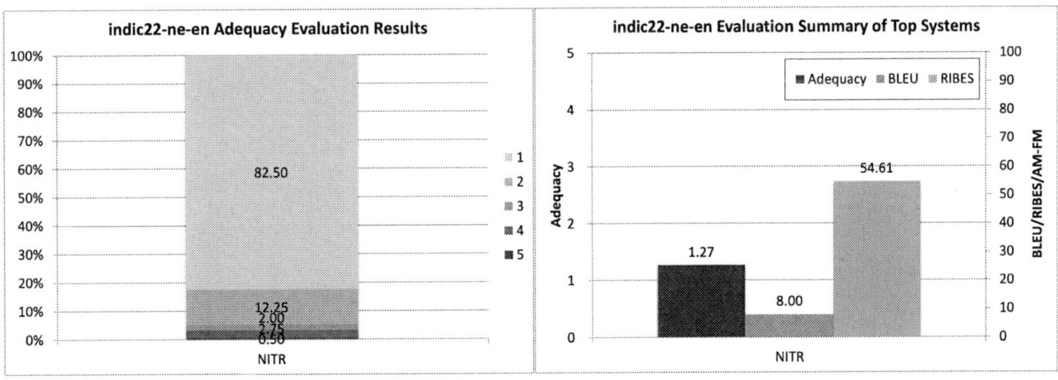

Figure 9: Official evaluation results of indic22-ne-en.

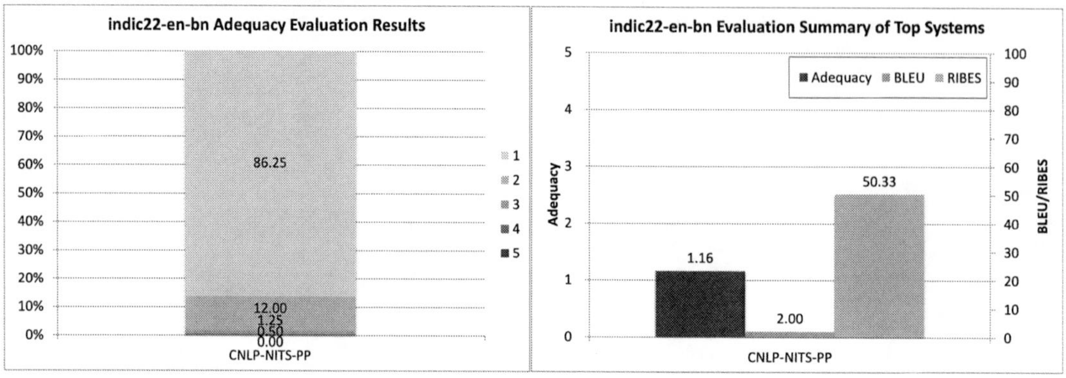

Figure 10: Official evaluation results of indic22-en-bn.

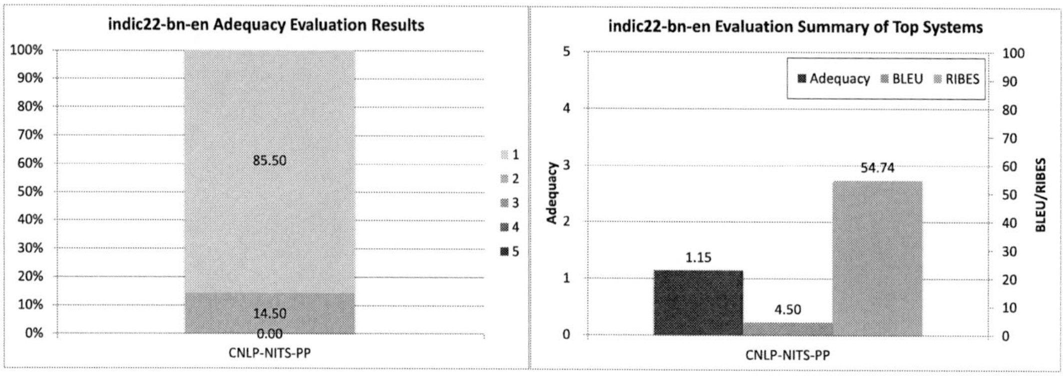

Figure 11: Official evaluation results of indic22-bn-en.

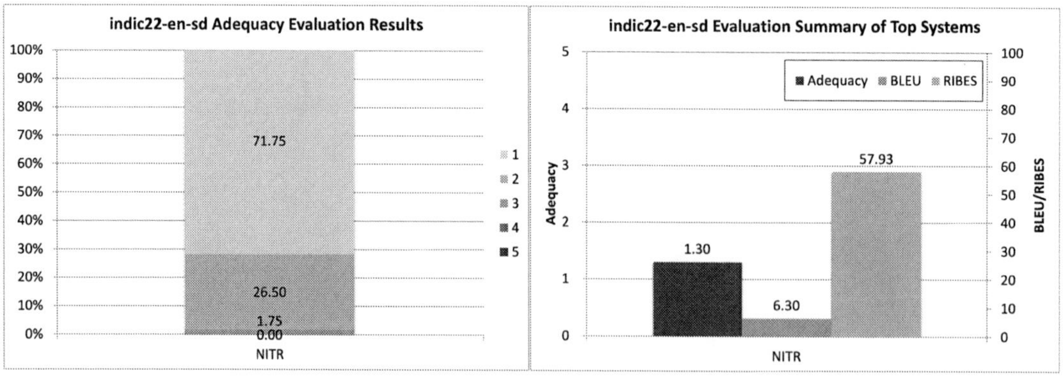

Figure 12: Official evaluation results of indic22-en-sd.

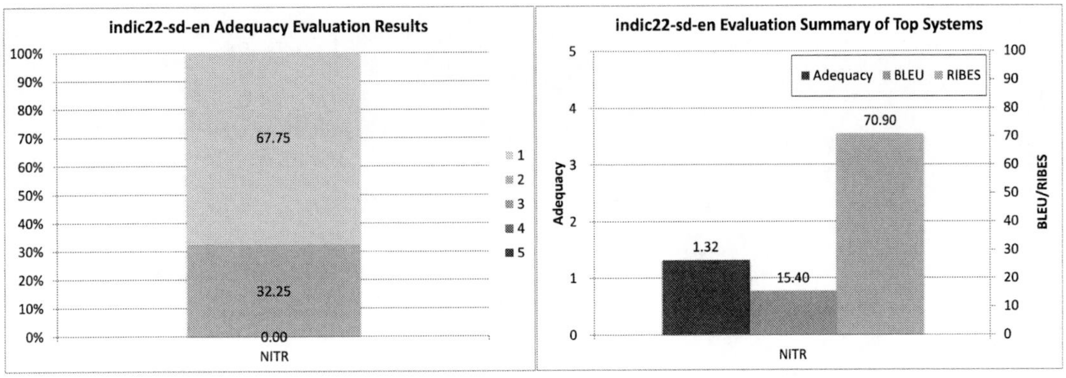

Figure 13: Official evaluation results of indic22-sd-en.

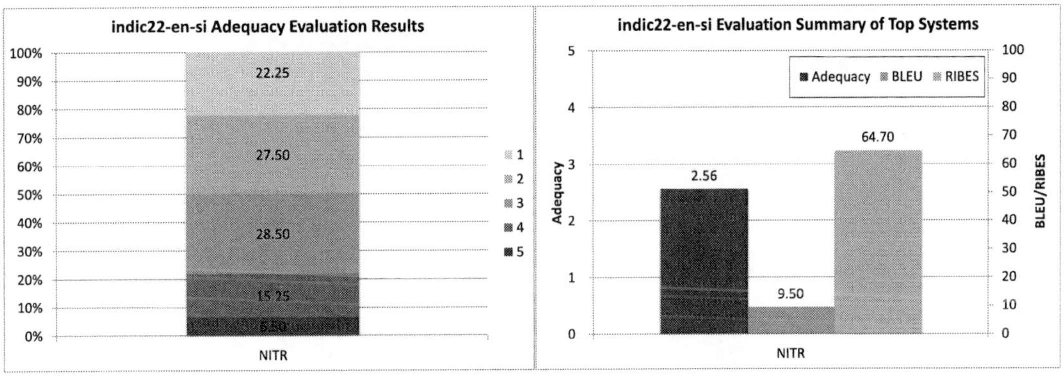

Figure 14: Official evaluation results of indic22-en-si.

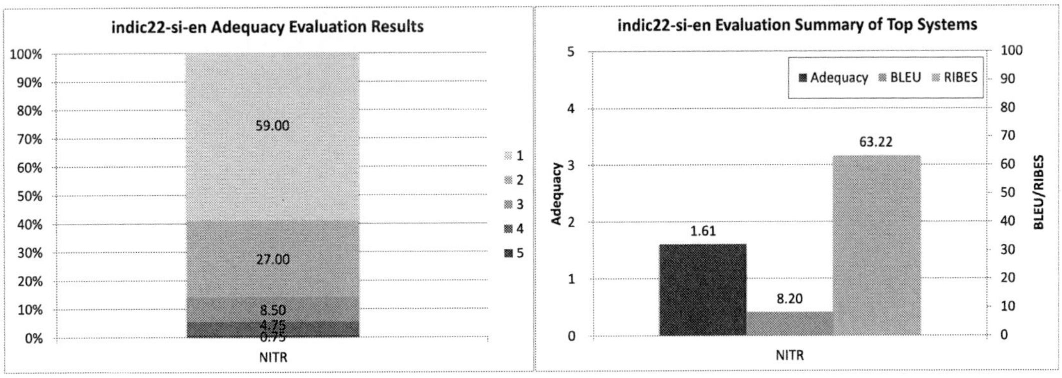

Figure 15: Official evaluation results of indic22-si-en.

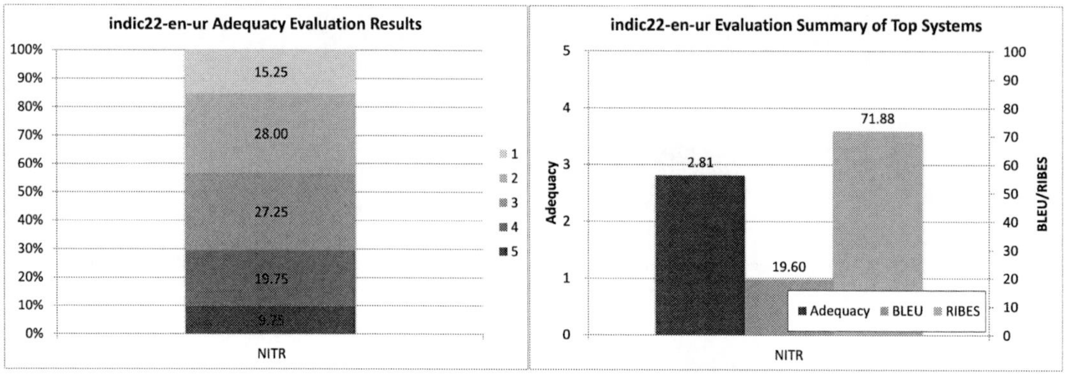

Figure 16: Official evaluation results of indic22-en-ur.

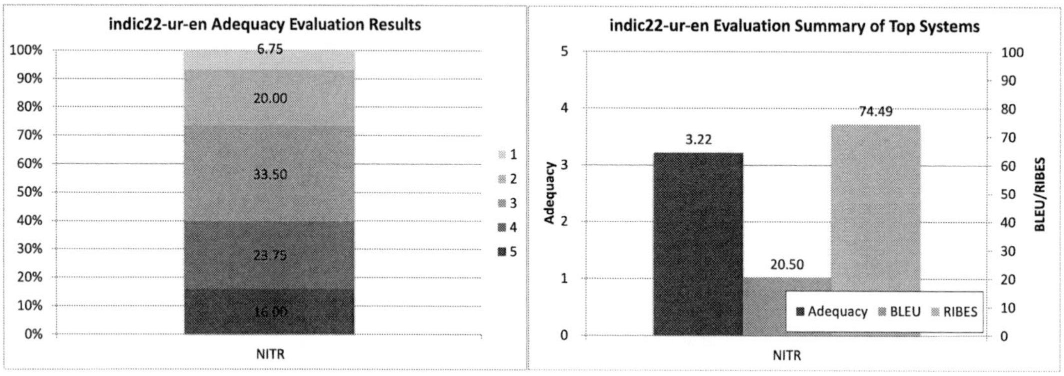

Figure 17: Official evaluation results of indic22-ur-en.

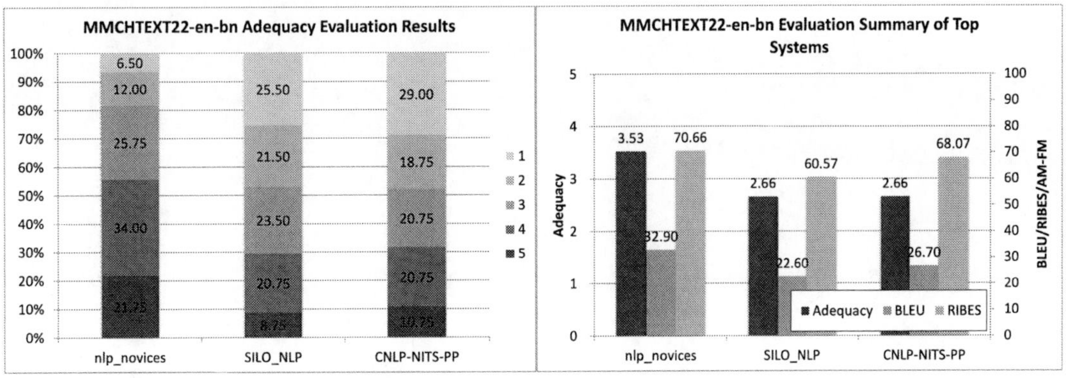

Figure 18: Official evaluation results of mmchtext22-en-bn.

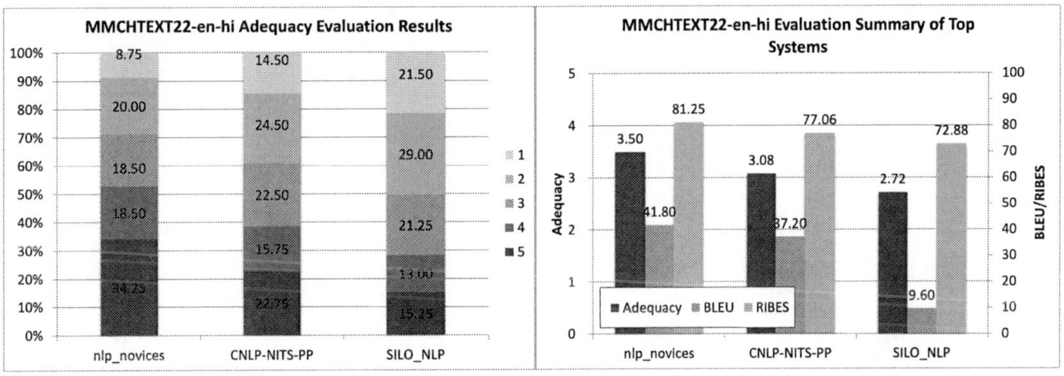

Figure 19: Official evaluation results of mmchtext22-en-hi.

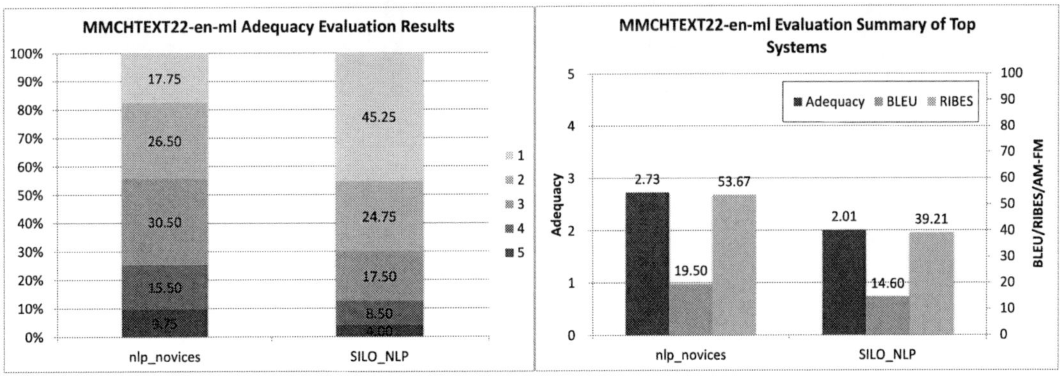

Figure 20: Official evaluation results of mmchtext22-en-ml.

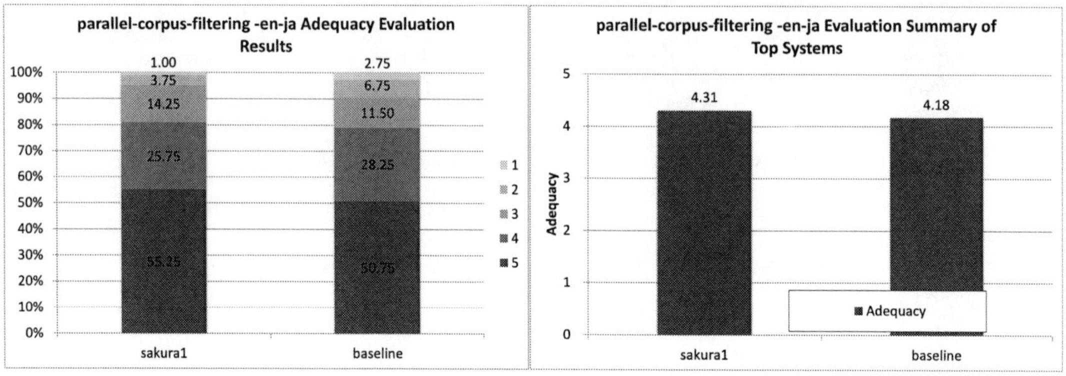

Figure 21: Official evaluation results of parallel-corpus-filtering-en-ja.

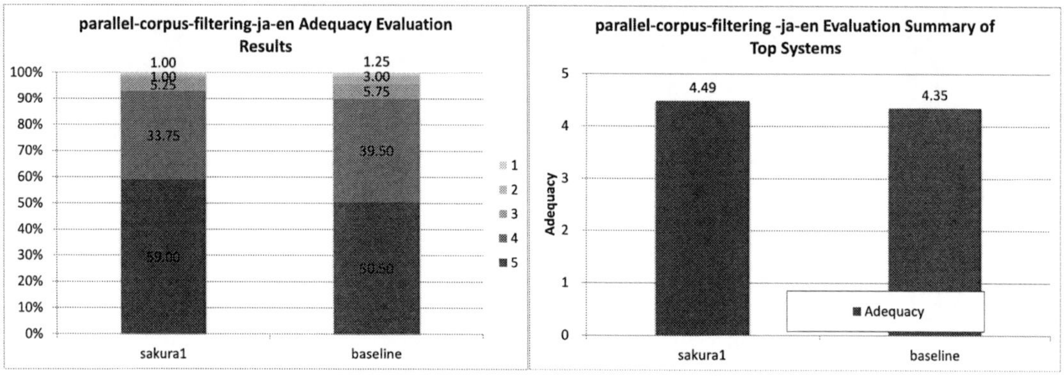

Figure 22: Official evaluation results of parallel-corpus-filtering-ja-en.

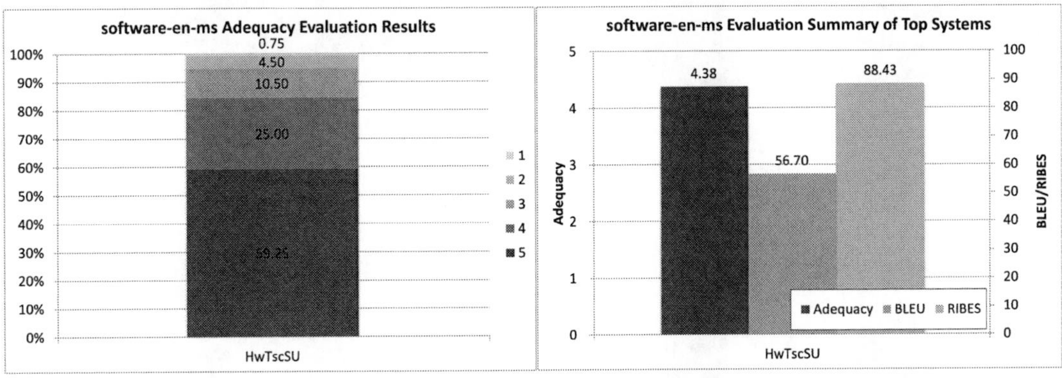

Figure 23: Official evaluation results of software-en-ms.

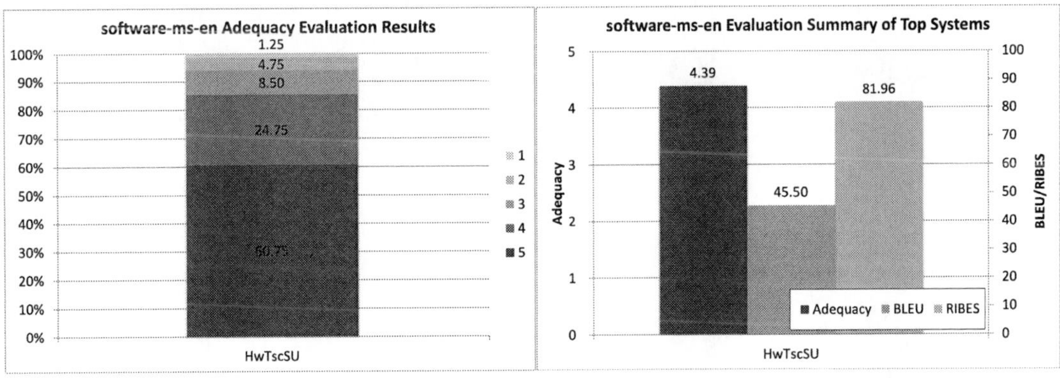

Figure 24: Official evaluation results of software-ms-en.

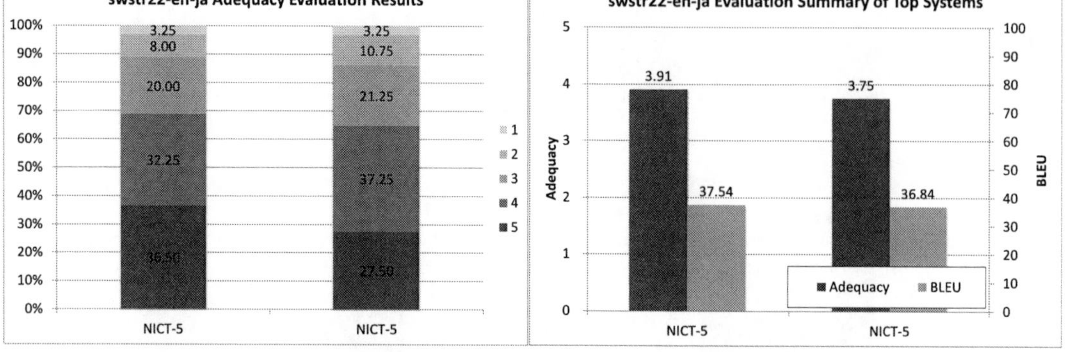

Figure 25: Official evaluation results of swstr22-en-ja.

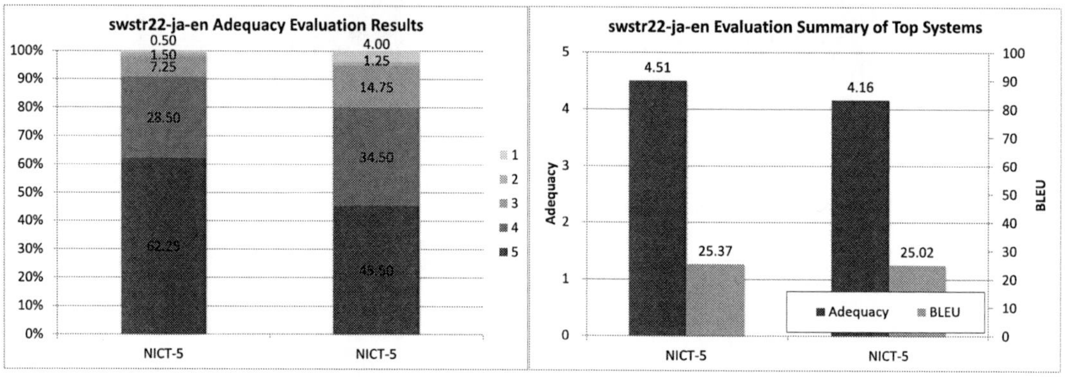

Figure 26: Official evaluation results of swstr22-ja-en.

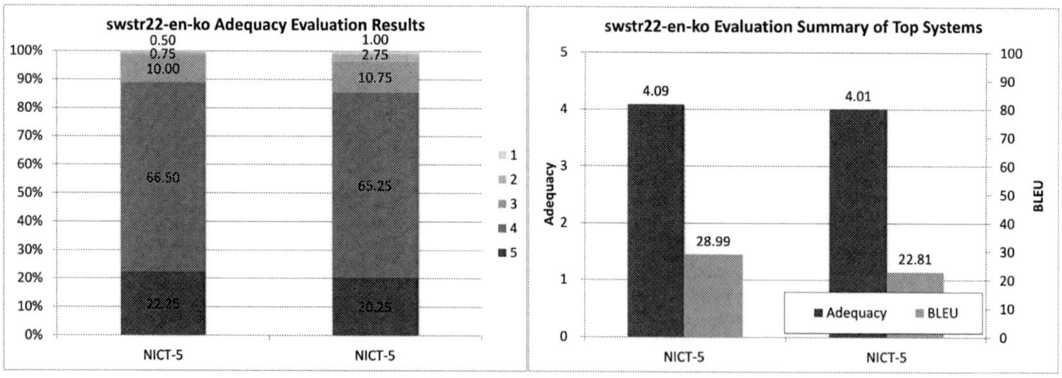

Figure 27: Official evaluation results of swstr22-en-ko.

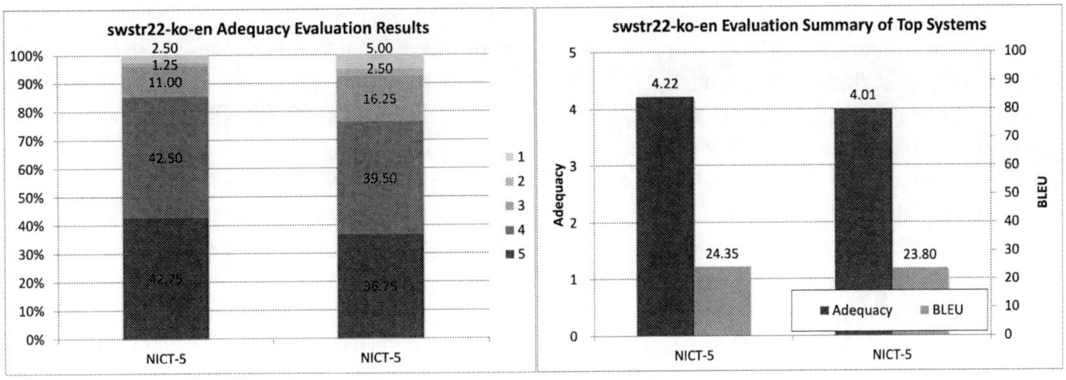

Figure 28: Official evaluation results of swstr22-ko-en.

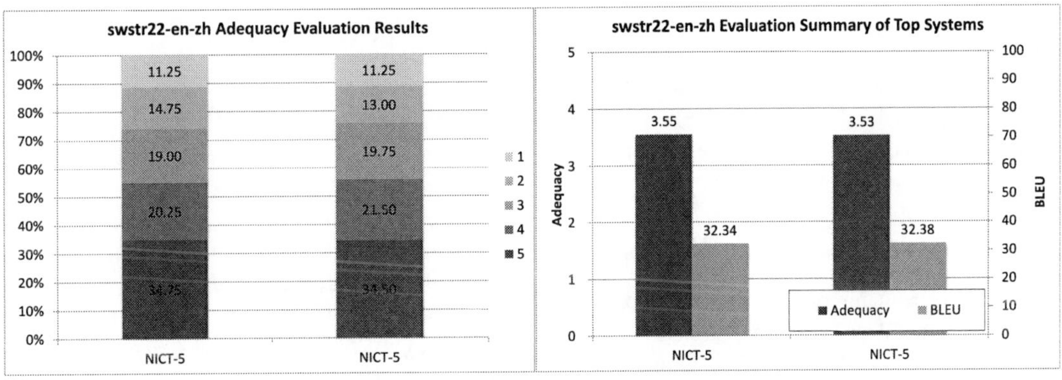

Figure 29: Official evaluation results of swstr22-en-zh.

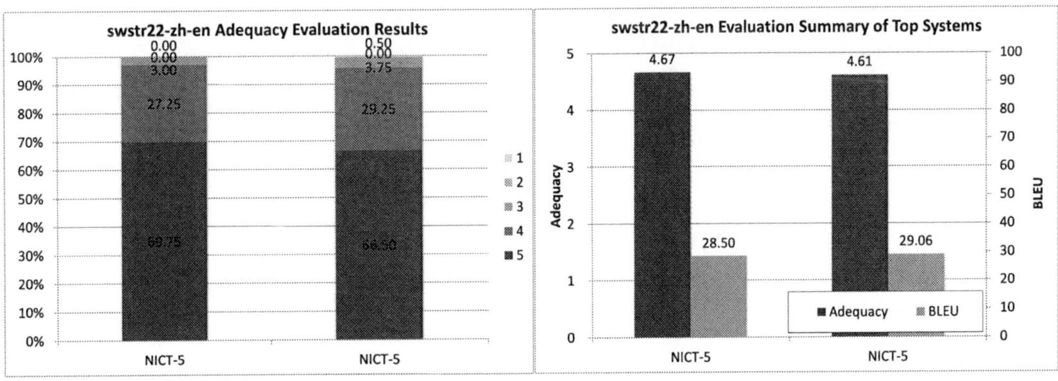

Figure 30: Official evaluation results of swstr22-zh-en.

49, 50.

For English to Malayalam text-only translation the team "Silo_NLP" obtained a BLEU score of *30.80* fine-tuning with pre-trained mBART-50 model for the evaluation test set and team "nlp_novices" obtained a BLEU score of *19.60* using the *Simple Transformer* model. For multimodal, the team "Silo_NLP" obtained a BLEU score of *41.00* for the evaluation test set and a BLEU score of *20.40* for the challenge test set. They extracted the object tags from the images with fine-tuning *mBART* for the multimodal task.

Human evaluation was done for the challenge test set text-only translation (TEXT) as shown in Figure 20. Automatic (both BLEU and RIBES) scores agree with the manual judgement on the JPO adequacy scale (see Table 13), but it is important to mention that even for the better system ("nlp_novices") only a little less than 10% of sentences have all information transmitted correctly. If we consider Adequacy ranks 3–5 together (i.e. about a half or more of information transmitted correctly), "nlp_novices" can produce about 55% of sentences like that while "Silo_NLP" has only 30% of sentences in these levels.

8.6 English→Bengali Multi-Modal Task

This year three teams participated in the different sub-tasks (TEXT, MM) of the English→Bengali Multi-Modal task. The WAT2022 automatic evaluation scores are shown in the Table 51, 52, 53, 54.

The team "Silo_NLP" obtained the highest BLEU score for the text-only translation (TEXT) for the evaluation (E-Test) set by using *Transformer* model and utilizing BNLIT Corpus as an additional resource. The team "nlp_novices" obtained the highest BLEU score on the challenge (C-Test) test set by fine-tuning the *Transformer* model. For the multimodal sub-task (MM), we received two submissions from the teams "CNLP-NITS-PP", and "Silo_NLP", respectively. The team "CNLP-NITS-PP" obtained the highest BLEU score for the evaluation (E-Test) test set following transliteration-based phrase pairs augmentation and visual features in training using BRNN encoder and doubly-attentive-rnn decoder. The team "Silo_NLP" and "nlp_novices" obtained the same BLEU score for the challenge (C-Test) test set. The team "nlp_novices" followed the same approach as that for E-Test while team "Silo_NLP" extracted the object tags from images and fine-tuned *mBART*.

Human evaluation was done for the challenge test set text-only translation (TEXT) as shown in Figure 18. Automatic scores (both BLEU and RIBES) agree on the best system ("nlp_novices") with the manual judgement on the JPO adequacy scale (see Table 13) but they diverge for "Silo_NLP" and "CNLP-NITS-PP" where both receive Adequacy of 2.66 and differ in BLEU and RIBES. "CNLP-NITS-PP" scores higher in automatic metrics and actually very close to the winning "nlp_novices", see RIBES of 70.66 ("nlp_novices") vs. 68.07 ("CNLP-NITS-PP"). This suggests a problem with RIBES because the difference in Adequacy is important: 3.53 vs 2.66. One can also see a striking difference in the distribution of Adequacy levels between the winning "CNLP-NITS-PP" (55% of sentences reach Adequacy of 4 or 5) and its competitors (only 30% of sentences reach 4 or 5), see the left part of Figure 18.

8.7 Restricted Translation Task

In this year, we received system submissions from the team "TMU" for the English→ Japanese and Japanese→ English tasks, and no systems submitted to the Chinese↔Japanese tasks. The TMU team employed a soft-constrained system that combined two methods, namely the Lexical Constraint Aware NMT (LeCA; Chen et al., 2020) and the Multi-Source Levenshtein Transformer (MSLevT Susanto et al., 2020). In case the soft constrained method of LeCA does not satisfy the target-side term requirements, the authors applied one of the automatic post-editing methods to compensate for those terms in the system outputs, such as MSLevT, and achieved 100% performance on the output of the constrained phrase pairs.

Table 14 reports the final score and two distinct human evaluation results[46]. Regarding the final automatic evaluation score, we used SacreBLEU[47] to calculate BLEU scores. More details are described in Section 2.15. Moreover, we asked human bilingual speakers to assess three systems on

[46]In the final automatic score for En-Ja, we received an inquiry from TMU that the specification of the submission form included backslashes before quotations, and they were detrimental to the evaluation of some constrained terms. The final score without the backslash is as follows; LeCA+LevT (*ensemble*): 42.1, LeCA+LevT: 39.3, LeCA only: 23.8.

[47]Detail settings: case.mixed, numrefs=1, smooth.exp, version.1.5.1, (en-ja) lang=en-ja, tok=ja-mecab-0.996-IPA, (ja-en) lang=ja-en.

the English↔Japanese translation tasks.[48] Two annotators were asked to assess the systems' translation accuracy, and we also conducted another system assessment by the source-based direct assessment (src-based DA) (Cettolo et al., 2017; Federmann, 2018), with two bilingual annotators.

In the English→Japanese direction (En-Ja), we do not observe any consistent tendency among three results. LeCA only is the most preferred system by annotators in terms of translation accuracy. However, the other two systems also achieve higher evaluation scores as well as src-based DA scores. These systems can not be statistically distinguished from the human reference. On the other hand, the LeCA+LevT ensemble model achieved the top performance in all metrics in the Japanese→English direction (Ja-En), while LeCA+LevT is less preferred in the src-based DA.

According to the HE (accuracy) results, we observe that the LeCA+LevT (ensemble) system achieves both the highest number of outputs with score=5 (58%) and score=1 (6%) in the human evaluation. For the outputs with score=1 in LeCA+LevT (ensemble), texts other than the constrained terms were often omitted. This indicates that the lack of the effects from the brevity penalty in our final score can not capture under-generation problems on the ensemble model. Therefore, we eventually need to consider an alternative scoring to address this issue in future work. Another observation is that annotators do not necessarily have specific domain knowledge that would be required to provide more accurate assessment. To address this issue, we need to allow annotators to look up the generated dictionaries during the assessment. In conclusion, the trade-off between completing vocabulary constraints and achieving high translation performance remains challenging, even in the soft-constrained model.

8.8 Parallel Corpus Filtering Task

We received a single submission from team 'sakura', Rakuten Institute of Technology. They submitted two systems, one leverages feature decay algorithms(FDA) and the other one uses probability scores of the NMT model trained on the ASPEC corpus. They submitted the top 5M-scored sentence pairs as a clean dataset.

Table 15 summarized the evaluation results. We carried out human evaluation only for the baseline and the FDA-based method since the NMT probability-based model was inferior to the baseline in terms of the BLEU scores.

The results show that the submission based on the FDA surpasses the baseline in both language directions on both BLEU and human evaluation while reducing the data size to 20%.

9 Conclusion and Future Perspective

This paper summarizes the shared tasks of WAT2022. We had 8 participants worldwide who submitted their translation results for the human evaluation, and collected a large number of useful submissions for improving the current machine translation systems by analyzing the submissions and identifying the issues.

This year we had smaller number of participants compared to the last year. For the next WAT workshop, we want attract much more people to join our shared tasks.

Acknowledgement

The English→Hindi English→Malayalam, and English→Bengali Multi-Modal shared tasks were supported by the following grants at Silo AI and Charles University. The authors do not see any significant ethical or privacy concerns that would prevent the processing of the data used in the study. The datasets do not contain any personal data. Personal data of annotators needed when the datasets were prepared and when the outputs were evaluated were processed in compliance with the GDPR and national law.

- At Silo AI, the work was supported by the NLP Innovation.
- At Charles University, the work was supported by the grant 19-26934X (NEUREM3) of the Czech Science Foundation and using language resources distributed by the LINDAT/CLARIN project of the Ministry of Education, Youth and Sports of the Czech Republic (projects LM2015071 and OP VVV VI CZ.02.1.01/0.0/0.0/16013/0001781).

The Restricted Translation is supported by Microsoft.

[48]Two systems, that is "LeCA only" and "LeCA+LevT", were originally designated by the team "TMU" for human evaluation, however, none of those systems are top-ranked on our metrics. Therefore, we decided to additionally include each top-ranked system (LeCA+LevT (*ensemble*)) to the human evaluation.

En-Ja Outputs	final	HE (Accuracy)	HE (src-based DA)
LeCA+LevT (*ensemble*)	**52.7**	4.18	**76.4***
LeCA+LevT	50.5	4.19	**76.6***
LeCA only	37.6	**4.24**	74.9
Human Reference	–	–	76.6
Ja-En Outputs	**final**	**HE (Accuracy)**	**HE (src-based DA)**
LeCA+LevT (*ensemble*)	**40.8**	**4.31**	**74.1***
LeCA+LevT	38.1	4.22	72.0
LeCA only	23.0	4.14	73.3
Human Reference	–	–	74.7

Table 14: Human evaluation results of translation accuracy run by WAT and source-based direct assessments, ranging $[0, 5]$ and $[0, 100]$, respectively. The "final" column reports the final score of the automatic evaluation metric described in the Section 2.15. * indicates that the systems and Human Reference are not statistically distinguishable to the annotators.

En-Ja Team	BLEU	Human Eval.
sakura (FDA)	**28.8**	**4.31**
baseline	27.4	4.18
sakura (NMT Prob.)	26.7	—
Ja-En Team	**final**	**Human Eval.**
sakura (FDA)	**21.8**	**4.49**
sakura (NMT Prob.)	19.9	—
baseline	19.4	4.35

Table 15: Results of the parallel corpus filtering task evaluated on the ASPEC test set.

References

Rafael E. Banchs, Luis F. D'Haro, and Haizhou Li. 2015a. Adequacy-fluency metrics: Evaluating mt in the continuous space model framework. *IEEE/ACM Trans. Audio, Speech and Lang. Proc.*, 23(3):472–482.

Rafael E. Banchs, Luis F. D'Haro, and Haizhou Li. 2015b. Adequacy–fluency metrics: Evaluating mt in the continuous space model framework. *IEEE/ACM Transactions on Audio, Speech, and Language Processing*, 23(3):472–482.

Bianka Buschbeck and Miriam Exel. 2020. A parallel evaluation data set of software documentation with document structure annotation.

M. Cettolo, Marcello Federico, L. Bentivogli, Niehues Jan, Stüker Sebastian, Sudoh Katsuitho, Yoshino Koichiro, and Federmann Christian. 2017. Overview of the iwslt 2017 evaluation campaign.

Guanhua Chen, Yun Chen, Yong Wang, and Victor O.K. Li. 2020. Lexical-constraint-aware neural machine translation via data augmentation. In *Proceedings of the Twenty-Ninth International Joint Conference on Artificial Intelligence, IJCAI-20*, pages 3587–3593. International Joint Conferences on Artificial Intelligence Organization. Main track.

Raj Dabre, Chenhui Chu, and Anoop Kunchukuttan. 2020. A survey of multilingual neural machine translation. *ACM Comput. Surv.*, 53(5).

Luis Fernando D'Haro, Rafael E. Banchs, Chiori Hori, and Haizhou Li. 2019. Automatic evaluation of end-to-end dialog systems with adequacy-fluency metrics. *Computer Speech and Language*, 55:200–215.

Chenchen Ding, Hnin Thu Zar Aye, Win Pa Pa, Khin Thandar Nwet, Khin Mar Soe, Masao Utiyama, and Eiichiro Sumita. 2019. Towards Burmese (Myanmar) morphological analysis: Syllable-based tokenization and part-of-speech tagging. *ACM Transactions on Asian and Low-Resource Language Information Processing (TALLIP)*, 19(1):5.

Chenchen Ding, Masao Utiyama, and Eiichiro Sumita. 2018. NOVA: A feasible and flexible annotation system for joint tokenization and part-of-speech tagging. *ACM Transactions on Asian and Low-Resource Language Information Processing (TALLIP)*, 18(2):17.

Christian Federmann. 2018. Appraise evaluation framework for machine translation. In *Proceedings of the 27th International Conference on Computational Linguistics: System Demonstrations*, pages 86–88, Santa Fe, New Mexico. Association for Computational Linguistics.

Weiqi Gu, Haiyue Song, Chenhui Chu, and Sadao Kurohashi. 2021. Video-guided machine translation with spatial hierarchical attention network. In *Proceedings of the 59th Annual Meeting of the Association for Computational Linguistics and the 11th International Joint Conference on Natural Language Processing: Student Research Workshop*, pages 87–92.

Kazuma Hashimoto, Raffaella Buschiazzo, James Bradbury, Teresa Marshall, Richard Socher, and Caiming Xiong. 2019. A high-quality multilingual dataset for structured documentation translation. In *Proceedings of the Fourth Conference on Machine Translation (Volume 1: Research Papers)*, pages 116–127,

Florence, Italy. Association for Computational Linguistics.

Aizhan Imankulova, Raj Dabre, Atsushi Fujita, and Kenji Imamura. 2019. Exploiting out-of-domain parallel data through multilingual transfer learning for low-resource neural machine translation. In *Proceedings of Machine Translation Summit XVII: Research Track*, pages 128–139, Dublin, Ireland. European Association for Machine Translation.

Hideki Isozaki, Tsutomu Hirao, Kevin Duh, Katsuhito Sudoh, and Hajime Tsukada. 2010. Automatic evaluation of translation quality for distant language pairs. In *Proceedings of the 2010 Conference on Empirical Methods in Natural Language Processing*, EMNLP '10, pages 944–952, Stroudsburg, PA, USA. Association for Computational Linguistics.

Melvin Johnson, Mike Schuster, Quoc V. Le, Maxim Krikun, Yonghui Wu, Zhifeng Chen, Nikhil Thorat, Fernanda Viégas, Martin Wattenberg, Greg Corrado, Macduff Hughes, and Jeffrey Dean. 2017. Google's multilingual neural machine translation system: Enabling zero-shot translation. *Transactions of the Association for Computational Linguistics*, 5:339–351.

Huda Khayrallah and Philipp Koehn. 2018. On the impact of various types of noise on neural machine translation. In *Proceedings of the 2nd Workshop on Neural Machine Translation and Generation*, pages 74–83, Melbourne, Australia. Association for Computational Linguistics.

Guillaume Klein, Yoon Kim, Yuntian Deng, Jean Senellart, and Alexander Rush. 2017. Opennmt: Open-source toolkit for neural machine translation. In *Proceedings of ACL 2017, System Demonstrations*, pages 67–72. Association for Computational Linguistics.

Philipp Koehn, Vishrav Chaudhary, Ahmed El-Kishky, Naman Goyal, Peng-Jen Chen, and Francisco Guzmán. 2020. Findings of the WMT 2020 shared task on parallel corpus filtering and alignment. In *Proceedings of the Fifth Conference on Machine Translation*, pages 726–742, Online. Association for Computational Linguistics.

T. Kudo. 2005. Mecab : Yet another part-of-speech and morphological analyzer. *http://mecab.sourceforge.net/*.

Anoop Kunchukuttan. 2020. The IndicNLP Library. `https://github.com/anoopkunchukuttan/indic_nlp_library/blob/master/docs/indicnlp.pdf`.

Sadao Kurohashi, Toshihisa Nakamura, Yuji Matsumoto, and Makoto Nagao. 1994. Improvements of Japanese morphological analyzer JUMAN. In *Proceedings of The International Workshop on Sharable Natural Language*, pages 22–28.

Mike Lewis, Yinhan Liu, Naman Goyal, Marjan Ghazvininejad, Abdelrahman Mohamed, Omer Levy, Veselin Stoyanov, and Luke Zettlemoyer. 2020. BART: Denoising sequence-to-sequence pre-training for natural language generation, translation, and comprehension. In *Proceedings of the 58th Annual Meeting of the Association for Computational Linguistics*, pages 7871–7880, Online. Association for Computational Linguistics.

Yihang Li, Shuichiro Shimizu, Weiqi Gu, Chenhui Chu, and Sadao Kurohashi. 2022. Visa: An ambiguous subtitles dataset for visual scene-aware machine translation. In *Proceedings of the 13th Language Resources and Evaluation Conference*, pages 6735–6743.

Yinhan Liu, Jiatao Gu, Naman Goyal, Xian Li, Sergey Edunov, Marjan Ghazvininejad, Mike Lewis, and Luke Zettlemoyer. 2020. Multilingual denoising pre-training for neural machine translation. *Transactions of the Association for Computational Linguistics*, 8:726–742.

Andrew Merritt, Chenhui Chu, and Yuki Arase. 2020. A corpus for english-japanese multimodal neural machine translation with comparable sentences.

Makoto Morishita, Jun Suzuki, and Masaaki Nagata. 2020. JParaCrawl: A large scale web-based English-Japanese parallel corpus. In *Proceedings of the 12th Language Resources and Evaluation Conference*, pages 3603–3609, Marseille, France. European Language Resources Association.

Toshiaki Nakazawa, Nobushige Doi, Shohei Higashiyama, Chenchen Ding, Raj Dabre, Hideya Mino, Isao Goto, Win Pa Pa, Anoop Kunchukuttan, Yusuke Oda, Shantipriya Parida, Ondřej Bojar, and Sadao Kurohashi. 2019. Overview of the 6th workshop on Asian translation. In *Proceedings of the 6th Workshop on Asian Translation*, pages 1–35, Hong Kong, China. Association for Computational Linguistics.

Toshiaki Nakazawa, Shohei Higashiyama, Chenchen Ding, Hideya Mino, Isao Goto, Hideto Kazawa, Yusuke Oda, Graham Neubig, and Sadao Kurohashi. 2017. Overview of the 4th workshop on asian translation. In *Proceedings of the 4th Workshop on Asian Translation (WAT2017)*, pages 1–54. Asian Federation of Natural Language Processing.

Toshiaki Nakazawa, Hideki Nakayama, Chenchen Ding, Raj Dabre, Shohei Higashiyama, Hideya Mino, Isao Goto, Win Pa Pa, Anoop Kunchukuttan, Shantipriya Parida, et al. 2021a. Overview of the 8th workshop on asian translation. In *Proceedings of the 8th Workshop on Asian Translation (WAT2021)*, pages 1–45.

Toshiaki Nakazawa, Hideki Nakayama, Chenchen Ding, Raj Dabre, Shohei Higashiyama, Hideya Mino, Isao Goto, Win Pa Pa, Anoop Kunchukuttan, Shantipriya Parida, Ondřej Bojar, Chenhui Chu, Akiko Eriguchi, Kaori Abe, Yusuke Oda, and Sadao Kurohashi.

2021b. Overview of the 8th workshop on Asian translation. In *Proceedings of the 8th Workshop on Asian Translation (WAT2021)*, pages 1–45, Online. Association for Computational Linguistics.

Toshiaki Nakazawa, Hideki Nakayama, Chenchen Ding, Raj Dabre, Shohei Higashiyama, Hideya Mino, Isao Goto, Win Pa Pa, Anoop Kunchukuttan, Shantipriya Parida, Ondřej Bojar, and Sadao Kurohashi. 2020. Overview of the 7th workshop on Asian translation. In *Proceedings of the 7th Workshop on Asian Translation*, pages 1–44, Suzhou, China. Association for Computational Linguistics.

Toshiaki Nakazawa, Hideki Nakayama, Isao Goto, Hideya Mino, Chenchen Ding, Raj Dabre, Anoop Kunchukuttan, Shohei Higashiyama, Hiroshi Manabe, Win Pa Pa, Shantipriya Parida, Ondřej Bojar, Chenhui Chu, Akiko Eriguchi, Kaori Abe, Yusuke Oda, Katsuhito Sudoh, Sadao Kurohashi, and Pushpak Bhattacharyya, editors. 2021c. *Proceedings of the 8th Workshop on Asian Translation (WAT2021)*. Association for Computational Linguistics, Online.

Toshiaki Nakazawa, Katsuhito Sudoh, Shohei Higashiyama, Chenchen Ding, Raj Dabre, Hideya Mino, Isao Goto, Win Pa Pa, Anoop Kunchukuttan, and Sadao Kurohashi. 2018. Overview of the 5th workshop on Asian translation. In *Proceedings of the 32nd Pacific Asia Conference on Language, Information and Computation: 5th Workshop on Asian Translation: 5th Workshop on Asian Translation*, Hong Kong. Association for Computational Linguistics.

Toshiaki Nakazawa, Manabu Yaguchi, Kiyotaka Uchimoto, Masao Utiyama, Eiichiro Sumita, Sadao Kurohashi, and Hitoshi Isahara. 2016. ASPEC: Asian scientific paper excerpt corpus. In *Proceedings of the Tenth International Conference on Language Resources and Evaluation (LREC'16)*, pages 2204–2208, Portorož, Slovenia. European Language Resources Association (ELRA).

Graham Neubig, Yosuke Nakata, and Shinsuke Mori. 2011. Pointwise prediction for robust, adaptable japanese morphological analysis. In *Proceedings of the 49th Annual Meeting of the Association for Computational Linguistics: Human Language Technologies: Short Papers - Volume 2*, HLT '11, pages 529–533, Stroudsburg, PA, USA. Association for Computational Linguistics.

Kishore Papineni, Salim Roukos, Todd Ward, and Wei-Jing Zhu. 2002. Bleu: a method for automatic evaluation of machine translation. In *ACL*, pages 311–318.

Shantipriya Parida and Ondřej Bojar. 2021. Malayalam visual genome 1.0. LINDAT/CLARIAH-CZ digital library at the Institute of Formal and Applied Linguistics (ÚFAL), Faculty of Mathematics and Physics, Charles University.

Shantipriya Parida, Ondřej Bojar, and Satya Ranjan Dash. 2019a. Hindi visual genome: A dataset for multimodal english-to-hindi machine translation. *arXiv preprint arXiv:1907.08948*.

Shantipriya Parida, Ondřej Bojar, and Satya Ranjan Dash. 2019b. Hindi Visual Genome: A Dataset for Multimodal English-to-Hindi Machine Translation. *Computación y Sistemas*. In print. Presented at CICLing 2019, La Rochelle, France.

Matt Post. 2018. A call for clarity in reporting BLEU scores. In *Proceedings of the Third Conference on Machine Translation: Research Papers*, pages 186–191, Brussels, Belgium. Association for Computational Linguistics.

Gowtham Ramesh, Sumanth Doddapaneni, Aravinth Bheemaraj, Mayank Jobanputra, Raghavan AK, Ajitesh Sharma, Sujit Sahoo, Harshita Diddee, Mahalakshmi J, Divyanshu Kakwani, Navneet Kumar, Aswin Pradeep, Srihari Nagaraj, Kumar Deepak, Vivek Raghavan, Anoop Kunchukuttan, Pratyush Kumar, and Mitesh Shantadevi Khapra. 2022. Samanantar: The largest publicly available parallel corpora collection for 11 indic languages. *Transactions of the Association for Computational Linguistics*, 10:145–162.

Hammam Riza, Michael Purwoadi, Teduh Uliniansyah, Aw Ai Ti, Sharifah Mahani Aljunied, Luong Chi Mai, Vu Tat Thang, Nguyen Phuong Thai, Vichet Chea, Sethserey Sam, Sopheap Seng, Khin Mar Soe, Khin Thandar Nwet, Masao Utiyama, and Chenchen Ding. 2016. Introduction of the asian language treebank. In *In Proc. of O-COCOSDA*, pages 1–6.

Arghyadeep Sen, Shantipriya Parida, Ketan Kotwal, Subhadarshi Panda, Ondřej Bojar, and Satya Ranjan Dash. 2022. Bengali visual genome 1.0. LINDAT/CLARIAH-CZ digital library at the Institute of Formal and Applied Linguistics (ÚFAL), Faculty of Mathematics and Physics, Charles University.

Kak Soky, Masato Mimura, Tatsuya Kawahara, Sheng Li, Chenchen Ding, Chenhui Chu, and Sethserey Sam. 2021. Khmer speech translation corpus of the extraordinary chambers in the courts of cambodia (eccc). In *2021 24th Conference of the Oriental COCOSDA International Committee for the Coordination and Standardisation of Speech Databases and Assessment Techniques (O-COCOSDA)*, pages 122–127.

Raymond Hendy Susanto, Shamil Chollampatt, and Liling Tan. 2020. Lexically constrained neural machine translation with Levenshtein transformer. In *Proceedings of the 58th Annual Meeting of the Association for Computational Linguistics*, pages 3536–3543, Online. Association for Computational Linguistics.

Ye Kyaw Thu, Win Pa Pa, Masao Utiyama, Andrew Finch, and Eiichiro Sumita. 2016. Introducing the Asian language treebank (ALT). In *Proceedings of the Tenth International Conference on Language*

Resources and Evaluation (LREC'16), pages 1574–1578, Portorož, Slovenia. European Language Resources Association (ELRA).

Huihsin Tseng. 2005. A conditional random field word segmenter. In *In Fourth SIGHAN Workshop on Chinese Language Processing*.

Masao Utiyama and Hitoshi Isahara. 2007. A japanese-english patent parallel corpus. In *MT summit XI*, pages 475–482.

Ashish Vaswani, Samy Bengio, Eugene Brevdo, Francois Chollet, Aidan Gomez, Stephan Gouws, Llion Jones, Łukasz Kaiser, Nal Kalchbrenner, Niki Parmar, Ryan Sepassi, Noam Shazeer, and Jakob Uszkoreit. 2018. Tensor2tensor for neural machine translation. In *Proceedings of the 13th Conference of the Association for Machine Translation in the Americas (Volume 1: Research Papers)*, pages 193–199. Association for Machine Translation in the Americas.

Ashish Vaswani, Noam Shazeer, Niki Parmar, Jakob Uszkoreit, Llion Jones, Aidan N. Gomez, Lukasz Kaiser, and Illia Polosukhin. 2017. Attention is all you need. *CoRR*, abs/1706.03762.

Yi Mon Shwe Sin and Khin Mar Soe. 2018. Syllable-based myanmar-english neural machine translation. In *In Proc. of ICCA*, pages 228–233.

Chen Zhang, Luis Fernando D'Haro, Rafael E. Banchs, Thomas Friedrichs, and Haizhou Li. 2021a. *Deep AM-FM: Toolkit for Automatic Dialogue Evaluation*, pages 53–69. Springer Singapore, Singapore.

Chen Zhang, Grandee Lee, Luis Fernando D'Haro, and Haizhou Li. 2021b. D-score: Holistic dialogue evaluation without reference. *IEEE/ACM Transactions on Audio, Speech, and Language Processing*, pages 1–1.

Yuting Zhao, Mamoru Komachi, Tomoyuki Kajiwara, and Chenhui Chu. 2020. Double attention-based multimodal neural machine translation with semantic image regions. In *EAMT*, pages 105–114.

Appendix A Submissions

Tables 16 to 63 summarize translation results submitted to WAT2022. Type and RSRC columns indicate type of method and use of other resources.

System	ID	Type	RSRC	BLEU			RIBES			AMFM
				juman	kytea	mecab	juman	kytea	mecab	
TMU	6947	NMT	NO	49.80	49.80	50.00	0.864394	0.865434	0.869480	0.788640
TMU	6948	NMT	NO	50.80	51.60	51.30	0.867732	0.869859	0.873110	0.800450

Table 16: ASPECRT en-ja submissions

System	ID	Type	RSRC	BLEU	RIBES	AMFM
TMU	6942	NMT	NO	39.60	0.799376	0.640000
TMU	6949	NMT	NO	39.30	0.795787	0.653280

Table 17: ASPECRT ja-en submissions

System	ID	Type	RSRC	BLEU	RIBES	AMFM
ORGANIZER	6932	NMT	NO	1.70	0.222952	–

Table 18: ECCC km-en submissions

System	ID	Type	RSRC	BLEU	RIBES	AMFM
ORGANIZER	6933	SMT	NO	5.70	0.202578	–
ORGANIZER	6934	NMT	NO	5.70	0.202578	–

Table 19: ECCC km-fr submissions

System	ID	Type	RSRC	BLEU	RIBES	AMFM
CNLP-NITS-PP	6963	NMT	YES	3.50	0.537859	–
NITR	6998	NMT	NO	15.50	0.706743	–

Table 20: INDIC22 as-en submissions

System	ID	Type	RSRC	BLEU	RIBES	AMFM
CNLP-NITS-PP	6966	NMT	YES	4.50	0.547407	–

Table 21: INDIC22 bn-en submissions

System	ID	Type	RSRC	BLEU	RIBES	AMFM
CNLP-NITS-PP	6965	NMT	YES	1.10	0.359265	–
NITR	7016	NMT	NO	10.20	0.634631	–

Table 22: INDIC22 en-as submissions

System	ID	Type	RSRC	BLEU	RIBES	AMFM
CNLP-NITS-PP	6969	NMT	YES	2.00	0.503286	–

Table 23: INDIC22 en-bn submissions

System	ID	Type	RSRC	BLEU	RIBES	AMFM
NITR	7009	NMT	NO	6.30	0.579323	–

Table 24: INDIC22 en-sd submissions

System	ID	Type	RSRC	BLEU	RIBES	AMFM
NITR	7012	NMT	NO	9.50	0.647028	–

Table 25: INDIC22 en-si submissions

System	ID	Type	RSRC	BLEU	RIBES	AMFM
NITR	7014	NMT	NO	19.60	0.718763	–

Table 26: INDIC22 en-ur submissions

System	ID	Type	RSRC	BLEU	RIBES	AMFM
NITR	7007	NMT	NO	8.00	0.546125	–

Table 27: INDIC22 ne-en submissions

System	ID	Type	RSRC	BLEU	RIBES	AMFM
NITR	7005	NMT	NO	15.40	0.709039	–

Table 28: INDIC22 sd-en submissions

System	ID	Type	RSRC	BLEU	RIBES	AMFM
NITR	7003	NMT	NO	8.20	0.632228	–

Table 29: INDIC22 si-en submissions

System	ID	Type	RSRC	BLEU	RIBES	AMFM
NITR	7000	NMT	NO	20.50	0.744934	–

Table 30: INDIC22 ur-en submissions

System	ID	Type	RSRC	BLEU			RIBES			AMFM
				juman	kytea	mecab	juman	kytea	mecab	
ORGANIZER	6543	NMT	NO	47.04	48.86	46.96	0.870867	0.870604	0.869950	–

Table 31: JPC22 en-ja submissions

System	ID	Type	RSRC	BLEU	RIBES	AMFM
ORGANIZER	6544	NMT	NO	44.51	0.857963	–

Table 32: JPC22 ja-en submissions

System	ID	Type	RSRC	BLEU	RIBES	AMFM
ORGANIZER	6542	NMT	NO	72.79	0.952385	–

Table 33: JPC22 ja-ko submissions

System	ID	Type	RSRC	BLEU			RIBES			AMFM
				kytea	ctb	pku	kytea	ctb	pku	
ORGANIZER	6540	NMT	NO	44.73	45.77	45.48	0.871424	0.877354	0.875780	–

Table 34: JPC22 ja-zh submissions

System	ID	Type	RSRC	BLEU			RIBES			AMFM
				juman	kytea	mecab	juman	kytea	mecab	
ORGANIZER	6541	NMT	NO	73.55	74.58	73.89	0.956442	0.956203	0.956269	–

Table 35: JPC22 ko-ja submissions

System	ID	Type	RSRC	BLEU			RIBES			AMFM
				juman	kytea	mecab	juman	kytea	mecab	
ORGANIZER	6539	NMT	NO	51.03	51.64	51.14	0.887901	0.885180	0.887404	–

Table 36: JPC22 zh-ja submissions

System	ID	Type	RSRC	BLEU			RIBES			AMFM
				juman	kytea	mecab	juman	kytea	mecab	
ORGANIZER	6536	NMT	NO	58.87	60.50	58.83	0.905725	0.907156	0.904626	–

Table 37: JPCN4 en-ja submissions

System	ID	Type	RSRC	BLEU	RIBES	AMFM
ORGANIZER	6537	NMT	NO	54.86	0.880671	–

Table 38: JPCN4 ja-en submissions

System	ID	Type	RSRC	BLEU	RIBES	AMFM
ORGANIZER	6535	NMT	NO	74.73	0.958438	–

Table 39: JPCN4 ja-ko submissions

System	ID	Type	RSRC	BLEU			RIBES			AMFM
				kytea	ctb	pku	kytea	ctb	pku	
ORGANIZER	6538	NMT	NO	57.51	57.92	57.99	0.898847	0.906742	0.904318	–

Table 40: JPCN4 ja-zh submissions

System	ID	Type	RSRC	BLEU			RIBES			AMFM
				juman	kytea	mecab	juman	kytea	mecab	
ORGANIZER	6534	NMT	NO	76.69	78.17	77.09	0.963465	0.963548	0.963376	–

Table 41: JPCN4 ko-ja submissions

System	ID	Type	RSRC	BLEU			RIBES			AMFM
				juman	kytea	mecab	juman	kytea	mecab	
ORGANIZER	6532	NMT	NO	64.31	65.00	64.62	0.924617	0.922020	0.924463	–

Table 42: JPCN4 zh-ja submissions

System	ID	Type	RSRC	BLEU	RIBES	AMFM
CNLP-NITS-PP	6739	NMT	NO	37.00	0.795302	–
SILO_NLP	6836	NMT	NO	36.20	0.785673	–
nlp_novices	6733	NMT	YES	43.10	0.816860	–

Table 43: MMEVTEXT22 en-hi submissions

System	ID	Type	RSRC	BLEU	RIBES	AMFM
CNLP-NITS-PP	6740	NMT	NO	39.40	0.802635	–
SILO_NLP	6958	NMT	YES	42.00	0.796441	–

Table 44: MMEVMM22 en-hi submissions

System	ID	Type	RSRC	BLEU	RIBES	AMFM
CNLP-NITS-PP	6742	NMT	NO	37.20	0.770640	–
SILO_NLP	6838	NMT	NO	29.60	0.728801	–
nlp_novices	6725	NMT	YES	41.80	0.812500	–

Table 45: MMCHTEXT22 en-hi submissions

System	ID	Type	RSRC	BLEU	RIBES	AMFM
CNLP-NITS-PP	6741	NMT	NO	39.30	0.791468	–
SILO_NLP	6959	NMT	YES	39.10	0.784169	–

Table 46: MMCHMM22 en-hi submissions

System	ID	Type	RSRC	BLEU	RIBES	AMFM
SILO_NLP	6848	NMT	NO	30.80	0.589471	–
nlp_novices	6719	NMT	YES	30.60	0.643987	–

Table 47: MMEVTEXT22 en-ml submissions

System	ID	Type	RSRC	BLEU	RIBES	AMFM
SILO_NLP	6849	NMT	NO	14.60	0.392158	–
nlp_novices	6720	NMT	YES	19.60	0.535043	–

Table 48: MMCHTEXT22 en-ml submissions

System	ID	Type	RSRC	BLEU	RIBES	AMFM
SILO_NLP	6936	NMT	NO	41.00	0.705349	–

Table 49: MMEVMM22 en-ml submissions

System	ID	Type	RSRC	BLEU	RIBES	AMFM
SILO_NLP	6937	NMT	NO	20.40	0.533737	–

Table 50: MMCHMM22 en-ml submissions

System	ID	Type	RSRC	BLEU	RIBES	AMFM
ORGANIZER	6703	NMT	NO	40.90	0.758246	–
CNLP-NITS-PP	6746	NMT	NO	40.90	0.752543	–
SILO_NLP	6954	NMT	NO	41.00	0.767212	–

Table 51: MMEVTEXT22 en-bn submissions

System	ID	Type	RSRC	BLEU	RIBES	AMFM
ORGANIZER	6704	NMT	NO	22.50	0.614267	–
CNLP-NITS-PP	6745	NMT	NO	26.70	0.680655	–
SILO_NLP	6843	NMT	NO	22.60	0.605676	–
nlp_novices	6970	NMT	YES	32.90	0.706596	–

Table 52: MMCHTEXT22 en-bn submissions

System	ID	Type	RSRC	BLEU	RIBES	AMFM
CNLP-NITS-PP	6743	NMT	NO	43.90	0.780669	–
SILO_NLP	6939	NMT	NO	42.10	0.754291	–

Table 53: MMEVMM22 en-bn submissions

System	ID	Type	RSRC	BLEU	RIBES	AMFM
CNLP-NITS-PP	6744	NMT	NO	28.70	0.688931	–
SILO_NLP	6940	NMT	NO	28.70	0.666817	–

Table 54: MMCHMM22 en-bn submissions

System	ID	Type	RSRC	BLEU	RIBES	AMFM
HwTscSU	6751	NMT	NO	56.70	0.884286	–

Table 55: SOFTWARE en-ms submissions

System	ID	Type	RSRC	BLEU	RIBES	AMFM
HwTscSU	6752	NMT	NO	45.50	0.819582	–

Table 56: SOFTWARE ms-en submissions

System	ID	Type	RSRC	BLEU			RIBES			AMFM
				juman	kytea	mecab	juman	kytea	mecab	
ORGANIZER	6806	NMT	NO	–	–	40.27	–	–	–	–
NICT-5	6821	NMT	NO	–	–	36.84	–	–	–	–
NICT-5	6974	NMT	NO	–	–	37.54	–	–	–	–

Table 57: SWSTR22 en-ja submissions

System	ID	Type	RSRC	BLEU	RIBES	AMFM
ORGANIZER	6809	NMT	NO	21.87	–	–
NICT-5	6823	NMT	NO	22.81	–	–
NICT-5	6976	NMT	NO	28.99	–	–

Table 58: SWSTR22 en-ko submissions

System	ID	Type	RSRC	BLEU			RIBES			AMFM
				kytea	ctb	pku	kytea	ctb	pku	
ORGANIZER	6811	NMT	NO	28.03	–	–	–	–	–	–
NICT-5	6827	NMT	NO	32.34	–	–	–	–	–	–
NICT-5	6978	NMT	NO	32.38	–	–	–	–	–	–

Table 59: SWSTR22 en-zh submissions

System	ID	Type	RSRC	BLEU	RIBES	AMFM
ORGANIZER	6807	NMT	NO	28.20	–	–
NICT-5	6822	NMT	NO	25.02	–	–
NICT-5	6975	NMT	NO	25.37	–	–

Table 60: SWSTR22 ja-en submissions

System	ID	Type	RSRC	BLEU	RIBES	AMFM
ORGANIZER	6810	NMT	NO	10.80	–	–
NICT-5	6824	NMT	NO	23.80	–	–
NICT-5	6977	NMT	NO	24.35	–	–

Table 61: SWSTR22 ko-en submissions

System	ID	Type	RSRC	BLEU	RIBES	AMFM
ORGANIZER	6812	NMT	NO	29.14	–	–
NICT-5	6826	NMT	NO	28.50	–	–
NICT-5	6979	NMT	NO	29.06	–	–

Table 62: SWSTR22 zh-en submissions

System	ID	Type	RSRC	BLEU	RIBES	AMFM
ORGANIZER	6706	OTHER	NO	14.50	0.465183	–

Table 63: VIDEOGAS ja-en submissions

Comparing BERT-based Reward Functions for Deep Reinforcement Learning in Machine Translation

Yuki Nakatani **Tomoyuki Kajiwara** **Takashi Ninomiya**
Graduate School of Science and Engineering, Ehime University, Japan
{nakatani@ai., kajiwara@, ninomiya@}cs.ehime-u.ac.jp

Abstract

In text generation tasks such as machine translation, models are generally trained using cross-entropy loss. However, mismatches between the loss function and the evaluation metric are often problematic. It is known that this problem can be addressed by direct optimization to the evaluation metric with reinforcement learning. In machine translation, previous studies have used BLEU to calculate rewards for reinforcement learning, but BLEU is not well correlated with human evaluation. In this study, we investigate the impact on machine translation quality through reinforcement learning based on metrics that are more highly correlated with human evaluation. Experimental results show that reinforcement learning with BERT-based rewards can improve various evaluation metrics.

1 Introduction

Sequence-to-sequence models based on deep learning, such as attention-based LSTM (Bahdanau et al., 2015; Luong et al., 2015) and Transformer (Vaswani et al., 2017), are capable of generating fluent sentences and have been used successfully in many text generation tasks, such as machine translation (Tan et al., 2020) and text simplification (Alva-Manchego et al., 2020). Most previous studies on text generation use cross-entropy loss between references and output sentences to train the models based on maximum likelihood estimation for each token. Differentiability of cross-entropy loss enables gradient-based estimation in a supervised learning framework, but it has a *Loss-Evaluation Mismatch* problem (Ranzato et al., 2016; Wiseman and Rush, 2016) in case of machine translation, where loss functions and evaluation metrics are not consistent, e.g., cross-entropy loss vs. BLEU (Papineni et al., 2002). That is, an output sentence that is semantically adequate may receive an unfairly low evaluation due to a superficial disagreement with the reference sentence.

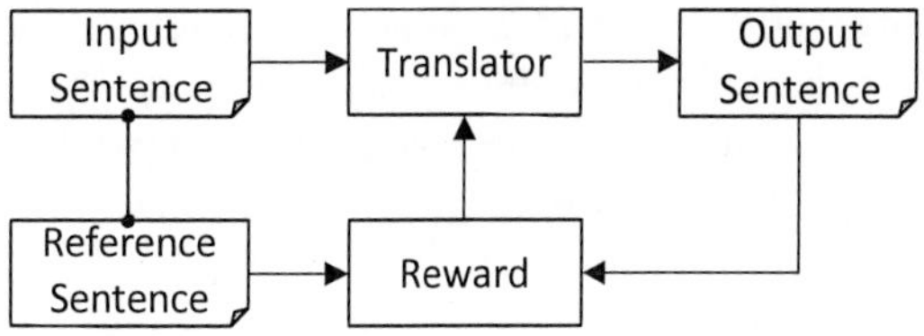

Figure 1: Machine translation based on deep reinforcement learning.

Such a Loss-Evaluation Mismatch problem (Ranzato et al., 2016; Wiseman and Rush, 2016) can be addressed by direct optimization of the evaluation metric through reinforcement learning (Williams, 1992). Since non-differentiable functions can be used as rewards in reinforcement learning, arbitrary evaluation metrics such as BLEU (Papineni et al., 2002), a word n-gram-based evaluation metric, and BLEURT (Sellam et al., 2020), an embedding-based evaluation metric, can be employed for the rewards of reinforcement learning. Performance improvements by using reinforcement learning have been reported in deep learning-based text generation, such as machine translation (Ranzato et al., 2016; Hashimoto and Tsuruoka, 2019; Yasui et al., 2019) and text simplification (Zhang and Lapata, 2017; Nakamachi et al., 2020).

In machine translation, many previous studies (Ranzato et al., 2016; Wu et al., 2018; Hashimoto and Tsuruoka, 2019; Kiegeland and Kreutzer, 2021) have used BLEU as rewards in reinforcement learning, but BLEU does not have a sufficiently high correlation with human evaluation. For machine translation metric tasks (Bojar et al., 2017), evaluation metrics have been proposed that correlate better with human evaluation than BLEU, such as chrF (Popović, 2017) and embedding-based evaluation metrics (Shimanaka et al., 2019; Zhang et al., 2020; Sellam et al., 2020) based on BERT (Devlin et al., 2019). Therefore, reward calculation using these evaluation metrics is expected to achieve further improvements in ma-

Proceedings of the 9th Workshop on Asian Translation, pages 37–43
October 17, 2022.

chine translation based on reinforcement learning.

This paper investigates the effectiveness of using surface-matching-based metrics and BERT-based metrics as the rewards for reinforcement learning in machine translation. Transformer-based machine translation models are trained in the reinforcement learning framework as shown in Figure 1. However, the action space for reinforcement learning of machine translation is very large because it deals with a vocabulary consisting of tens of thousands of tokens. Therefore, as in previous studies (Ranzato et al., 2016; Hashimoto and Tsuruoka, 2019), reinforcement learning is applied as fine-tuning to machine translation models that have been pre-trained by minimizing the cross-entropy loss. We then examine multiple metrics for both reward calculation and quality evaluation of machine translation, and investigate suitable reward functions for reinforcement learning of machine translation.

Experimental results on the IWSLT-2014 De-En translation task (Cettolo et al., 2014) revealed that reinforcement learning with BLEU as a reward function can only improve evaluation metrics based on surface matching, BLEU and chrF. On the other hand, reinforcement learning using BERT-based metrics as reward functions, such as BLEURT and BERT fine-tuned on the Semantic Textual Similarity (STS) estimation tasks (Cer et al., 2017), improved various metrics.

2 Reinforcement Learning for Machine Translation

In this study, pre-trained machine translation models are fine-tuned by deep reinforcement learning using various evaluation metrics as rewards. Section 2.1 describes pre-training of the machine translation model, followed by fine-tuning with reinforcement learning in Section 2.2, and finally, Section 2.3 outlines a machine translation metrics as a reward function for reinforcement learning.

2.1 Pre-training

The neural machine translation model consists of an encoder that encodes input sentences and a decoder that generates output sentences. The encoder is given a sequence of tokens of the input sentence $x = (x_0, x_1, ..., x_L)$ and outputs the hidden state $h = (h_0, h_1, ..., h_L)$. The decoder outputs the token sequence of the output sentence $y = (y_0, y_1, ..., y_M)$, given the hidden state h generated by the encoder. The probability of token y_t generation is maximized subject to x and $y_{<t} = (y_1, ..., y_{t-1})$. The log-likelihood of the output prediction is computed as follows.

$$\log p(y^i|x^i) = \sum_{t=1}^{M} \log p(y_t^i|y_{<t}^i, x^i) \qquad (1)$$

Pre-training minimizes the following cross-entropy loss for a dataset $D = (x^1, y^1), ..., (x^N, y^N)$ consisting of input sentences x and output sentences y of length M or less.

$$L_{\text{MLE}} = -\sum_{i=1}^{N}\sum_{t=1}^{M} \log p(y_t^i|y_{<t}^i, x^i) \qquad (2)$$

2.2 Fine-tuning

REINFORCE (Williams, 1992) is used for fine-tuning machine translation models based on reinforcement learning. REINFORCE is a type of policy gradient algorithm in which a machine translation model is trained to maximize the expected reward.

The loss function for fine-tuning is obtained by weighting the log-likelihood by the reward.

$$L_R = \sum_{i=1}^{N}\sum_{t=1}^{M} (R(\hat{y}^i) - R_b) \log p(\hat{y}_t^i|\hat{y}_{<t}^i, x^i), \qquad (3)$$

where h_t is the hidden state of the decoder at time t, R is the reward function, R_b is the baseline reward, and $\hat{y}^i$ is the output sentence from the decoder. In this study, the average reward within a mini-batch is used as the baseline reward.

To stabilize the training, the following loss function is used during reinforcement learning as in previous studies (Hashimoto and Tsuruoka, 2019).

$$L = \lambda L_{\text{MLE}} + (1 - \lambda) L_R \qquad (4)$$

2.3 Rewards for Reinforcement Learning

In this study, the following evaluation metrics are used as rewards for reinforcement learning.

- BLEU[1] (Papineni et al., 2002) evaluates the surface token similarity between the output and reference sentences, using the word n-gram agreement rate.

[1] https://github.com/mjpost/sacrebleu

Reward	BLEU	Sent. BERT	BERT Reg.	SimCSE	chrF	BERTScore	BLEURT	STS BERT	Mean rank
None	33.73	75.66	0.0478	82.10	54.27	58.47	0.0639	3.654	7.75
BLEU	**34.26**	74.91	0.0202	81.93	**54.39**	58.01	0.0234	3.641	7.50
Sent. BERT	**33.78**	**75.79**	**0.0513**	**82.24**	**54.38**	**58.72**	**0.0649**	**3.656**	6.00
BERT Reg.	33.47	**75.80**	**0.0557**	**82.32**	54.25	**58.64**	**0.0681**	3.650	5.75
SimCSE	33.73	**75.84**	**0.0512**	**82.25**	**54.37**	**58.76**	**0.0669**	**3.659**	5.13
chrF	**33.90**	**75.81**	**0.0517**	**82.24**	**54.45**	**58.69**	**0.0671**	**3.657**	4.63
BERTScore	**33.96**	**75.80**	**0.0511**	**82.30**	**54.48**	**58.80**	**0.0677**	**3.658**	4.00
BLEURT	**33.85**	**75.90**	**0.0572**	**82.33**	**54.44**	**58.92**	**0.0759**	**3.660**	2.38
STS BERT	**34.09**	**76.11**	**0.0528**	**82.52**	**54.62**	**59.10**	**0.0700**	**3.684**	1.50

Table 1: Reinforcement learning performance of machine translation on IWSLT-2014 De→En task (bold indicates improvement by reinforcement learning, underlined indicates the highest value)

- chrF[1] (Popović, 2017) evaluates the surface token similarity between the output and reference sentences, using F1 scores of character n-grams and word n-grams.
- BERTScore[2] (Zhang et al., 2020) evaluates the semantic similarity between the output and reference sentences, using maximum matching of contextualized token embeddings obtained from pre-trained RoBERTa (`roberta-large`) (Liu et al., 2019).
- STS BERT (Yasui et al., 2019) evaluates the semantic similarity between the output and reference sentences, using BERT (Devlin et al., 2019) fine-tuned on the STS task (Cer et al., 2017).
- Sentence BERT[3] (Reimers and Gurevych, 2019) evaluates the semantic similarity between the output and reference sentences, using BERT fine-tuned on Natural Language Inference (NLI) task (Bowman et al., 2015).
- SimCSE[4] (Gao et al., 2021) evaluates the semantic similarity between the output and reference sentences, using RoBERTa fine-tuned by contrastive learning on sentence pairs with entailment labels in the NLI corpus as positive examples.
- BERT Regressor (Shimanaka et al., 2019) evaluates the semantic similarity between the output and reference sentences, using BERT fine-tuned on the metric task (Bojar et al., 2017).
- BLEURT[5] (Sellam et al., 2020) evaluates the semantic similarity between the output and reference sentences, using BERT pre-trained on an augmented data generated automatically by round-trip translation, and then fine-tuned on the metric task (Bojar et al., 2017).

3 Evaluation Experiments

3.1 Settings

IWSLT-2014 German-to-English task (Cettolo et al., 2014) was used for both pre-training and fine-tuning by reinforcement learning. The training dataset consists of $159,392$ sentence pairs, the validation dataset consists of $7,245$ sentence pairs, and the test dataset consists of $6,750$ sentence pairs.

Transformer (Vaswani et al., 2017) was used as the machine translation model, with 6 layers, 4 heads, 256 dimensions, and dropout rate of 0.3. In the pre-training, the optimization method was Adam (Kingma and Ba, 2015) (learning rate of 0.0003), the batch size was set to $2,048$, and the training was stopped by early stopping for BLEU on the validation data. In reinforcement learning, the optimization method was Adam (learning rate of 0.00001), $\lambda = 0.3$, batch size was 512, and training was stopped by early stopping for the evaluation metrics used as the reward. Reinforce-Joey[6] (Kiegeland and Kreutzer, 2021) was used for implementation.

The evaluation metrics in Section 2.3 were used for the reward calculation and the performance evaluation. STS BERT (Yasui et al., 2019) and BERT Regressor (Shimanaka et al., 2019) were im-

[2] `https://github.com/Tiiiger/bert_score`

[3] `https://huggingface.co/sentence-transformers/all-mpnet-base-v2`

[4] `https://huggingface.co/princeton-nlp/sup-simcse-roberta-large`

[5] `https://storage.googleapis.com/bleurt-oss/bleurt-large-512.zip`

[6] `https://github.com/samuki/reinforce-joey`

	cs-en	de-en	fi-en	lv-en	ru-en	tr-en	zh-en	Mean
BLEU	0.412	0.413	0.565	0.393	0.460	0.531	0.524	0.471
chrF	0.517	0.531	0.671	0.525	0.599	0.607	0.591	0.577
STS BERT	0.535	0.597	0.667	0.637	0.611	0.589	0.608	0.606
Sentence BERT	0.632	0.621	0.692	0.685	0.690	0.657	0.635	0.659
SimCSE	0.696	0.628	0.684	0.696	0.713	0.660	0.672	0.678
BERTScore	0.710	0.745	0.833	0.756	0.746	0.751	0.775	0.759
BERT Regressor	0.712	0.732	0.858	0.804	0.775	0.789	0.765	0.776
BLEURT	**0.845**	**0.845**	**0.870**	**0.865**	**0.861**	**0.846**	**0.860**	**0.856**

Table 2: Pearson correlations with human evaluation in the WMT-2017 Metrics task (bold indicates the best score)

plemented using $\text{BERT}_{\text{BASE}}$[7] from HuggingFace Transformers[8] (Wolf et al., 2020).

3.2 Results

Table 1 shows the experimental results. The first line, "None", is the baseline where only pre-training was performed without reinforcement learning. The comparison between the baseline and the reinforcement learning after the second line shows that the performance of all methods improved with reinforcement learning when the same evaluation metrics were used for both rewards and evaluation.

When BLEU was used as the reward, reinforcement learning improved only BLEU and chrF, i.e., surface-matching-based metrics, while performance deteriorated for the other BERT-based metrics. On the other hand, when chrF, also based on surface matching, was used as the reward, all evaluation metrics were improved by reinforcement learning.

Among the BERT-based rewards, reinforcement learning with Sentence BERT shows small improvement from the baseline model across the board, indicating that Sentence BERT is less effective. Reinforcement learning with SimCSE as the reward did not improve BLEU, and reinforcement learning with BERT Regressor as the reward resulted in worse BLEU than the baseline model.

Among the BERT-based rewards, we confirmed that the use of BERTScore, BLEURT, and STS BERT improved the performance of all the evaluation metrics tested in this study. In particular, STS BERT achieved the best performance on the majority of the evaluation metrics and was the most suitable reward function for reinforcement learning of machine translation.

[7]https://huggingface.co/bert-base-uncased

[8]https://github.com/huggingface/transformers

4 Analysis

4.1 Meta-Evaluation of Evaluation Metrics

In this section, we examine whether the evaluation metrics that were effective as rewards for reinforcement learning in the experiments in Table 1 are highly correlated with the human evaluation of machine translation. In this analysis, we investigate the Pearson correlations between evaluation metrics and human evaluation for to-English language pairs in the WMT-2017 metrics task (Bojar et al., 2017). This task covers 7 language pairs: cs-en, de-en, fi-en, lv-en, ru-en, tr-en, and zh-en. Each 560 sentence pair (output and reference sentence pairs) is evaluated by human experts.

The results of the analysis are shown in Table 2. It can be seen that BERT-based evaluation metrics have a higher correlation with human evaluation than surface-matching metrics, BLEU and chrF. In particular, BLEURT shows the best correlation with human evaluation for all language pairs. However, contrary to expectations, STS BERT, which was the best reward for reinforcement learning, had a low correlation with human evaluation.

4.2 Correlations among Evaluation Metrics

In this section, we examine whether the correlations among the evaluation metrics affect the performance evaluation of reinforcement learning. As in Section 4.1, this section investigates the Pearson correlations among the metrics for to-English language pairs in the WMT-2017 metrics task.

The results are shown in Table 3. First, it can be seen that the correlation between BLEU and the other metrics was low. Although the correlation of BLEU with chrF, based on word n-gram match-

	BLEU	STS BERT	chrF	SimCSE	Sent. BERT	BERT Reg.	BLEURT	BERTScore	Mean
BLEU	-	0.449	0.788	0.417	0.428	0.517	0.496	0.641	0.534
STS BERT	0.449	-	0.671	0.772	0.788	0.648	0.665	0.636	0.661
chrF	0.788	0.671	-	0.616	0.635	0.608	0.613	0.715	0.664
SimCSE	0.417	0.772	0.616	-	0.856	0.653	0.717	0.664	0.671
Sent. BERT	0.428	0.788	0.635	0.856	-	0.674	0.712	0.662	0.679
BERT Reg.	0.517	0.648	0.608	0.653	0.674	-	0.866	0.798	0.681
BLEURT	0.496	0.665	0.613	0.717	0.712	0.866	-	0.805	0.696
BERTScore	0.641	0.636	0.715	0.664	0.662	0.798	0.805	-	0.703

Table 3: Pearson's correlation coefficient between evaluation metrics

ing, and BERTScore, based on token-embedding matching, was relatively high, the correlation with sentence embedding-based metrics was low. These results indicates that BLEU may not be suitable sentence-based global evaluation. These characteristics of BLEU might have had effects on the low performance of BLEU in Tables 1 and 2.

Table 3 also indicates that the high performance of STS BERT in many of metrics as shown in Table 1 was unlikely due to the effect of compatibility between metrics because STS BERT tended to have relatively low correlations with other metrics.

5 Conclusion

In this study, we investigated BERT-based evaluation metrics as rewards for reinforcement learning in machine translation. The evaluation metrics can be used for both reward calculation and performance evaluation of machine translation. In the experiments, we examined the evaluation metrics in the total combination of using it as a reward and using it as a performance evaluation.

Experimental results on German-to-English translation of IWSLT-2014 show that reinforcement learning using BERT fine-tuned on STS task as a reward (STS BERT) can improve performance on many of evaluation metrics. The correlation between STS BERT and other evaluation metrics was relatively low, and this indicates that the high performance of STS BERT was unlikely due to the effect of metric compatibility. However, STS BERT has a relatively low correlation with human evaluation in the WMT-2017 metrics task and is not a good evaluation metric from this perspective.

BERTScore and BLEURT have high correlations with human evaluation and relatively high correlations with other evaluation metrics, and also improved all metrics as rewards for reinforcement learning. Therefore these metrics can also be considered good rewards.

As future work, we plan to use quality estimation (Specia et al., 2018) without reference sentences as a reward for reinforcement learning of machine translation. Rewards based on quality estimation have the potential to improve machine translation models in an unsupervised manner.

Acknowledgment

This work was supported by JSPS KAKENHI Grant Number JP20K19861. This research was also obtained from the commissioned research (No. 225) by National Institute of Information and Communications Technology (NICT), Japan.

References

Fernando Alva-Manchego, Carolina Scarton, and Lucia Specia. 2020. Data-Driven Sentence Simplification: Survey and Benchmark. *Computational Linguistics*, pages 135–187.

Dzmitry Bahdanau, Kyunghyun Cho, and Yoshua Bengio. 2015. Neural machine translation by jointly learning to align and translate. In *3rd International Conference on Learning Representations, ICLR 2015, San Diego, CA, USA, May 7-9, 2015, Conference Track Proceedings*.

Ondřej Bojar, Yvette Graham, and Amir Kamran. 2017. Results of the WMT17 Metrics Shared Task. In *Proceedings of the Second Conference on Machine Translation*, pages 489–513.

Samuel R. Bowman, Gabor Angeli, Christopher Potts, and Christopher D. Manning. 2015. A Large Annotated Corpus for Learning Natural Language Inference. In *Proceedings of the 2015 Conference on Empirical Methods in Natural Language Processing*, pages 632–642.

Daniel Cer, Mona Diab, Eneko Agirre, Iñigo Lopez-Gazpio, and Lucia Specia. 2017. SemEval-2017 Task 1: Semantic Textual Similarity Multilingual and Crosslingual Focused Evaluation. In *Proceedings of the 11th International Workshop on Semantic Evaluation*, pages 1–14.

Mauro Cettolo, Jan Niehues, Sebastian Stüker, Luisa Bentivogli, and Marcello Federico. 2014. Report on the 11th IWSLT Evaluation Campaign. In *Proceedings of the 11th International Workshop on Spoken Language Translation: Evaluation Campaign*, pages 2–17.

Jacob Devlin, Ming-Wei Chang, Kenton Lee, and Kristina Toutanova. 2019. BERT: Pre-training of Deep Bidirectional Transformers for Language Understanding. In *Proceedings of the 2019 Conference of the North American Chapter of the Association for Computational Linguistics: Human Language Technologies*, pages 4171–4186.

Tianyu Gao, Xingcheng Yao, and Danqi Chen. 2021. SimCSE: Simple Contrastive Learning of Sentence Embeddings. In *Proceedings of the 2021 Conference on Empirical Methods in Natural Language Processing*, pages 6894–6910.

Kazuma Hashimoto and Yoshimasa Tsuruoka. 2019. Accelerated Reinforcement Learning for Sentence Generation by Vocabulary Prediction. In *Proceedings of the 2019 Conference of the North American Chapter of the Association for Computational Linguistics: Human Language Technologies*, pages 3115–3125.

Samuel Kiegeland and Julia Kreutzer. 2021. Revisiting the Weaknesses of Reinforcement Learning for Neural Machine Translation. In *Proceedings of the 2021 Conference of the North American Chapter of the Association for Computational Linguistics: Human Language Technologies*, pages 1673–1681.

Diederik P. Kingma and Jimmy Lei Ba. 2015. Adam: A Method for Stochastic Optimization. In *Proceedings of the 3rd International Conference on Learning Representations*.

Yinhan Liu, Myle Ott, Naman Goyal, Jingfei Du, Mandar Joshi, Danqi Chen, Omer Levy, Mike Lewis, Luke Zettlemoyer, and Veselin Stoyanov. 2019. RoBERTa: A Robustly Optimized BERT Pretraining Approach. *arXiv:1907.11692*.

Thang Luong, Hieu Pham, and Christopher D. Manning. 2015. Effective approaches to attention-based neural machine translation. In *Proceedings of the 2015 Conference on Empirical Methods in Natural Language Processing*, pages 1412–1421, Lisbon, Portugal. Association for Computational Linguistics.

Akifumi Nakamachi, Tomoyuki Kajiwara, and Yuki Arase. 2020. Text Simplification with Reinforcement Learning Using Supervised Rewards on Grammaticality, Meaning Preservation, and Simplicity. In *Proceedings of the 1st Conference of the Asia-Pacific Chapter of the Association for Computational Linguistics and the 10th International Joint Conference on Natural Language Processing: Student Research Workshop*, pages 153–159.

Kishore Papineni, Salim Roukos, Todd Ward, and Wei-Jing Zhu. 2002. BLEU: a Method for Automatic Evaluation of Machine Translation. In *Proceedings of the 40th Annual Meeting of the Association for Computational Linguistics*, pages 311–318.

Maja Popović. 2017. chrF++: Words Helping Character N-grams. In *Proceedings of the second conference on machine translation*, pages 612–618.

Marc'Aurelio Ranzato, Sumit Chopra, Michael Auli, and Wojciech Zaremba. 2016. Sequence Level Training with Recurrent Neural Networks. In *Proceedings of the 4th International Conference on Learning Representations*.

Nils Reimers and Iryna Gurevych. 2019. Sentence-BERT: Sentence Embeddings using Siamese BERT-Networks. In *Proceedings of the 2019 Conference on Empirical Methods in Natural Language Processing and the 9th International Joint Conference on Natural Language Processing*, pages 3982–3992.

Thibault Sellam, Dipanjan Das, and Ankur Parikh. 2020. BLEURT: Learning Robust Metrics for Text Generation. In *Proceedings of the 58th Annual Meeting of the Association for Computational Linguistics*, pages 7881–7892.

Hiroki Shimanaka, Tomoyuki Kajiwara, and Mamoru Komachi. 2019. Machine Translation Evaluation with BERT Regressor. *arXiv:1907.12679*.

Lucia Specia, Carolina Scarton, and Gustavo Henrique Paetzold. 2018. Quality Estimation for Machine Translation. *Synthesis Lectures on Human Language Technologies*, 11(1):1–162.

Zhixing Tan, Shuo Wang, Zonghan Yang, Gang Chen, Xuancheng Huang, Maosong Sun, and Yang Liu. 2020. Neural machine translation: A review of methods, resources, and tools. *AI Open*, 1:5–21.

Ashish Vaswani, Noam Shazeer, Niki Parmar, Jakob Uszkoreit, Llion Jones, Aidan N Gomez, Łukasz Kaiser, and Illia Polosukhin. 2017. Attention is All you Need. In *Advances in Neural Information Processing Systems*, pages 5998–6008.

Ronald J. Williams. 1992. Simple Statistical Gradient-Following Algorithms for Connectionist Reinforcement Learning. *Machine Learning*, pages 229–256.

Sam Wiseman and Alexander M. Rush. 2016. Sequence-to-Sequence Learning as Beam-Search Optimization. In *Proceedings of the 2016 Conference on Empirical Methods in Natural Language Processing*, pages 1296–1306.

Thomas Wolf, Lysandre Debut, Victor Sanh, Julien Chaumond, Clement Delangue, Anthony Moi, Pierric Cistac, Tim Rault, Rémi Louf, Morgan Funtowicz, Joe Davison, Sam Shleifer, Patrick von Platen, Clara Ma, Yacine Jernite, Julien Plu, Canwen Xu, Teven Le Scao, Sylvain Gugger, Mariama Drame, Quentin

Lhoest, and Alexander M. Rush. 2020. Transformers: State-of-the-Art Natural Language Processing. In *Proceedings of the 2020 Conference on Empirical Methods in Natural Language Processing: System Demonstrations*, pages 38–45.

Lijun Wu, Fei Tian, Tao Qin, Jianhuang Lai, and Tie-Yan Liu. 2018. A Study of Reinforcement Learning for Neural Machine Translation. In *Proceedings of the 2018 Conference on Empirical Methods in Natural Language Processing*, pages 3612–3621.

Go Yasui, Yoshimasa Tsuruoka, and Masaaki Nagata. 2019. Using Semantic Similarity as Reward for Reinforcement Learning in Sentence Generation. In *Proceedings of the 57th Annual Meeting of the Association for Computational Linguistics: Student Research Workshop*, pages 400–406.

Tianyi Zhang, Varsha Kishore, Felix Wu, Kilian Q. Weinberger, and Yoav Artzi. 2020. BERTScore: Evaluating Text Generation with BERT. In *Proceedings of the 8th International Conference on Learning Representations*, pages 1–43.

Xingxing Zhang and Mirella Lapata. 2017. Sentence Simplification with Deep Reinforcement Learning. In *Proceedings of the 2017 Conference on Empirical Methods in Natural Language Processing*, pages 584–594.

Improving Jejueo-Korean Translation With Cross-Lingual Pretraining Using Japanese and Korean

Francis Zheng, Edison Marrese-Taylor, Yutaka Matsuo
Graduate School of Engineering
The University of Tokyo
{francis, emarrese, matsuo}@weblab.t.u-tokyo.ac.jp

Abstract

Jejueo is a critically endangered language spoken on Jeju Island and is closely related to but mutually unintelligible with Korean. Parallel data between Jejueo and Korean is scarce, and translation between the two languages requires more attention, as current neural machine translation systems typically rely on large amounts of parallel training data. While low-resource machine translation has been shown to benefit from using additional monolingual data during the pretraining process, not as much research has been done on how to select languages other than the source and target languages for use during pretraining. We show that using large amounts of Korean and Japanese data during the pretraining process improves translation by 2.16 BLEU points for translation in the Jejueo → Korean direction and 1.34 BLEU points for translation in the Korean → Jejueo direction compared to the baseline.

1 Introduction

Low-resource machine translation has recently attracted more attention in the field of natural language processing, as neural machine translation (NMT) systems typically do not perform well for low-resource languages, where parallel data are lacking (Koehn and Knowles, 2017). Current machine translation systems typically use tens or even hundreds of millions of parallel sentences as training data, but this type of data is only available for a small number of language pairs (Haddow et al., 2022). However, there are many examples of low-resource languages that have many speakers (Haddow et al., 2022), so more attention is needed in the field of machine translation to serve speakers of these languages. Additionally, for the purpose of helping to preserve language and culture and providing equitable access to technology, it is important to improve machine translation for speakers of all languages, even those that have a small number of speakers.

Jejueo (Jeju language, ISO 639-3 language code *jje*) is a language spoken on Jeju Island, located just south of the Korean Peninsula. It is closely related to but mutually unintelligible with Korean (ISO 639-3 language code: *kor*) (Yang et al., 2020b). It was also classified as a critically endangered language by UNESCO in 2010, meaning that its youngest fluent speakers are grandparents or great-grandparents (Yang et al., 2020b). Despite academic efforts to preserve Jejueo (Yang et al., 2017; Saltzman, 2017; Yang et al., 2020a, 2018), data-driven approaches have not been explored deeply (Park et al., 2020). There are only 5,000 - 10,000 fluent speakers of Jejueo, and most of these speakers are more than 70 years old (Park et al., 2020), so it is hard to acquire Jejueo data itself, let alone parallel data between Jejueo and Korean. Despite this scarcity of data, translation between Jejueo and Korean is an important task due to their lack of mutual intelligibility.

We propose a method that uses an mBART (Liu et al., 2020) implementation of FAIRSEQ[1] (Ott et al., 2019) and leverages the use of large amounts of linguistically similar languages during pretraining to improve the accuracy of translation between Korean and Jejueo. We show that using large amounts of Japanese and Korean monolingual data during pretraining improves translation by 2.16 BLEU points in the Jejueo → Korean direction and 1.34 BLEU points in the Korean → Jejueo direction over the baseline.

2 Related Work

Park et al. (2020) published a parallel dataset for Korean and Jejueo, described later in Section 3.1.2, and used a Transformer (Vaswani et al., 2017) with six encoder and decoder blocks and eight attention heads for translation in both directions between Korean and Jejueo. The authors used FAIRSEQ (Ott

[1]https://github.com/pytorch/fairseq

Proceedings of the 9th Workshop on Asian Translation, pages 44–50
October 17, 2022.

Table 1: Monolingual Dataset Statistics

Dataset	Description	Size	Tokens
JA	Japanese	6.6 GB	1,638,553,045
KO	Korean	5.7 GB	1,603,938,119
ZH	Chinese (written in traditional characters) data	5.9 GB	2,257,606,300
MIX	A mix of monolingual data from Bulgarian, English, French, Irish, Korean, Latin, Spanish, Sundanese, Vietnamese, and Yoruba	11.5 GB	3,206,224,170

Table 2: JIT Dataset Statistics (Park et al., 2020)

	Total	Train	Dev	Test
Parallel sentences	170,356	160,356	5,000	5,000
Jejueo words	1,421,723	1,298,672	61,448	61,603
Korean words	1,421,836	1,300,489	61,541	61,806
Jejueo word forms	161,200	151,699	17,828	18,029
Korean word forms	110,774	104,874	14,362	14,595

et al., 2019) to run their experiments and SentencePiece [2] (Kudo and Richardson, 2018) for byte-pair encoding (BPE) segmentation. They experimented with different vocabulary sizes and found that a vocabulary size of 4,000 produced the best results, establishing a new baseline for translation between Jejueo and Korean. They achieved BLEU (Papineni et al., 2002) scores of 67.70 for the Jejueo → Korean direction and 43.31 for the Korean → Jejueo direction on the test set of their parallel dataset. Then, they followed an approach by Sennrich et al. (2016), who showed that machine translation models can be improved with monolingual data, and augmented "both the source and target sides of the training set with the same number of randomly sampled Korean sentences from a Wikidump" (Park et al., 2020). This improved their BLEU scores to 67.94 for the Jejueo → Korean direction and 44.19 for the Korean → Jejueo direction on the test set of their parallel dataset.

Zheng et al. (2021) explored the use of large amounts of monolingual data during the pretraining process to improve translation between low-resource languages from the Americas and Spanish. Instead of monolingual data from either the source or target language, languages from all over the world were used in this training process to expose the model to a wide variety of linguistic features, allowing for improvements of BLEU scores that were 1.64 higher and CHRF scores that were 0.0749 higher on average than the baseline for those language pairs.

We build on this work by taking a closer look at how the selection of language for these monolingual data used during the pretraining process affects translation quality in the case of translation between Jejueo and Korean. Our methods are described in the following section.

3 Methods

3.1 Data

We experimented with four sets of monolingual data described in Table 1 and Jejueo-Korean parallel data described in Table 2. Tokenization was performed as described in Section 3.2. Details on the size of and amount of tokens used from each language in the MIX dataset can be found in Table 6 in Appendix A.

3.1.1 Monolingual Data

The monolingual datasets JA, KO, ZH, and MIX were obtained from CC100[3] (Wenzek et al., 2020; Conneau et al., 2020). The Japanese dataset JA was chosen for its similarity in syntax and vocabulary to Korean and Jejueo, and the Korean dataset KO was chosen to provide more data for one side of translation between Korean and Jejueo. The Chinese dataset ZH was selected because both Korean and Jejueo (and Japanese, for that matter) have

[2] https://github.com/google/sentencepiece

[3] http://data.statmt.org/cc-100/

Table 3: Datasets Used in Pretraining

Model 1	Model 2	Model 3	Model 4	Model 5	Model 6
MIX	JA, KO, ZH	JA, KO	KO	JA	ZH

loanwords from Chinese even though Chinese has a vastly different syntax and writing system.

The dataset MIX compiles data from a variety of widely-spoken languages across the Americas, Asia, Europe, Africa, and Oceania and was included in hopes of allowing the model to learn from a wider range of language families and linguistic features.

We use these monolingual data as part of our pretraining, as this has been shown to improve results with smaller parallel datasets (Conneau and Lample, 2019; Liu et al., 2020; Song et al., 2019). Different combinations of these datasets are used in our pretraining to examine the effect of language similarity on translation accuracy after finetuning.

3.1.2 Parallel Data

Parallel data between Korean and Jejueo are from the Jejueo Interview Transcripts (JIT) dataset[4] (Park et al., 2020). These data were compiled from data from the Center for Jeju Studies, which collected data by interviewing senior Jeju citizens in Jejueo and having these interviews transcribed and translated into Korean by experts (Park et al., 2020).

3.2 Preprocessing

All data were tokenized using a unigram (Kudo, 2018) implementation of SentencePiece (Kudo and Richardson, 2018) in preparation for our multilingual model. We used a vocabulary size of 6,000 and a character coverage of 0.9995, as the languages used have a rich character set, especially the JA, KO, and ZH datasets. Separate SentencePiece models were trained for each combination of datasets shown in Table 3.

All data were then sharded for faster processing. With our SentencePiece model and vocabulary, we used FAIRSEQ (Ott et al., 2019) to build vocabularies and binarize our data.

The Jejueo-Korean parallel training, development, and test sets for finetuning and evaluating our models were the same as those used by the authors of the JIT dataset (Park et al., 2020) and are described in Table 2.

3.3 Pretraining

We pretrained six different models on different combinations (Table 3) of the datasets described in Section 3.1.1 using an mBART (Liu et al., 2020) implementation of FAIRSEQ (Ott et al., 2019). We also included 8.7 MB (160,356 sentences) of Jejeuo training data from the JIT dataset as part of the pretraining process for each combination of datasets. Each model was pretrained on 32 NVIDIA V100 GPUs for two hours.

Balancing data across languages

Due to the large variability in size amongst the different datasets used in pretraining, we used an exponential sampling technique used in Conneau and Lample (2019); Liu et al. (2020) to re-sample text according to smoothing parameter α as follows:

$$q_i = \frac{p_i^\alpha}{\sum_{j=1}^{N} p_j^\alpha} \tag{1}$$

In equation 1, q_i refers to the resampling probability for language i given a multinomial distribution $\{q_i\}_{i=1...N}$ with original sampling probability p_i.

Because we want our model to work well with low-resource languages such as Jejueo, we set the smoothing parameter α to 0.25 (instead of 0.7 as used in mBART (Liu et al., 2020)) to reduce model bias towards the higher proportion of data from high-resource languages.

Hyperparameters

Using FAIRSEQ (Ott et al., 2019), we trained our models using a Transformer (Vaswani et al., 2017) with six encoder and decoder layers with eight attention heads each, a hidden dimension of 512, a feed-forward size of 2048, and a learning rate of 0.0003. Each model was optimized using Adam (Kingma and Ba, 2015) with hyperparameters $\beta = (0.9, 0.98)$ and $\epsilon = 10^{-6}$. For regularization, we used a dropout rate of 0.1 and a weight decay of 0.01.

[4]https://www.kaggle.com/datasets/bryanpark/jit-dataset

3.4 Finetuning

We performed finetuning using the best checkpoints (chosen using loss as a metric) from each of our pretrained models on the Jejueo → Korean translation task and Korean → Jejueo translation task. Using FAIRSEQ (Ott et al., 2019), we finetuned our models using the same hyperparameters used during pretraining, except for the dropout rate, which we changed to 0.5. We found that a higher dropout rate improved the translation output from our models.

3.5 Evaluation

We evaluated translations outputted by our models with detokenized BLEU (Papineni et al., 2002; Post, 2018) using the SacreBLEU library[5] (Post, 2018) on the test data from the parallel dataset JIT. We also used CHRF (Popović, 2015) to measure performance at the character level.

4 Results and Analysis

Table 4: Jejueo → Korean Results

		BLEU	CHRF
Baseline		67.94	
Model 1	MIX	65.79	0.7664
Model 2	JA, KO, ZH	64.04	0.7542
Model 3	JA, KO	**70.10**	**0.8009**
Model 4	KO	67.61	0.7788
Model 5	JA	66.90	0.7739
Model 6	ZH	62.95	0.7436

Table 5: Korean → Jejueo Results

		BLEU	CHRF
Baseline		44.19	
Model 1	MIX	42.97	0.5665
Model 2	JA, KO, ZH	41.17	0.5553
Model 3	JA, KO	**45.53**	**0.5867**
Model 4	KO	42.58	0.5626
Model 5	JA	42.35	0.5573
Model 6	ZH	42.47	0.5608

We compiled our results in Table 4 and Table 5. The best BLEU scores on the test data achieved by the authors who published the Korean and Jejueo parallel dataset (Park et al., 2020) are displayed as a baseline. To the best of our knowledge, these baseline BLEU scores are the highest published for this dataset, and there are no existing baseline CHRF scores.

Model 3, primarily trained on Japanese and Korean data (in addition to a small amount of Jejeuo training data, as described in Section 3.3), performed the best, beating the baseline by 2.16 BLEU points for translation in the Jejueo → Korean direction and 1.34 BLEU points for translation in the Korean → Jejueo direction. Model 4, which made use of only Korean and Jejeuo data, performed similarly to the baseline, despite having employed a much larger amount of Korean data. Model 1 and Model 2 performed even worse, which suggests that pretraining using languages that are more different from Korean and Jejeuo can be detrimental to model quality. Though Model 1's Korean → Jejueo score is a bit higher than that of Model 4, there is a marked drop in score for the the Korean → Jejueo direction in Model 2 and the Jejueo → Korean direction for both Model 1 and Model 2.

Though Park et al. (2020) did not publish CHRF scores, we calculated CHRF scores to see if a similar trend could still be seen. When using CHRF scores, we can still see that Model 3 performed the best. Additionally, it still holds true that Model 4 performed better than Model 1 and Model 2 in the Jejueo → Korean direction and that Model 1 slightly beats Model 4 in the Korean → Jejueo direction followed by a steeper drop in score for Model 2 in this direction.

The similar trends in CHRF scores and BLEU scores amongst the six models suggest that the selection of languages used in the pretraining stage has a marked effect on model quality. Japanese, Korean, and Jejueo share many similar characteristics, such as having a similar syntax and having a high proportion of vocabulary of Chinese origin. While Chinese shares some vocabulary with Japanese, Korean, and Jejueo, it operates under a vastly different syntax and has a much lower degree of linguistic similarity. As can be seen from the results for Model 2, the addition of the Chinese dataset ZH may have thus hampered model quality. Model 1, which incorporates languages from all over the world, suffers from a similar issue, but the sheer variety of languages used may have helped it perform better than Model 2, as the model was exposed to a larger variety of linguistic features.

Model 4, however, also did not perform as well as Model 3 and achieved close, but not higher

[5] https://github.com/mjpost/sacrebleu

scores compared to the baseline, as it did not have enough linguistic variety from which to learn. Thus, while it is important to introduce linguistic variety to the model during pretraining, data must be selected carefully such that there is still a relatively high degree of linguistic similarity, perhaps most particularly in terms of syntax.

Model 5 and Model 6 both performed worse than Model 4, which was expected, as Korean is used in translation between Jejueo and Korean and is closely related to Jejueo itself. Model 6's performance displayed a more pronounced drop in translation quality in the Jejueo $\rightarrow$ Korean direction, performing nearly 5 BLEU points worse than the baseline and more than 7 BLEU points worse than Model 3. This marked difference is also reflected in the CHRF scores. Model 5 performed more similarly to Model 4, which may be due to the linguistic similarity between Korean and Japanese.

Model 4, Model 5, and Model 6 all performed similarly, however, in the Korean $\rightarrow$ Jejueo direction. Their performance is also similar to that of Model 1 and that of Model 2 in this direction, indicating that only a particular combination of languages can bring about a marked improvement in translation quality. Additionally, the fact that Model 1 and Model 2 achieved similar performance despite having used much more data than Model 4, Model 5, and Model 6 shows that Model 3's higher translation quality may not be due to simply having more data but instead be due to having a more advantageous combination of languages, though this needs more exploration in future work.

It is also worth noting that translation from Jejueo to Korean performs significantly better than translation from Korean to Jejueo. This is likely due to the fact that a single Korean word may have multiple translations in the Jejueo dataset while a single word in Jejueo typically corresponds to just one word in Korean. Thus, translation quality as measured by BLEU and CHRF is higher for translation in the Jejueo $\rightarrow$ Korean direction. This was also observed in Park et al. (2020)'s baseline translations. Another potential reason for this difference is the fact that Korean data outside of the parallel data was used during the pretraining process, where as no additional Jejueo data was used, giving the model overwhelmingly more exposure to Korean vocabulary and a relatively small amount of exposure to Jejueo vocabulary. Perhaps more Jejueo data is needed for the model to better learn how different Jejueo words are used in different contexts.

5 Conclusions and Future Work

We have shown how pretraining on a large amount of carefully selected monolingual data can improve the quality of translation between Korean and Jejueo, a low-resource language pair. By using Japanese and Korean data during the pretraining process, our model was exposed to some linguistic diversity beyond Korean and Jejueo from a language of relatively high linguistic similarity, allowing our model to improve translation by 2.16 BLEU points for translation in the Jejueo $\rightarrow$ Korean direction and 1.34 BLEU points for translation in the Korean $\rightarrow$ Jejueo direction in comparison to the baseline.

If enough is known linguistically about the source and target languages, it is important to carefully select additional but similar languages to use during the pretraining process. Pretraining with Korean alone and pretraining with other languages of low linguistic similarity generated models that performed worse than the baseline. Syntactic similarity may be of particular importance, as Korean, Jejueo, and Japanese all share a similar syntax while differing mostly in vocabulary. Korean, Japanese, and Jejueo are all considered synthetic SOV (subject-object-verb) languages, while Chinese is an analytic SVO language. This drastic difference in syntax may explain how using Chinese during the pretraining process resulted in a marked drop in translation quality.

Japanese, Jejueo, and Korean, however, do share many words that come from Chinese origins. For future work, we are interested in better leveraging these cognates found amongst Korean, Jejueo, and Japanese as shared representations that can be used as additional linguistic information for improving translation quality.

References

Alexis Conneau, Kartikay Khandelwal, Naman Goyal, Vishrav Chaudhary, Guillaume Wenzek, Francisco Guzmán, Edouard Grave, Myle Ott, Luke Zettlemoyer, and Veselin Stoyanov. 2020. Unsupervised cross-lingual representation learning at scale. In *Proceedings of the 58th Annual Meeting of the Association for Computational Linguistics*, pages 8440–8451, Online. Association for Computational Linguistics.

Alexis Conneau and Guillaume Lample. 2019. Cross-lingual language model pretraining. In *Advances in Neural Information Processing Systems 32: Annual Conference on Neural Information Processing Systems 2019, NeurIPS 2019, December 8-14, 2019, Vancouver, BC, Canada*, pages 7057–7067.

Barry Haddow, Rachel Bawden, Antonio Valerio Miceli Barone, Jindřich Helcl, and Alexandra Birch. 2022. Survey of Low-Resource Machine Translation. *Computational Linguistics*, pages 1–67.

Diederik P. Kingma and Jimmy Ba. 2015. Adam: A method for stochastic optimization. In *3rd International Conference on Learning Representations, ICLR 2015, San Diego, CA, USA, May 7-9, 2015, Conference Track Proceedings*.

Philipp Koehn and Rebecca Knowles. 2017. Six challenges for neural machine translation. In *Proceedings of the First Workshop on Neural Machine Translation*, pages 28–39, Vancouver. Association for Computational Linguistics.

Taku Kudo. 2018. Subword regularization: Improving neural network translation models with multiple subword candidates. In *Proceedings of the 56th Annual Meeting of the Association for Computational Linguistics (Volume 1: Long Papers)*, pages 66–75, Melbourne, Australia. Association for Computational Linguistics.

Taku Kudo and John Richardson. 2018. SentencePiece: A simple and language independent subword tokenizer and detokenizer for neural text processing. In *Proceedings of the 2018 Conference on Empirical Methods in Natural Language Processing: System Demonstrations*, pages 66–71, Brussels, Belgium. Association for Computational Linguistics.

Chunxi Liu, Qiaochu Zhang, Xiaohui Zhang, Kritika Singh, Yatharth Saraf, and Geoffrey Zweig. 2020. Multilingual graphemic hybrid ASR with massive data augmentation. In *Proceedings of the 1st Joint Workshop on Spoken Language Technologies for Under-resourced languages (SLTU) and Collaboration and Computing for Under-Resourced Languages (CCURL)*, pages 46–52, Marseille, France. European Language Resources association.

Myle Ott, Sergey Edunov, Alexei Baevski, Angela Fan, Sam Gross, Nathan Ng, David Grangier, and Michael Auli. 2019. fairseq: A fast, extensible toolkit for sequence modeling. In *Proceedings of the 2019 Conference of the North American Chapter of the Association for Computational Linguistics (Demonstrations)*, pages 48–53, Minneapolis, Minnesota. Association for Computational Linguistics.

Kishore Papineni, Salim Roukos, Todd Ward, and Wei-Jing Zhu. 2002. Bleu: a method for automatic evaluation of machine translation. In *Proceedings of the 40th Annual Meeting of the Association for Computational Linguistics*, pages 311–318, Philadelphia, Pennsylvania, USA. Association for Computational Linguistics.

Kyubyong Park, Yo Joong Choe, and Jiyeon Ham. 2020. Jejueo datasets for machine translation and speech synthesis. In *Proceedings of the 12th Language Resources and Evaluation Conference*, pages 2615–2621, Marseille, France. European Language Resources Association.

Maja Popović. 2015. chrF: character n-gram F-score for automatic MT evaluation. In *Proceedings of the Tenth Workshop on Statistical Machine Translation*, pages 392–395, Lisbon, Portugal. Association for Computational Linguistics.

Matt Post. 2018. A call for clarity in reporting BLEU scores. In *Proceedings of the Third Conference on Machine Translation: Research Papers*, pages 186–191, Brussels, Belgium. Association for Computational Linguistics.

Moira Saltzman. 2017. Jejueo talking dictionary: A collaborative online database for language revitalization. In *Proceedings of the 2nd Workshop on the Use of Computational Methods in the Study of Endangered Languages*, pages 122–129, Honolulu. Association for Computational Linguistics.

Rico Sennrich, Barry Haddow, and Alexandra Birch. 2016. Improving neural machine translation models with monolingual data. In *Proceedings of the 54th Annual Meeting of the Association for Computational Linguistics (Volume 1: Long Papers)*, pages 86–96, Berlin, Germany. Association for Computational Linguistics.

Kaitao Song, Xu Tan, Tao Qin, Jianfeng Lu, and Tie-Yan Liu. 2019. MASS: Masked sequence to sequence pre-training for language generation. In *Proceedings of the 36th International Conference on Machine Learning, ICML 2019, 9-15 June 2019, Long Beach, California, USA*, volume 97 of *Proceedings of Machine Learning Research*, pages 5926–5936. PMLR.

Ashish Vaswani, Noam Shazeer, Niki Parmar, Jakob Uszkoreit, Llion Jones, Aidan N Gomez, Ł ukasz Kaiser, and Illia Polosukhin. 2017. Attention is all you need. In *Advances in Neural Information Processing Systems*, volume 30. Curran Associates, Inc.

Guillaume Wenzek, Marie-Anne Lachaux, Alexis Conneau, Vishrav Chaudhary, Francisco Guzmán, Armand Joulin, and Edouard Grave. 2020. CCNet: Extracting high quality monolingual datasets from web crawl data. In *Proceedings of the 12th Language Resources and Evaluation Conference*, pages 4003–4012, Marseille, France. European Language Resources Association.

Changyong Yang, William O'Grady, and Sejung Yang. 2017. Toward a linguistically realistic assessment of language vitality: The case of Jejueo.

Changyong Yang, William O'Grady, Sejung Yang, Nanna Haug Hilton, Sang-Gu Kang, and So-Young Kim. 2020a. *Revising the Language Map of Korea*, pages 215–229. Springer International Publishing, Cham.

Changyong Yang, Sejung Yang, and William O'Grady. 2018. Integrating analysis and pedagogy in the revitalization of Jejueo. *Japanese-Korean Linguistics*, 25.

Changyong Yang, Sejung Yang, and William O'Grady. 2020b. *Jejueo: The Language of Korea's Jeju Island*. University of Hawai'i Press.

Francis Zheng, Machel Reid, Edison Marrese-Taylor, and Yutaka Matsuo. 2021. Low-resource machine translation using cross-lingual language model pretraining. In *Proceedings of the First Workshop on Natural Language Processing for Indigenous Languages of the Americas*, pages 234–240, Online. Association for Computational Linguistics.

A MIX Dataset Details

Table 6: MIX Dataset Statistics

	Size	Tokens
Bulgarian	2.7 GB	637,886,934
English	1.2 GB	378,524,430
French	1.3 GB	406,561,356
Irish	0.5 GB	121,007,968
Korean	1.6 GB	448,758,999
Latin	1.6 GB	496,141,311
Spanish	1.3 GB	401,305,855
Sudanese	49 MB	15,355,568
Vietnamese	1.2 GB	299,449,330
Yoruba	4.1 MB	1,232,419
Total	11.5 GB	3,206,224,170

TMU NMT System with Automatic Post-Editing by Multi-Source Levenshtein Transformer for the Restricted Translation Task of WAT 2022

Seiichiro Kondo and **Mamoru Komachi**
Tokyo Metropolitan University
kondo-seiichiro@ed.tmu.ac.jp, komachi@tmu.ac.jp

Abstract

In this paper, we describe our TMU English–Japanese systems submitted to the restricted translation task at WAT 2022 (Nakazawa et al., 2022). In this task, we translate an input sentence with the constraint that certain words or phrases (called restricted target vocabularies (RTVs)) should be contained in the output sentence. To satisfy this constraint, we address this task using a combination of two techniques. One is lexical-constraint-aware neural machine translation (LeCA) (Chen et al., 2020), which is a method of adding RTVs at the end of input sentences. The other is multi-source Levenshtein transformer (MSLevT) (Wan et al., 2020), which is a non-autoregressive method for automatic post-editing. Our system generates translations in two steps. First, we generate the translation using LeCA. Subsequently, we filter the sentences that do not satisfy the constraints and post-edit them with MSLevT. Our experimental results reveal that 100% of the RTVs can be included in the generated sentences while maintaining the translation quality of the LeCA model on both English to Japanese (En→Ja) and Japanese to English (Ja→En) tasks. Furthermore, the method used in previous studies requires an increase in the beam size to satisfy the constraints, which is computationally expensive. In contrast, the proposed method does not require a similar increase and can generate translations faster.

1 Introduction

We participated in the restricted translation task at WAT 2022. In this task, we were given pairs of an input sentence and a list of restricted target vocabularies (RTVs), wherein words or phrases are stored in a random order. Next, we were asked to generate a translated sentence for the input sentence that contained all the RTVs in the corresponding list. This setting is intended for cases where a user wishes to translate technical terms or proper nouns consistently by specifying these words in advance.

Previous studies have shown that neural machine translation (NMT) models (Sutskever et al., 2014; Bahdanau et al., 2015; Vaswani et al., 2017) exhibit high translation performance in machine translation. Additionally, studies to control output in NMT under terminological constraints have been conducted (Hasler et al., 2018; Dinu et al., 2019; Chen et al., 2020; Song et al., 2020). However, several of these studies were set up to be available a bilingual dictionary rather than only the desired words to output.

In the previous year, the first shared task of restricted translation was performed, for which Chousa and Morishita (2021) achieved the highest score (Nakazawa et al., 2021). Their proposed method combines a "soft" method (which does not ensure constraint satisfaction using data augmentation (Chen et al., 2020)) and a "hard" method (which ensures constraint word satisfaction using grid beam search (Hokamp and Liu, 2017; Post and Vilar, 2018)). Their results revealed that certain constraint terms could be satisfied with only soft methods. We speculated whether the constraints could be satisfied by correcting those that were not satisfied by automatic post-editing.

In this study, we tackled this task in two generation steps. First, we generated the translation by a soft method (lexical-constraint-aware NMT (LeCA)). Next, we filtered the sentences that did not satisfy the constraints and post-edited those with multi-source Levenshtein transformer (MSLevT) (Wan et al., 2020). In general, hard methods employs a computationally expensive decoding algorithm compared with conventional beam search. We adopted MSLevT, an efficient non-autoregressive model, as the automatic post-editting from the perspective of computational complexity. In addition, while performing post-editing in MSLevT, RTVs were provided as initial values. Subsequently, the sentences were generated with repeated modifications according to the Levenshtein

Proceedings of the 9th Workshop on Asian Translation, pages 51–58
October 17, 2022.

transformer process. The restriction of delete and insert operations to RTVs ensured that RTVs would appear in the output in the order provided as the initial value. Consequently, we had to determine the order of the RTVs in advance. We used the cosine similarity of the embedding of each word in LeCA's generated text and RTVs, which were obtained using fasttext (Bojanowski et al., 2017), to determine the order of the RTVs.

We submitted the system outputs to the En→Ja task and Ja→En tasks. We successfully included 100% of the constraint words in the system's output without significantly compromising the BLEU score of the LeCA model. We confirmed the effectiveness of the proposed method in reordering constraint words by calculating Spearman's rank correlation coefficient for the reordered constraint words and the constraint words in the reference.

2 System Overview

First, we used a baseline model called lexical-constraint-aware NMT (Chen et al., 2020), for translation that considers constraint words. However, because this method did not ensure that constraint words would appear in the generated text, automatic post-processing correction was performed on the sentences that failed to satisfy the constraints in the LeCA output to ensure that the constraints were satisfied. The automatic correction was performed by reordering the RTVs using fasttext (Bojanowski et al., 2017) and then, using MSLevT (Wan et al., 2020).

2.1 Lexical-Constraint-Aware NMT

The LeCA model is designed to induce the model to include pre-specified words in the generated sentences by data augmentation. In particular, the RTVs are concatenated at the end of the input sentence, thus ensuring that LeCA obtains the source sentence and RTVs simultaneously before the decoding step and is expected to be able to start decoding, taking into account constraint words. Furthermore, LeCA employs a pointer network, which is expected to copy the constraint words concatenated in the input sentence at the appropriate places while generating the translation.

2.2 Sorting RTV with fasttext

Synonyms of the constraint words and those close to the surface form of the constraint words tended to appear in the output of LeCA when the constraint words were not included in the output. Therefore, we addressed the reordering of the constraint words under the assumption that the words corresponding to the constraint words are included in the output of LeCA.

En	Ja
0.664	0.718

Table 1: Evaluation of the proposed RTV-sorting method by Spearman's rank correlation coefficient between the order of sorted RTVs and that of references.

We adopted the following steps to align each RTV with a word in the LeCA outputs.

1. We obtained word embeddings of each word (both RTV and LeCA output) via fasttext.

2. If the RTV is a phrase consisting of multiple words, its embedding is the average of the embeddings of each word that constitutes the RTV. Assuming that the number of words in the output range of LeCA corresponding to an RTV is equal to the number of words in the RTV, the embedding of the output words of LeCA is summarized by taking the average over the n-gram of the number of words in the RTV. We call the n-gram "word block" and regard the first word in the word block as the representative word.

3. Cosine similarity ranking is considered for the RTV and all the word blocks.

4. Essentially, the RTV is considered to correspond to the word block with the highest ranking. However, if the corresponding word block (representative word) overlaps with other RTVs, the one with a higher cosine similarity is assigned priority. The RTV discarded here is considered to correspond to the next highest ranking word block.

Note that in a few cases, the number of output words of LeCA was smaller than the total number of words of RTVs. In such cases, the RTV was reordered randomly. [1]

Table 1 lists the Spearman's rank correlation coefficients. There were calculated from the RTV order when the proposed method used, and the RTV order that appeared in the reference in the entire

[1]In our experiments, we observed only one case in the Ja→En validation data set.

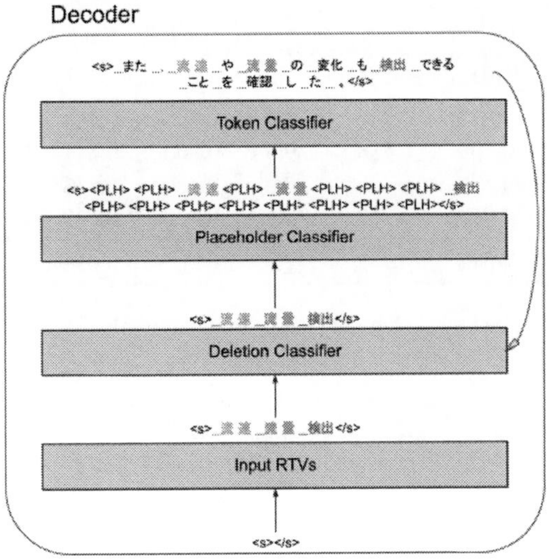

Figure 1: Decoder of Levenshtein transformers. The decoder repeats deletion, insertion, and replacement until the sentence is complete. This figure shows an example given three RTVs. The colored characters represent these. The generated Japanese sentence means "And, it was confirmed to enable also to detect change of flow rate and volume.", corresponding to "流速", "流量", and "体積" for "flow rate", "volume", and "detection", respectively.

test set. A positive correlation was observed, thus verifying the effectiveness of the proposed method.

2.3 Automatic Post-Editing by multi-source Levenshtein transformer

MSLevT has two encoders: one encoder is fed with the source sentence and the other with the output of the LeCA. Tebbifakhr et al. (2018) contends that in the APE task, a better representation of attention can be obtained by concatenating the outputs of two such encoders and subsequently passing them as an attention key.

Moreover, the decoder is provided with RTVs in parallel as initial values, and it operates similar to a Levenshtein transformer (Gu et al., 2019) (See Figure 1). The Levenshtein transformer generates sentences by repeating three phases, namely delete tokens, insert placeholders, and replace placeholders with new tokens, until the generated sentences stop varying or the number of iterations attains a pre-defined max-iteration. In the task setting in this study, both the deletion of RTVs given in the initial step and insertion of placeholders into the RTVs are undesirable. Therefore, we designed the model to prohibit these operations while generating the outputs.

2.4 Post-processing

We performed post-processing because the output of the model needed to be matched with that of the reference for submission. In particular, English words, certain symbols, and spaces in the Japanese text were normalized to full-width characters. In addition, in some cases, the model failed to recognize out-of-vocabulary characters in the constraint words that were not included in the training data and output special tokens. For these cases, we replaced the spans of constraint words that contained special tokens with constraint words.

3 Experimental Setup

3.1 Dataset

We used the provided ASPEC (Nakazawa et al., 2016) dataset. This dataset contains three million parallel sentences as training data; 1,790 parallel sentences as validation data; and 1,812 parallel sentences as test data. ASPEC training sentences are ordered by sentence alignment scores. Therefore, the sentences at the end are considered relatively noisy data. Morishita et al. (2017) reported that the translation quality of training with the original three million corpus is less than that of training with only the first two million sentences. Therefore, we used only the first two million sentences as training data.

Referring to Chousa and Morishita (2021) and Morishita et al. (2019), we tokenized both Japanese and English sentences using MeCab (Kudo et al., 2004) with the `mecab-ipadic-NEologd`[2] dictionary and `mosestokenizer` [3], respectively. Next we split these into subwords using sentencepiece (Kudo and Richardson, 2018), where the vocabulary size was set to 4,000.

3.2 Evaluation

Based on the official evaluation, we evaluated the outputs of our system using two metrics: the BLEU score (Papineni et al., 2002) and consistency score.

BLEU score. The BLEU score is calculated based on the n-gram matching rate between hypothesis and reference. We calculated it by SACREBLEU (Post, 2018).

[2] https://github.com/neologd/mecab-ipadic-neologd

[3] https://pypi.org/project/mosestokenizer/

	En→Ja			Ja→En		
	BLEU	RIBES	AMFM	BLEU	RIBES	AMFM
LeCA	51.3	0.873	0.800	39.3	0.796	0.653
LeCA + MSLevT	49.6	0.869	0.786	39.5	0.800	0.641
LeCA + MSLevT (dist→org)	49.9	0.870	0.786	39.6	0.800	0.638
LeCA + MSLevT (dist+org)	50.0	0.869	0.789	39.6	0.799	0.640
LeCA (× 5 ensemble) + MSLevT (dist+org)	52.2	0.877	0.789	41.3	0.808	0.654

Table 2: Results of the official score. Herein, "dist→org" implies that the model is pretrained with distilled data for ten steps and then finetuned by original data; and "dist+org" implies that the model is trained with mixed data consisting of distilled and original data.

	En→Ja		Ja→En	
	FS	AS	FS	AS
LeCA	37.6	4.24	23.0	4.22
LeCA + MSLevT (dist+org)	50.5	4.19	38.1	4.14
LeCA (× 5 ensemble) + MSLevT (dist+org)	52.7	4.18	40.8	4.31

Table 3: Results of human evaluation. Herein, FS denotes final score; and AS denotes adequacy scores on a 5-point scale.

Consistency score. The consistency score is the percentage of sentences in the test corpus that could be translated by including the given RTVs in the output. Whether or not an RTV is included in a sentence is determined by an exact match. While evaluating English sentences, we lowercased hypotheses and references, and performed character-based sequence matching (including white spaces).

Final score. For the final ranking, the score was calculated by combining the BLEU and consistency scores. In particular, the BLEU score was calculated with only the exact match sentences. Essentially, translations that did not satisfy the constraints were replaced to empty the string before measuring the BLEU score.

3.3 Model

LeCA. We used the Transformer big model. The implementation was based on that of Chen et al. (2020). The hyperparameters were based on the previous work of Chousa and Morishita (2021), with a learning rate of 0.001, max-token of 4,000, mini-batch size of 512,000 tokens, and the Adam optimizer.

fasttext. We used fasttext, which is available as a Python module. [4] Fasttext was learned from scratch using three million sentences of training data for Japanese and English.

multi-source LevT. We used an almost identical model and hyperparameters used in the previous study of Wan et al. (2020). However, their implementation could adversely affect the RTV when LevT performs delete and insert operations. Therefore, we modified the implementation to prohibit delete and insert operations on the RTV, referring to the implementation of Susanto et al. (2020).

In general, non-autoregressive models are known to improve the BLEU score by performing knowledge distillation (Gu et al., 2018; Zhou et al., 2020). Therefore, we prepared distilled data (which is LeCA's output as reference) for the training step. We used distilled data in two strategies, as follows. One is wherein the model is pretrained on the distilled data for ten steps and then finetuned by the original data. The other is wherein the model is trained with mixed data consisting of the distilled and original data.

4 Results

4.1 Official Evaluation

Official score Table 2 lists the official BLEU, RIBES (Isozaki et al., 2010), and AMFM (Banchs et al., 2015) scores, calculated in the evaluation server for our submissions. The results revealed

[4] `https://fasttext.cc/docs/en/python-module.html`

Model	En→Ja BLEU	En→Ja CS	En→Ja FS	Ja→En BLEU	Ja→En CS	Ja→En FS
LeCA	**52.0**	0.805	36.0	39.0	0.719	19.6
MSLevT	35.8	**1.000**	35.8	32.6	**1.000**	32.6
MSLevT (dist→org)	37.5	**1.000**	37.5	32.2	**1.000**	32.2
MSLevT (dist + org)	44.4	**1.000**	44.4	**39.4**	**1.000**	**39.4**
LeCA + MSLevT	50.1	**1.000**	50.1	39.3	**1.000**	39.3
LeCA + MSLevT (dist + org)	50.5	**1.000**	**50.5**	39.3	**1.000**	39.3

Table 4: Results of our evaluation. Herein, "dist→org" implies that the model is pretrained on the distilled data for ten steps and then, finetuned by the original data; "dist+org" implies that the model is trained with mixed data consisting of the distilled and original data; and CS and FS denote consistency score and final score, respectively.

	beam size	En→Ja sec/sent	En→Ja ratio	Ja→En sec/sent	Ja→En ratio
LeCA	5	0.094	×1.00	0.099	×1.00
	30	0.221	×2.35	0.228	×2.30
LeCA + MSLevT (proposed)	5	0.115	×1.22	0.126	×1.27

Table 5: Inference time on GPU.

that LeCA's scores were higher than those of LeCA+MSLevT. However, LeCA's output did not include 100% constraints. The use of distilled data for training MSLevT tended to be marginally more effective. The reason for the marginal improvement in scores may be that few sentences required automatic post-processing in MSLevT.

Human Evaluation Table 3 lists the human evaluation and official final scores (Nakazawa et al., 2022). Human evaluation performed adequacy scores on a 5-point scale by the WAT organization. Our proposed method has higher Final Scores [5] because it reliably includes RTVs in the output, but the adequacy of the human evaluation tends to be marginally lower.

4.2 Our Evaluation

Table 4 lists the scores obtained in our evaluation.

English to Japanese Although LeCA achieved the highest BLEU score, the consistency score was 0.805, and the final score was significantly lower by 16.0. In contrast, "MSLevT" (which is the result of passing the LeCA's output through MSLevT) exhibited a significant decrease in BLEU, although all the RTVs could be output. However, our proposed combined approach ("LeCA + MSLevT") maintained BLEU scores comparable to those of LeCA and the consistency score was 1.000.

With regard to the effectiveness of the distillation data for MSLevT, training the model with mixed data consisting of the distilled and original data is the most effective approach for improving the BLEU score. However, MSLevT's improvement by distilled data had a negligible impact on "LeCA + MSLevT" (by 0.4 points). The likely cause of this is that the revision of only the 20% texts by MSLevT is not influenced by the presence or absence of distilled data. An analysis of this aspect is for future work.

Japanese to English Although LeCA achieved a BLEU score of 39.0, the consistency score was 0.719, and the final score was significantly lower by 19.4. In contrast, "MSLevT" exhibited a decrease in BLEU, although all the RTVs could be output. However, our proposed combined approach ("LeCA + MSLevT") maintained BLEU scores comparable to those of LeCA and the consistency score was 1.000 (similar to En→Ja).

Moreover, the effectiveness of the distillation data for MSLevT exhibited a trend similar to that of En→Ja. However, the BLEU score of "MSLevT" was higher than those of "LeCA" and "LeCA +

[5]The evaluation by the organizer in the ja-en test set showed that consistency score did not reach 100%. We found that this was due to the inclusion of escape sequences in 39 sentences at submission.

MSLevT (dist + org)." This implies that for English texts, applying all the LeCA outputs to MSLevT is more effective compared with being selective.

4.3 Inference Time

In the previous study by Chousa and Morishita (2021), the authors used grid beam search to generate translations. However, they reported that the method generated repetitions when the beam size was small and could not generate all the constraint words. Therefore, they performed a preliminary experiment and determined the beam size as 30 to generate a translation that included all the constraint words. However, larger beam sizes require more inference time. In contrast, our method can satisfy the RTVs without increasing the beam size.

Table 5 lists the time required for inference by LeCA with beam sizes of 5 and 30, and that by the proposed method with 5. The experiments verified that the time required to generate the translations by the proposed method was significantly shorter than that by LeCA with a beam size of 30.

5 Related Work

NMT with terminology constraints have been studied widely. In particular, the Machine Translation using Terminologies task in WMT2021 (Akhbardeh et al., 2021) had a setting that was highly similar to that in this study. Unlike this study, WMT's task provided terminology dictionaries. Consequently, such setting-specific approaches were observed. For example, Wang et al. (2021) employed a method of replacing words in the input sentence that corresponded to constrained source words with the constrained target words. Furthermore, Ailem et al. (2021) used a selective constraint word selection method during training based on dictionaries.

Bergmanis and Pinnis (2021) worked on a similar task in a setting that was marginally looser than that in this study. They differed from the other studies in that they focused on word conjugation as well, although their approach was to replace the constraining words in the input sentence with words from the target side. They added a process of lemmatizing the words to be replaced on the target side to ensure that the model could flexibly learn conjugations.

In the previous year, Chousa and Morishita (2021) achieved the highest score in the restricted translation task in WAT2021 (Nakazawa et al., 2021). Their proposed method combines LeCA and grid beam search (Hokamp and Liu, 2017; Post and Vilar, 2018). Although grid beam search can consistently output constraint words, it incurs high computational cost and is known to adversely affect translation accuracy if a sufficient beam width is not adopted. Chousa and Morishita (2021) demonstrated that this problem can be mitigated by combining grid beam search with LeCA.

6 Conclusion

We introduced an automatic post-editing approach for the restricted translation task of WAT 2022. In our experiments, 100% of the RTVs could be included in the generated sentences while maintaining the translation quality of LeCA. Furthermore, our method does not require any preliminary experiments to determine the beam size and can generate translations faster while satisfying constraints compared with existing methods using grid beam search.

References

Melissa Ailem, Jingshu Liu, and Raheel Qader. 2021. Lingua custodia's participation at the WMT 2021 machine translation using terminologies shared task. In *Proceedings of the Sixth Conference on Machine Translation*, pages 799–803, Online. Association for Computational Linguistics.

Farhad Akhbardeh, Arkady Arkhangorodsky, Magdalena Biesialska, Ondřej Bojar, Rajen Chatterjee, Vishrav Chaudhary, Marta R. Costa-jussa, Cristina España-Bonet, Angela Fan, Christian Federmann, Markus Freitag, Yvette Graham, Roman Grundkiewicz, Barry Haddow, Leonie Harter, Kenneth Heafield, Christopher Homan, Matthias Huck, Kwabena Amponsah-Kaakyire, Jungo Kasai, Daniel Khashabi, Kevin Knight, Tom Kocmi, Philipp Koehn, Nicholas Lourie, Christof Monz, Makoto Morishita, Masaaki Nagata, Ajay Nagesh, Toshiaki Nakazawa, Matteo Negri, Santanu Pal, Allahsera Auguste Tapo, Marco Turchi, Valentin Vydrin, and Marcos Zampieri. 2021. Findings of the 2021 conference on machine translation (WMT21). In *Proceedings of the Sixth Conference on Machine Translation*, pages 1–88, Online. Association for Computational Linguistics.

Dzmitry Bahdanau, Kyunghyun Cho, and Yoshua Bengio. 2015. Neural machine translation by jointly learning to align and translate. In *Proceedings of the 3rd International Conference on Learning Representations*, San Diego, California.

Rafael E. Banchs, Luis F. D' Haro, and Haizhou Li. 2015. Adequacy–fluency metrics: Evaluating MT in the continuous space model framework. *IEEE/ACM Transactions on Audio, Speech, and Language Processing*, 23(3):472–482.

Toms Bergmanis and Mārcis Pinnis. 2021. Facilitating terminology translation with target lemma annotations. In *Proceedings of the 16th Conference of the European Chapter of the Association for Computational Linguistics: Main Volume*, pages 3105–3111, Online. Association for Computational Linguistics.

Piotr Bojanowski, Edouard Grave, Armand Joulin, and Tomas Mikolov. 2017. Enriching word vectors with subword information. *Transactions of the Association for Computational Linguistics*, 5:135–146.

Guanhua Chen, Yun Chen, Yong Wang, and Victor O.K. Li. 2020. Lexical-constraint-aware neural machine translation via data augmentation. In *Proceedings of the Twenty-Ninth International Joint Conference on Artificial Intelligence*, pages 3587–3593. International Joint Conferences on Artificial Intelligence Organization.

Katsuki Chousa and Makoto Morishita. 2021. Input augmentation improves constrained beam search for neural machine translation: NTT at WAT 2021. In *Proceedings of the 8th Workshop on Asian Translation (WAT2021)*, pages 53–61, Online. Association for Computational Linguistics.

Georgiana Dinu, Prashant Mathur, Marcello Federico, and Yaser Al-Onaizan. 2019. Training neural machine translation to apply terminology constraints. In *Proceedings of the 57th Annual Meeting of the Association for Computational Linguistics*, pages 3063–3068, Florence, Italy. Association for Computational Linguistics.

Jiatao Gu, James Bradbury, Caiming Xiong, Victor O.K. Li, and Richard Socher. 2018. Non-autoregressive neural machine translation. In *Proceedings of the 6th International Conference on Learning Representations*, Vancouver, Canada. OpenReview.net.

Jiatao Gu, Changhan Wang, and Junbo Zhao. 2019. Levenshtein transformer. In *Advances in Neural Information Processing Systems*, volume 32, pages 11181–11191. Curran Associates, Inc.

Eva Hasler, Adrià de Gispert, Gonzalo Iglesias, and Bill Byrne. 2018. Neural machine translation decoding with terminology constraints. In *Proceedings of the 2018 Conference of the North American Chapter of the Association for Computational Linguistics: Human Language Technologies, Volume 2 (Short Papers)*, pages 506–512, New Orleans, Louisiana. Association for Computational Linguistics.

Chris Hokamp and Qun Liu. 2017. Lexically constrained decoding for sequence generation using grid beam search. In *Proceedings of the 55th Annual Meeting of the Association for Computational Linguistics (Volume 1: Long Papers)*, pages 1535–1546, Vancouver, Canada. Association for Computational Linguistics.

Hideki Isozaki, Tsutomu Hirao, Kevin Duh, Katsuhito Sudoh, and Hajime Tsukada. 2010. Automatic evaluation of translation quality for distant language pairs. In *Proceedings of the 2010 Conference on Empirical Methods in Natural Language Processing*, pages 944–952, Cambridge, MA. Association for Computational Linguistics.

Taku Kudo and John Richardson. 2018. SentencePiece: A simple and language independent subword tokenizer and detokenizer for neural text processing. In *Proceedings of the 2018 Conference on Empirical Methods in Natural Language Processing: System Demonstrations*, pages 66–71, Brussels, Belgium. Association for Computational Linguistics.

Taku Kudo, Kaoru Yamamoto, and Yuji Matsumoto. 2004. Applying conditional random fields to Japanese morphological analysis. In *Proceedings of the 2004 Conference on Empirical Methods in Natural Language Processing*, pages 230–237, Barcelona, Spain. Association for Computational Linguistics.

Makoto Morishita, Jun Suzuki, and Masaaki Nagata. 2017. NTT neural machine translation systems at WAT 2017. In *Proceedings of the 4th Workshop on Asian Translation (WAT2017)*, pages 89–94, Taipei, Taiwan. Asian Federation of Natural Language Processing.

Makoto Morishita, Jun Suzuki, and Masaaki Nagata. 2019. NTT neural machine translation systems at WAT 2019. In *Proceedings of the 6th Workshop on Asian Translation*, pages 99–105, Hong Kong, China. Association for Computational Linguistics.

Toshiaki Nakazawa, Hideya Mino, Isao Goto, Raj Dabre, Shohei Higashiyama, Shantipriya Parida, Anoop Kunchukuttan, Makoto Morishita, Ondřej Bojar, Chenhui Chu, Akiko Eriguchi, Kaori Abe, Yusuke Oda, and Sadao Kurohashi. 2022. Overview of the 9th workshop on Asian translation. In *Proceedings of the 9th Workshop on Asian Translation (WAT2022)*, Gyeongju, Republic of Korea. Association for Computational Linguistics.

Toshiaki Nakazawa, Hideki Nakayama, Chenchen Ding, Raj Dabre, Shohei Higashiyama, Hideya Mino, Isao Goto, Win Pa Pa, Anoop Kunchukuttan, Shantipriya Parida, Ondřej Bojar, Chenhui Chu, Akiko Eriguchi, Kaori Abe, Yusuke Oda, and Sadao Kurohashi. 2021. Overview of the 8th workshop on Asian translation. In *Proceedings of the 8th Workshop on Asian Translation (WAT2021)*, pages 1–45, Online. Association for Computational Linguistics.

Toshiaki Nakazawa, Manabu Yaguchi, Kiyotaka Uchimoto, Masao Utiyama, Eiichiro Sumita, Sadao Kurohashi, and Hitoshi Isahara. 2016. ASPEC: Asian scientific paper excerpt corpus. In *Proceedings of the Tenth International Conference on Language Resources and Evaluation (LREC'16)*, pages 2204–2208, Portorož, Slovenia. European Language Resources Association (ELRA).

Kishore Papineni, Salim Roukos, Todd Ward, and Wei-Jing Zhu. 2002. Bleu: a method for automatic evaluation of machine translation. In *Proceedings of the 40th Annual Meeting of the Association for Computational Linguistics*, pages 311–318, Philadelphia, Pennsylvania, USA. Association for Computational Linguistics.

Matt Post. 2018. A call for clarity in reporting BLEU scores. In *Proceedings of the Third Conference on Machine Translation: Research Papers*, pages 186–191, Brussels, Belgium. Association for Computational Linguistics.

Matt Post and David Vilar. 2018. Fast lexically constrained decoding with dynamic beam allocation for neural machine translation. In *Proceedings of the 2018 Conference of the North American Chapter of the Association for Computational Linguistics: Human Language Technologies, Volume 1 (Long Papers)*, pages 1314–1324, New Orleans, Louisiana. Association for Computational Linguistics.

Kai Song, Kun Wang, Heng Yu, Yue Zhang, Zhongqiang Huang, Weihua Luo, Xiangyu Duan, and Min Zhang. 2020. Alignment-enhanced transformer for constraining NMT with pre-specified translations. In *Proceedings of the Thirty-Fourth AAAI Conference on Artificial Intelligence*, pages 8886–8893, New York City, New York. Association for the Advancement of Artificial Intelligence.

Raymond Hendy Susanto, Shamil Chollampatt, and Liling Tan. 2020. Lexically constrained neural machine translation with Levenshtein transformer. In *Proceedings of the 58th Annual Meeting of the Association for Computational Linguistics*, pages 3536–3543, Online. Association for Computational Linguistics.

Ilya Sutskever, Oriol Vinyals, and Quoc V Le. 2014. Sequence to sequence learning with neural networks. In *Advances in Neural Information Processing Systems 27*, pages 3104–3112, Montreal, Canada. Curran Associates, Inc.

Amirhossein Tebbifakhr, Ruchit Agrawal, Matteo Negri, and Marco Turchi. 2018. Multi-source transformer with combined losses for automatic post editing. In *Proceedings of the Third Conference on Machine Translation: Shared Task Papers*, pages 846–852, Belgium, Brussels. Association for Computational Linguistics.

Ashish Vaswani, Noam Shazeer, Niki Parmar, Jakob Uszkoreit, Llion Jones, Aidan N Gomez, Łukasz Kaiser, and Illia Polosukhin. 2017. Attention is all you need. In *Advances in Neural Information Processing Systems 30*, pages 5998–6008, Long Beach, California. Curran Associates, Inc.

David Wan, Chris Kedzie, Faisal Ladhak, Marine Carpuat, and Kathleen McKeown. 2020. Incorporating terminology constraints in automatic post-editing. In *Proceedings of the Fifth Conference on Machine Translation*, pages 1193–1204, Online. Association for Computational Linguistics.

Ke Wang, Shuqin Gu, Boxing Chen, Yu Zhao, Weihua Luo, and Yuqi Zhang. 2021. TermMind: Alibaba's WMT21 machine translation using terminologies task submission. In *Proceedings of the Sixth Conference on Machine Translation*, pages 851–856, Online. Association for Computational Linguistics.

Chunting Zhou, Jiatao Gu, and Graham Neubig. 2020. Understanding knowledge distillation in non-autoregressive machine translation. In *International Conference on Learning Representations*.

Domain Fine-tuning Narrows the Gap: HwTscSU's Submissions on WAT 2022 Shared Tasks

Yilun Liu[1], **Zhen Zhang**[2], **Shimin Tao**[1], **Junhui Li**[2], **Hao Yang**[1]

[1]2012 Lab, Huawei

[2]School of Computer Science and Technology, Soochow University, Suzhou, China

{liuyilun3,taoshimin,yanghao30}@huawei.com

zzhang99@stu.suda.edu.cn, lijunhui@suda.edu.cn

Abstract

In this paper we describe our submission to the shared tasks of the 9th Workshop on Asian Translation (WAT 2022) on NICT–SAP Task under the team name "HwTscSU". The tasks involve translations from 5 languages into English and vice-versa in two domains: IT domain and Wikinews domain. The purpose is to determine the feasibility of multilingualism, domain adaptation or document-level knowledge given very little to none clean parallel corpora for training. Our approach for all translation tasks mainly focus on pre-training NMT models on general datasets and fine-tuning them on domain-specific datasets. Due to the scarcity of parallel corpora, we collect and clean the OPUS dataset, including three IT domain corpora, i.e., GNOME, KDE4, and Ubuntu. We then train Transformer models on the collected datasets and fine-tune them on corresponding dev sets. The BLEU scores are greatly improved in comparison with other systems.

1 Introduction

Explorations on machine translation have come far since the era of neural machine translation (NMT) (Kalchbrenner and Blunsom, 2013). Owing to the incorporation of novel structures such as CNN (Gehring et al., 2017) and Transformer (Vaswani et al., 2017), modern NMT models are able to compete with human translation.

However, the performance of neural machine translation is often highly relevant to the size of available datasets. When the training datasets are small in quantity, performances of NMT models are often poor, especially for low-resource languages. Considering that it is often helpful, in such low-resource scenarios, to leverage monolingual or bilingual corpora from multiple languages and domains to boost translation quality, we collected a large amount of web-crawled datasets for training models in the task.

The Workshop on Asian Translation[1] (Nakazawa et al., 2022) is an open machine translation evaluation campaign focusing on Asian languages. WAT gathers and shares the resources and knowledge of Asian language translation to understand the problems to be solved for the practical tasks of machine translation technologies among all Asian countries. Among those tasks, we participated on NICT-SAP tasks which evaluate Hindi/Thai/Malay/Indonesian/Vietnamese $\leftrightarrow$ English translation in two domains: IT domain (Software Documentation) and Wikinews domain (ALT). IT domain and Wikinews are two extremely low-resource domains for machine translation, especially when concerning languages such as Hindi, Thai, Malay, Indonesian and Vietnamese. Often, in these domains, there is no clean bilingual parallel corpus at all (the IT domain), or the size of available corpora is extremely small (the Wikinews).

Both two corpora contain a lot of technical terms. Moreover, some technical terms are domain-specific and do not exist in general dictionaries. Therefore, we focus on domain adaptation for translations of both IT and Wikinews domains.

In this paper, we describe our simple approach involving Transformer pre-training and fine-tuning. We first collected and cleaned rich sentence pairs from public dataset. Following Berling Lab (Park and Lee, 2021), for both NICT-SAP IT domain and ALT domain tasks we first collected public dataset from OPUS (Tiedemann, 2012) such as but not limited to GNOME, KDE4 and Ubuntu. Then we chose G-Transformer (Bao et al., 2021) as our model and pre-train the baseline with these datasets. Finally, as fine-tuning on domain-specific dataset greatly boosts translation performance in WMT evaluation (Barrault et al., 2020; Akhbardeh et al., 2021), we fine-tuned the pre-trained models on corresponding dev set officially provided for

[1]https://lotus.kuee.kyoto-u.ac.jp/WAT/WAT2022/index.html

Proceedings of the 9th Workshop on Asian Translation, pages 59–63
October 17, 2022.

high performance for all sub-tasks. Our method obtained the new state-of-the-art results on IT-domain tasks. We ranked first place on all NICT-SAP IT domain tasks, especially achieving 10.74 improvement for English to Malay. On ALT domain tasks, we ranked first in one out of eight sub-tasks.

2 Task Description

2.1 NICT-SAP Shared Task

The NICT-SAP shared task is to translate texts between English and other five languages, that is, Hindi (Hi), Thai (Th), Malay (Ms), Indonesian (Id), and Vietnamese (Vi) in extremely low-resource conditions. The task contains two domains: IT domain and ALT domain.

The data in the Asian Language Translation (ALT) domain (Thu et al., 2016) consists of translations obtained from WikiNews which is a multilingual parallel corpus. The training, development, and test sets are provided by the WAT organizers. We filter translations that are longer than 512 tokens, resulting in fewer than 20K training sentences in all languages.

The data in the IT domain consist of translations of software documents. However, there is no clean corpus from the IT domain for training. Different from ALT domain, the WAT organizers only provide the development and test sets (Buschbeck and Exel, 2020). In this case, we collected and cleaned parallel corpora available through OPUS for training, where the domain is not fully identical with the domains of the provided dev/test sets.

The dataset sizes of two given corpora are shown in Table 1.

2.2 Evaluation Metric

We report the performance in BLEU (Papineni et al., 2002) and RIBES (Isozaki et al., 2010), which are official evaluation metrics.

3 Our Approaches

For our submissions we focus on training G-Transformer (Bao et al., 2021) on OPUS dataset from scratch and fine-tuning on dev sets. G-Transformer is developed on FairSeq (Ott et al., 2019) for document-level translation, and also supports Transformer-based sentence-level translation.

3.1 Data crawling and preprocessing

For all tasks, we pre-trained the sentence-level Transformer models on web-crawled dataset as baselines. Since the WAT organizers do not provide the training dataset for IT domain, we collect it from public dataset including GNOME, KDE4, Ubuntu,Tateoba, Tanzil, QED (Abdelali et al., 2014), tico-19, OpenSubtitles, ELRC. We download all the dataset from OPUS site and filter translations that are longer than 512 tokens. Table 2 shows the statistics of the data obtained from the site. Note that, the data obtained from GNOME, KDE4 and Ubuntu are all in the IT domain, while others are not.

3.2 Model configuration

For the NMT system, we use G-Transformer (Bao et al., 2021) to train Transformer (Vaswani et al., 2017) architecture models. We use Transformer-base as our basic model setting, which has 6 layers in both the encoder and decoder, respectively. For each layer, it consists of a multi-head attention sublayer with 8 heads. We set the max sequence length as 512 for both source and target sides. We use an effective batch size of 8192 tokens. We chose Adam (Kingma and Ba, 2015) as our optimizer, with parameters settings $\beta_1 = 0.9$, $\beta_2 = 0.98$, and warm-up steps 4000. The learning rate is set to be $5e^{-4}$ for NMT pre-training and domain fine-tuning. We set the data type to the floating point 16 for fast computation. Following Berling Lab (Park and Lee, 2021), we change the hidden layer size from 512 to 1024 and the feed forward networks from 2048 to 4096 for better performances. In both pre-training and fine-tuning, we save the checkpoints every epoch and set the early-stop patience as 10 by evaluating the loss on the dev set. Each model was trained on 2 V100 (32GB).

In preprocessing, we use Google sentencepiece library[2] to train separate SentencePiece models (Kudo, 2018) for each source-side and target-side language. Then following Berling Lab (Park and Lee, 2021), we set vocabulary size to 8,000 for English, Malaysian and Vietnamese and to 16,000 for Hindi, Indonesian and Thai. We set a character coverage to 0.995. Specifically, we only use IT domain datasets (Ubuntu, GNOME, KDE4) to train SentencePiece models.

[2] https://github.com/google/sentencepiece

Domain	Set	En-Hi	En-Th	En-Ms	En-Id	En-Vi
ALT	Train	18,088	18,088	18,088	18,087	18,088
	Test	1,018	1,018	1,018	1,018	1,018
	Dev	1,000	1,000	1,000	1,000	1,000
IT	Train	-	-	-	-	-
	Test	2,073	2,050	2,050	2,037	2,000
	Dev	2,016	2,048	2,050	2,023	2,003

Table 1: Data sizes (number of sentence pairs) for the NICT-SAP domain task provided officially after filtering.

Pair	GNOME	KDE4	Ubuntu	ELRC	TANZIL	Opensubtitles	tico-19	QED	Tatoeba
En-Hi	145,706	97,227	11,309	245	187,080	93,016	3,071	11,314	10,900
En-Th	78	70,634	3,785	236	93,540	3,281,533	-	264,677	1,162
En-Ms	299,601	87,122	120,016	1,697	122,483	1,928,345	3,071	79,697	-
En-Id	47,234	14,782	96,456	2,679	393,552	926,8181	3,071	274,581	9,967
En-Vi	149	42,782	5,056	4,273	-	3,505,276	-	338,024	5,693

Table 2: Statistics (number of sentence pairs) of parallel corpora from OPUS. The data from GNOME, KDE4, Ubuntu are IT domain.

Tasks	Pre-training	Fine-tuning
En→Hi	13.05	41.85
Hi→En	14.79	40.42
En→Th	15.81	40.44
Th→En	7.92	31.95
En→Ms	31.35	56.75
Ms→En	27.97	45.65
En→Id	42.77	59.36
Id→En	37.02	58.20
En→Vi	13.09	10.68
Vi→En	25.40	50.90

Table 3: BLEU's comparison of pre-training and fine-tuning in IT domain tasks.

4 Result

4.1 Pre-training and Fine-tuning

We pre-train the Transformer with the clean data shown in Table 2. Then we fine-tune on corresponding dev set for each sub-task. Table 3 shows the comparison of their performances in IT domain. Note that the BLEU scores are obtained by the Mosesdecoder[3] scripts rather than official results because the official would evaluate Thai language using character level BLEU. Except En→Vi, domain fine-tuning could get better performance.

4.2 NICT-SAP IT Domain Translation Task

We submitted the fine-tuned models which show the best performance. Table 4 shows the overall results on NICT-SAP IT domain. For multilingual translation, it is popular to fine-tune mBART (Liu et al., 2020) which is pre-trained on large-scale monolingual corpora in many languages. However, we simply pre-trained the models from scratch and used relatively small corpus from OPUS. Domain fine-tuning makes a huge improvement in performance and we rank first in all sub-tasks in IT domain, as shown in Table 4. After submitting the translations, we noticed that the improvement was partially due to the overlaps between the dev set and test set.

Tasks	BLEU	RIBES	Rank
En→Hi	41.70	0.74	1
Hi→En	40.20	0.73	1
En→Th	70.10	0.89	1
Th→En	31.80	0.71	1
En→Ms	56.70	0.88	1
Ms→En	45.50	0.82	1
En→Id	58.80	0.78	1
Id→En	57.20	0.78	1
En→Vi	32.70	0.68	1
Vi→En	61.50	0.84	1

Table 4: Official BLEU/RIBES scores for NICT-SAP IT domain tasks on leader-board. The rank is sorted by BLEU score.

[3]https://github.com/moses-smt/mosesdecoder

Tasks	BLEU	RIBES	Rank
En→Hi	20.30	0.74	7
Hi→En	21.30	0.76	3
En→Th	49.70	0.79	3
Th→En	16.10	0.75	3
En→Ms	43.10	0.91	3
Ms→En	38.90	0.89	3
En→Id	42.40	0.91	1
Id→En	40.00	0.89	3

Table 5: Official BLEU/RIBES scores for NICT-SAP ALT domain tasks on leader-board. The rank is sorted by BLEU score.

4.3 NICT-SAP ALT Domain Translation Task

Table 5 shows official results on NICT-SAP ALT domain. We fine-tune the pre-trained models showed in Table 3 on corresponding dev set. Although the models are not pre-trained with in-domain corpus, the performances are better than other Transformer-base models. However, there is still a gap between our models and other models which are fine-tuned from mBART (Liu et al., 2020).

4.4 Fine-tuning on Document-Level Dataset

As G-Transformer (Bao et al., 2021) is designed for document-level translation, finally we try to fine-tune the pre-trained models on the dev sets at the document-level through G-Transformer. However, fine-tuning the document-level translation model on dev sets does not achieve good performance. For example, the dev set for En↔Ms contains 210 documents. And the performance changes from 31.35 to 29.14 in BLEU and 29.97 to 33.42 on the two tasks, respectively, when moving from sentence-level fine-tuning to document-level fine-tuning. Therefore, the document-level fine-tuning is less effective than the sentence-level fine-tuning. We attribute it to two reasons. First, the number of document in dev sets is too small to properly train the new added document-level parameters. Second, with small fine-tuning set, the model is not well adopted to accept long sequences as inputs.

5 Conclusion

In this paper, we have described our translation models to the NICT-SAP translation tasks on NICT-SAP track. We first pre-train our models from scratch on the datasets from OPUS. Then we fine-tune the models on corresponding dev sets. Experimental results have shown that our model ranked firsts place for NICT-SAP IT domain tasks and achieved good performance for NICT-SAP ALT domain tasks.

References

Ahmed Abdelali, Francisco Guzman, Hassan Sajjad, and Stephan Vogel. 2014. The amara corpus: Building parallel language resources for the educational domain. In *Proceedings of the Ninth International Conference on Language Resources and Evaluation*, pages 1044–1054. European Language Resources Association.

Farhad Akhbardeh, Arkady Arkhangorodsky, Magdalena Biesialska, Ondřej Bojar, Rajen Chatterjee, Vishrav Chaudhary, Marta R. Costa-jussa, Cristina España-Bonet, Angela Fan, Christian Federmann, Markus Freitag, Yvette Graham, Roman Grundkiewicz, Barry Haddow, Leonie Harter, Kenneth Heafield, Christopher Homan, Matthias Huck, Kwabena Amponsah-Kaakyire, Jungo Kasai, Daniel Khashabi, Kevin Knight, Tom Kocmi, Philipp Koehn, Nicholas Lourie, Christof Monz, Makoto Morishita, Masaaki Nagata, Ajay Nagesh, Toshiaki Nakazawa, Matteo Negri, Santanu Pal, Allahsera Auguste Tapo, Marco Turchi, Valentin Vydrin, and Marcos Zampieri. 2021. Findings of the 2021 conference on machine translation (WMT21). In *Proceedings of the Sixth Conference on Machine Translation*, pages 1–88. Association for Computational Linguistics.

Guangsheng Bao, Yue Zhang, Zhiyang Teng, Boxing Chen, and Weihua Luo. 2021. G-transformer for document-level machine translation. In *Proceedings of the 59th Annual Meeting of the Association for Computational Linguistics and the 11th International Joint Conference on Natural Language Processing (Volume 1: Long Papers)*, pages 3442–3455. Association for Computational Linguistics.

Loïc Barrault, Magdalena Biesialska, Ondřej Bojar, Marta R. Costa-jussà, Christian Federmann, Yvette Graham, Roman Grundkiewicz, Barry Haddow, Matthias Huck, Eric Joanis, Tom Kocmi, Philipp Koehn, Chi-kiu Lo, Nikola Ljubešić, Christof Monz, Makoto Morishita, Masaaki Nagata, Toshiaki Nakazawa, Santanu Pal, Matt Post, and Marcos Zampieri. 2020. Findings of the 2020 conference on machine translation (WMT20). In *Proceedings of the Fifth Conference on Machine Translation*, pages 1–55. Association for Computational Linguistics.

Bianka Buschbeck and Miriam Exel. 2020. A parallel evaluation data set of software documentation with document structure annotation. In *Proceedings of the 7th Workshop on Asian Translation*, pages 160–169. Association for Computational Linguistics.

Jonas Gehring, Michael Auli, David Grangier, Denis Yarats, and Yann N. Dauphin. 2017. Convolutional sequence to sequence learning. In *Proceedings of the*

34th International Conference on Machine Learning, pages 1243–1252. PMLR.

Hideki Isozaki, Tsutomu Hirao, Kevin Duh, Katsuhito Sudoh, and Hajime Tsukada. 2010. Automatic evaluation of translation quality for distant language pairs. In *Proceedings of the 2010 Conference on Empirical Methods in Natural Language Processing*, pages 944–952. Association for Computational Linguistics.

Nal Kalchbrenner and Phil Blunsom. 2013. Recurrent continuous translation models. In *Proceedings of the 2013 Conference on Empirical Methods in Natural Language Processing*, pages 1700–1709. Association for Computational Linguistics.

Diederik P. Kingma and Jimmy Ba. 2015. Adam: A method for stochastic optimization. In *Proceedings of the 3rd International Conference on Learning Representations*.

Taku Kudo. 2018. Subword regularization: Improving neural network translation models with multiple subword candidates. In *Proceedings of the 56th Annual Meeting of the Association for Computational Linguistics (Volume 1: Long Papers)*, pages 66–75. Association for Computational Linguistics.

Yinhan Liu, Jiatao Gu, Naman Goyal, Xian Li, Sergey Edunov, Marjan Ghazvininejad, Mike Lewis, and Luke Zettlemoyer. 2020. Multilingual denoising pretraining for neural machine translation. *Transactions of the Association for Computational Linguistics*, 8:726–742.

Toshiaki Nakazawa, Hideya Mino, Isao Goto, Raj Dabre, Shohei Higashiyama, Shantipriya Parida, Anoop Kunchukuttan, Makoto Morishita, Ondřej Bojar, Chenhui Chu, Akiko Eriguchi, Kaori Abe, Yusuke Oda, and Sadao Kurohashi. 2022. Overview of the 9th workshop on Asian translation. In *Proceedings of the 9th Workshop on Asian Translation (WAT2022)*. Association for Computational Linguistics.

Myle Ott, Sergey Edunov, Alexei Baevski, Angela Fan, Sam Gross, Nathan Ng, David Grangier, and Michael Auli. 2019. fairseq: A fast, extensible toolkit for sequence modeling. In *Proceedings of the 2019 Conference of the North American Chapter of the Association for Computational Linguistics (Demonstrations)*, pages 48–53. Association for Computational Linguistics.

Kishore Papineni, Salim Roukos, Todd Ward, and Wei-Jing Zhu. 2002. Bleu: a method for automatic evaluation of machine translation. In *Proceedings of the 40th Annual Meeting of the Association for Computational Linguistics*, pages 311–318. Association for Computational Linguistics.

Heesoo Park and Dongjun Lee. 2021. Bering lab's submissions on WAT 2021 shared task. In *Proceedings of the 8th Workshop on Asian Translation (WAT2021)*, pages 141–145. Association for Computational Linguistics.

Ye Kyaw Thu, Win Pa Pa, Masao Utiyama, Andrew M. Finch, and Eiichiro Sumita. 2016. Introducing the asian language treebank (ALT). In *Proceedings of the Tenth International Conference on Language Resources and Evaluation LREC 2016, Portorož, Slovenia, May 23-28, 2016*. European Language Resources Association (ELRA).

Jörg Tiedemann. 2012. Parallel data, tools and interfaces in OPUS. In *Proceedings of the Eighth International Conference on Language Resources and Evaluation, LREC 2012, Istanbul, Turkey, May 23-25, 2012*, pages 2214–2218. European Language Resources Association (ELRA).

Ashish Vaswani, Noam Shazeer, Niki Parmar, Jakob Uszkoreit, Llion Jones, Aidan N. Gomez, Łukasz Kaiser, and Illia Polosukhin. 2017. Attention is all you need. In *Proceedings of NIPS*, pages 6000–6010.

NICT's Submission to the WAT 2022 Structured Document Translation Task

Raj Dabre
National Institute of Information and Communications Technology (NICT),
Kyoto, Japan
raj.dabre@nict.go.jp

Abstract

We present our submission to the structured document translation task organized by WAT 2022. In structured document translation, the key challenge is the handling of inline tags, which annotate text. Specifically, the text that is annotated by tags, should be translated in such a way that in the translation should contain the tags annotating the translation. This challenge is further compounded by the lack of training data containing sentence pairs with inline XML tag annotated content. However, to our surprise, we find that existing multilingual NMT systems are able to handle the translation of text annotated with XML tags without any explicit training on data containing said tags. Specifically, massively multilingual translation models like M2M-100 perform well despite not being explicitly trained to handle structured content. This direct translation approach is often either as good as if not better than the traditional approach of "remove tag, translate and re-inject tag" also known as the "detag-and-project" approach.

1 Introduction

Neural machine translation (Bahdanau et al., 2015) using transformers (Vaswani et al., 2017) is gradually beginning to reach a saturation point in terms of translation quality for major languages like English, French, Japanese, Chinese (Fan et al., 2021). Most existing work focus on the translation of plain text, where the sentence is translated individually or by considering its context via a document level translation approach (Miculicich et al., 2018). However, this does not directly address an important real life application: "web page translation". Web pages are structured documents containing formatted or annotated text, where the annotation is done via inline tags or XML tags. When translating web pages, care must be taken to translate not only the text but also the XML tags. For example, *This is a <b>sentence</b>.* is an example of a sentence in a structured document. Its translation in Spanish should be: *Esta es una <b>frase</b>.* where the <b> and </b> tags appropriately enclose the translation of the word *sentence* which is *frase*. The structured document translation task[1] in WAT 2022 aims at evaluating approaches for the translation of text with XML tags or inline tags. For a detailed overview of the task, kindly refer to the overview paper (Nakazawa et al., 2022).

Since NMT models are sensitive to what they are trained on, it is natural to assume that they should be exposed to examples of how to handle XML tags. Unfortunately, there is a scarcity of training data containing XML tags to train NMT models to handle structured content. Hashimoto et al. (2019) provide training data for 7 languages, but this is not possible for all languages. Therefore, the most viable solution would be the "remove tag, translate and re-inject tag" approach also known as the detag-and-project approach (Zenkel et al., 2021) shortened to DnP. The main problem with DnP is that it needs high quality word alignments and heuristic algorithms when reinserting the tags into the translation. Therefore, poor translations, poor alignments and heuristics lead to compounding errors which can negatively affect the injection process leading to poor transfer of structure.

In WAT 2022, we participated under the team name "NICT-5" where we applied the DnP approach to the structured document translation task for English to Japanese/Chinese/Korean as well as Japanese/Chinese/Korean to English translation. Given the large availability of pre-trained translation models, we decided to use the M2M-100 model. In order to compare against the DnP approach, we translated sentences containing XML tags using this model and to our surprise, this approach was able to outperform the DnP approach in some instances. Our analyses reveal that the

[1] https://lotus.kuee.kyoto-u.ac.jp/WAT/NICT-SAP-Task/index.2022.struc.html

Proceedings of the 9th Workshop on Asian Translation, pages 64–67
October 17, 2022.

DnP approach is better at transferring the XML tag structure but gives poor automatic evaluation scores in some cases as it fails to handle cases such as non-closing tags and the tag injection for words and phrases for which word alignment fails.

2 Related Work

Hashimoto et al. (2019) present a dataset from the IT domain, same as the domain of the evaluation set used in the task, that features XML markup, and corresponding results using a constrained beam search approach for decoding. They create and use training data with XML tags but we do not and instead opt to use direct translation and the detag-and-project (DnP) approaches Hanneman and Dinu (2020). The methods for tag transfer in Zenkel et al. (2021) are relevant, although their focus is on inserting tags into a fixed human translation. Although the task evaluation sets contain complete documents which can allow for context-sensitive translation, such as in Miculicich et al. (2018), and in-context evaluation (Läubli et al., 2018, amongst others), we do not focus on these aspects in our submission.

In terms of methods, according to our knowledge, we are the first to report results on tag transfer using a massively multilingual translation model like M2M-100 (Tang et al., 2021; Fan et al., 2021) which surprisingly lead to reasonable automatic evaluation scores. We also submit results for the DnP approach, but find that it does not always outperform the direct translation approach. For evaluation, WAT uses the XML-BLEU metric in accordance with Hashimoto et al. (2019) but we additionally report on the XML tag structure accuracy to better understand the limitations of the approaches we used.

3 Approaches

We use the direct translation (DiT) and the detag-and-project (DnP) approaches for our submissions.

a. Direct translation: In this approach, we directly translate the sentences with XML content in them.

b. Detag-and-project: In this approach, we use the following steps:

1. Remove the XML tags from the sentence and make a list of words and phrases which are wrapped with XML tags. In case of non-closing tags, we do not handle them.
2. Translate the plain sentences.
3. Use a word aligner to align the words between the plain sentence and its translation.
4. For each sentence, for each word or phrase obtained in step 1, get its aligned target word and phrase and wrap it with the applicable tag.

Note that the following considerations are to be made:

- For translation, the NMT model's tokenizer can handle subword segmentation.
- For word alignment, tokenizers should be used for unsegmented languages prior to alignment.
- To infer phrase alignment, we use the inside-outside algorithm from Zenkel et al. (2021) who also used an alternative approach called the min-max algorithm, but we do not use it in our submissions as we found the former to be slightly better.
- When translating content wrapped hierarchically in XML tags, the innermost tags are dealt with first.

4 Experiments

4.1 Dataset

We only use the official development and test sets (located here) provided by the organizers. We focus on translation to and from English and Japanese/Korean/Chinese. We do not consider traditional Chinese due to lack of reliable models and word aligners.

4.2 Implementation

We implement the inside-outside approach in Python along with other pre-processing scripts. For word alignment we use awesome-align (Dou and Neubig, 2021).[2] as we do not have reliable training data for word alignment. awesome-align uses mBERT[3] and is known to work well even without using fine-tuning to improve alignment quality. For tokenization prior to word alignment, we use mecab for Japanese[4] and Korean[5] and Stanford

[2]https://github.com/neulab/awesome-align

[3]https://github.com/google-research/bert/blob/master/multilingual.md

[4]https://taku910.github.io/mecab/

[5]https://github.com/SamuraiT/mecab-python3

XML-BLEU						
Approach	**en→ja**	**ja→en**	**en→ko**	**ko→en**	**en→zh**	**zh→en**
DnP	36.84	25.02	22.81	23.80	32.34	28.50
DiT	36.40	18.76	**28.99**	**24.35**	**32.38**	29.06
Organizer	**40.27**	**28.20**	21.87	10.80	28.03	**29.14**

XML structure transfer accuracy (%)						
Approach	**en→ja**	**ja→en**	**en→ko**	**ko→en**	**en→zh**	**zh→en**
DnP	**84.38**	**85.35**	**86.93**	**80.24**	**85.40**	**84.16**
DiT	81.66	23.51	82.34	77.85	83.53	81.26

Table 1: XML-BLEU and XML structure transfer accuracy scores for our submissions and the organizer submission. Best scores are in bold.

segmenter for Chinese[6].

4.3 Models Used

We use the M2M-100 (or M2M) 1.2 billion parameter model[7] (Fan et al., 2021) which supports 100 languages. To our knowledge, M2M was not trained to handle XML tags in sentences. We use beam search with beam size 4 and length penalty of 1.0.

4.4 Evaluation

WAT uses the XML-BLEU metric proposed by Hashimoto et al. (2019) using a modified version[8] of the publicly available repository. The modification was done to handle the XML tags specific to the evaluation sets. We use this modified code for our analyses as well. Specifically, we calculate the XML structure transfer accuracy, which indicates the number of sentences whose XML structures have been transferred into the translation. This only concerns the structure and not the content wrapped in the XML tags. There are 590 sentences in the test set with XML tags in them and the accuracy indicates the percentage of sentences with proper structure transfer.

5 Results

We present in Table 1 the XML-BLEU scores and the XML structure transfer accuracy for our submissions. In the last row, we give the organizer scores. According to their description, they seem to use am mBART model for direct translation (DiT). The results show that except for Japanese↔English translation and Chinese→English translation, our submissions are better than the organizer's submissions. The organizer scores for Japanese↔English translation are vastly better than ours for this direction, and this may be due to the ability of the mBART model they used to translate to/from Japanese better than M2M-100. Indeed, for Chinese→English translation, the gap between our best and organizers is 0.08 XML-BLEU which is negligible. For the remaining directions, our submissions are substantially better by at least 4.35 XML-BLEU.

Comparing the DnP and DiT rows for our submissions, it can be seen that except for Japanese↔English translation, DiT is slightly if not substantially better than DnP. This is quite surprising since the M2M model was never explicitly trained to handle XML tags. It is possible that the model treats the tags as rare or unknown English tokens which are usually copied as is in Japanese, Chinese and Korean translation. We leave this investigation for the future.

With regard to the XML structure transfer accuracy, it is interesting that although the XML-BLEU is higher for DnP, the structure transfer accuracy is lower. Upon some manual investigation we found the following:

- DnP is good at transferring structure but is bad at transferring it in the right place. This is due to the difficulty in aligning phrases which is affected by language divergence and word alignment quality. Using a high quality word aligner should help resolve this partially.

- Whenever DnP is unable to align words or phrases, the entire example wont count towards the structure match accuracy. This happens in case of non-closing tags which we do

[6]https://nlp.stanford.edu/software/stanford-segmenter-4.2.0.zip

[7]https://huggingface.co/facebook/m2m100_1.2B

[8]https://github.com/prajdabre/localization-xml-mt

not transfer as they do not wrap any word or phrase making it hard, if not impossible, to determine its position in the translation. However, this problem does not occur for DiP.

- DiP often hallucinates tags or discards them. Since our NMT model was not explicitly trained to handle tags, this makes sense. Some constrained decoding would be helpful here.

Overall, the DnP approach needs a lot of investment but the returns are not equivalent. Future work should focus more on the DiT approach which is end-to-end and hence more attractive.

6 Conclusion

In this paper, we describe our submissions as team "NICT-5" to the structured document translation task in WAT 2022. We used the direct translation and the detag-and-project approaches and to our surprise found that the direct translation approach outperforms detag-and-project approach slightly or substantially depending on the language pair. Our analyses reveal that the former approach has poorer tag structure transfer accuracy, but still is better than the latter approach, due to (a.) the latter's inability to handle the transfer of tags for content that can't be aligned with its translation and (b.) the latter's sensitivity to poor alignment. Rather than working to improve the detag-and-project approach, we plan to focus more on the direct translation approach with constrained generation and some additional training to handle structured content more effectively.

References

Dzmitry Bahdanau, Kyunghyun Cho, and Yoshua Bengio. 2015. Neural machine translation by jointly learning to align and translate. In *3rd International Conference on Learning Representations, ICLR 2015, San Diego, CA, USA, May 7-9, 2015, Conference Track Proceedings*.

Zi-Yi Dou and Graham Neubig. 2021. Word alignment by fine-tuning embeddings on parallel corpora. In *Proceedings of the 16th Conference of the European Chapter of the Association for Computational Linguistics: Main Volume*, pages 2112–2128, Online. Association for Computational Linguistics.

Angela Fan, Shruti Bhosale, Holger Schwenk, Zhiyi Ma, Ahmed El-Kishky, Siddharth Goyal, Mandeep Baines, Onur Celebi, Guillaume Wenzek, Vishrav Chaudhary, Naman Goyal, Tom Birch, Vitaliy Liptchinsky, Sergey Edunov, Michael Auli, and Armand Joulin. 2021. Beyond english-centric multilingual machine translation. *Journal of Machine Learning Research*, 22(107):1–48.

Greg Hanneman and Georgiana Dinu. 2020. How should markup tags be translated? In *Proceedings of the Fifth Conference on Machine Translation*, pages 1160–1173, Online. Association for Computational Linguistics.

Kazuma Hashimoto, Raffaella Buschiazzo, James Bradbury, Teresa Marshall, Richard Socher, and Caiming Xiong. 2019. A high-quality multilingual dataset for structured documentation translation. In *Proceedings of the Fourth Conference on Machine Translation (Volume 1: Research Papers)*, pages 116–127, Florence, Italy. Association for Computational Linguistics.

Samuel Läubli, Rico Sennrich, and Martin Volk. 2018. Has machine translation achieved human parity? a case for document-level evaluation. In *Proceedings of the 2018 Conference on Empirical Methods in Natural Language Processing*, pages 4791–4796, Brussels, Belgium. Association for Computational Linguistics.

Lesly Miculicich, Dhananjay Ram, Nikolaos Pappas, and James Henderson. 2018. Document-level neural machine translation with hierarchical attention networks. In *Proceedings of the 2018 Conference on Empirical Methods in Natural Language Processing*, pages 2947–2954, Brussels, Belgium. Association for Computational Linguistics.

Toshiaki Nakazawa, Hideya Mino, Isao Goto, Raj Dabre, Shohei Higashiyama, Shantipriya Parida, Anoop Kunchukuttan, Makoto Morishita, Ondřej Bojar, Chenhui Chu, Akiko Eriguchi, Kaori Abe, Yusuke Oda, and Sadao Kurohashi. 2022. Overview of the 9th workshop on Asian translation. In *Proceedings of the 9th Workshop on Asian Translation (WAT2022)*, Gyeongju, Republic of Korea. Association for Computational Linguistics.

Yuqing Tang, Chau Tran, Xian Li, Peng-Jen Chen, Naman Goyal, Vishrav Chaudhary, Jiatao Gu, and Angela Fan. 2021. Multilingual translation from denoising pre-training. In *Findings of the Association for Computational Linguistics: ACL-IJCNLP 2021*, pages 3450–3466, Online. Association for Computational Linguistics.

Ashish Vaswani, Noam Shazeer, Niki Parmar, Jakob Uszkoreit, Llion Jones, Aidan N Gomez, Ł ukasz Kaiser, and Illia Polosukhin. 2017. Attention is all you need. In *Advances in Neural Information Processing Systems*, volume 30. Curran Associates, Inc.

Thomas Zenkel, Joern Wuebker, and John DeNero. 2021. Automatic bilingual markup transfer. In *Findings of the Association for Computational Linguistics: EMNLP 2021*, pages 3524–3533, Punta Cana, Dominican Republic. Association for Computational Linguistics.

Rakuten's Participation in WAT 2022: Parallel Dataset Filtering by Leveraging Vocabulary Heterogeneity

Alberto Poncelas, Johanes Effendi, Ohnmar Htun, Sunil Kumar Yadav, Dongzhe Wang, Saurabh Jain
Rakuten Institute of Technology
Rakuten Group, Inc.
{alberto.poncelas, johanes.effendi, ohnmar.htun, sunilkumar.yadav, dongzhe.wang, saurabh.b.jain}@rakuten.com

Abstract

This paper introduces our neural machine translation system's participation in the WAT 2022 shared translation task (team ID: *sakura*). We participated in the Parallel Data Filtering Task. Our approach based on Feature Decay Algorithms achieved +1.4 and +2.4 BLEU points for English→Japanese and Japanese→English respectively compared to the model trained on the full dataset, showing the effectiveness of FDA on in-domain data selection.

1 Introduction

This paper introduces our neural machine translation (NMT) systems' participation in the 9th Workshop on Asian Translation (WAT-2022) shared translation tasks (Nakazawa et al., 2022). We participated in the Parallel Corpus Filtering Task[1] and our team id is *sakura*.

The task consists of domain specific data selection out of noisy parallel corpus mined from the web. The goal is to build English→Japanese and Japanese→English models with better performance on scientific domain. The constraint is to select the data from JParaCrawl v3.0 (Morishita et al., 2020). Only a subset of the data should be extracted and no other actions, such as transformation or augmentation, are allowed. The models built with this data are evaluated using the test set from ASPEC (Nakazawa et al., 2016), a scientific domain parallel corpus.

In our submissions, we used two independent techniques viz. feature decay algorithms (Biçici and Yuret, 2011; Biçici, 2013; Biçici and Yuret, 2015) (FDA) and log-likelihood scores. FDA based submission achieved +1.4 and +2.4 BLEU for English→Japanese and Japanese→English respectively. Log-likelihood based submission achieved +0.5 BLEU for Japanese→English direction only.

Our submission related scripts can be accessed through following public repository. [2]

2 Data Selection

In this section we detail our approach to select domain specific sentences. Our approach aimed to extract the sentences from JParaCrawl (Morishita et al., 2020) that were in-domain, based on the train set of ASPEC (Nakazawa et al., 2016).

2.1 Feature Decay Algorithms

FDA is an n-gram based data selection technique. It has shown a better performance when compared to other word-based data selection methods (Silva et al., 2018).The selection is based on n-grams, and has demonstrated good performance when used to train NMT models (Poncelas et al., 2018, 2019).

The strength of this technique is that it aims to find a balance between the number of n-grams that are present in the in-domain data and the heterogeneity of the n-grams. This is achieved by considering not only the relevance of each n-gram in the domain but also how frequently it has been selected already.

The technique iteratively selects the sentence s (from a set of candidates, initially being the full JParaCrawl set) with the highest score according to the Equation (1):

$$score(s, S_{ASPEC}, S_{sel}) = \frac{\sum_{ngr \in \{s \bigcap S_{ASPEC}\}} 0.5^{count(ngr, S_{sel})}}{\text{len(s)}} \quad (1)$$

and adding it to a set of selected sentences S_{sel}.

The in-domain n-grams of s are obtained by finding $\{s \bigcap S_{ASPEC}\}$ (i.e. the intersection with the in-domain set S_{ASPEC}). Each n-gram has a contribution towards the score inversely proportional to the number of instances in the selected set

[1] https://sites.google.com/view/wat-filtering/

[2] https://github.com/sukuya/wat2022-parallel-data-filtering

Proceedings of the 9th Workshop on Asian Translation, pages 68–72
October 17, 2022.

S_{sel}. By default, this is conducted by computing $0.5^{count(ngr,S_{sel})}$. In our system, we decided to follow this configuration although it is not necessarily the optimal (Poncelas et al., 2017; Poncelas, 2019). We leave for future work exploring different configurations and finding a better selection criterion.

The selection was executed considering the n-grams of order up to 3 on the English side only. Configurations where the selection is based on both source and target sides have been reported to achieve good results (Poncelas et al., 2022). However, on the Japanese side, it is unclear what should be considered as n-gram (e.g. character-wise or token-wise) to achieve the best performance.

Another important question is the number of sentences that should be selected. For our system, we selected 5M sentences. This decision is based on the scores of FDA presented in Figure 1. In the plot, there is a relatively sharp decrease in FDA scores after 10M. From top 10M sentences we selected 5M based purely on empirical observations by carrying out experiments using 1M, 3M, 5M and 7M sentences and ASPEC Dev set performance (see Figure 2). We were mainly focused on minimising the number of selected sentences without compromising on model performance in terms of BLEU.

2.2 Normalised Log Probability Scores

Our second submission for the task involves using the normalised log-probability scores, inspired by dual conditional cross entropy filtering (Junczys-Dowmunt, 2018). We train two separate models on ASPEC Train, one for each direction. We calculate normalised (by number of output tokens) log-probability scores using marian-scorer (Junczys-Dowmunt et al., 2018) for entire JParaCrawl using these models. We calculate the final score for a parallel sentence by summing these two log-likelihood scores. Finally, we sort the sentences based on final scores and take the top 5M (4.634M unique) sentences for our submission.

3 Model

We trained both English→Japanese and Japanese→English models. We follow the details from the organizers[3] and build transformer (Vaswani et al., 2017) models using Fairseq (Ott et al., 2019) framework. The sentences were tokenized with a SentencePiece model (Kudo and Richardson, 2018) based on BPE method with 32000 operations. We use train and dev test from ASPEC only. The size of the different datasets are reported in Table 1.

[3] https://github.com/MorinoseiMorizo/wat2022-filtering

Dataset	Size
JParaCrawl	25.7M
ASPEC Train	3M
ASPEC Dev	1.8K
ASPEC Devtest	1.8K
ASPEC Test	1.8K

Table 1: Size (number of lines) of the datasets.

Submission	BLEU		Adequacy
	Dev	Test	Test
FDA(5M)	28.8	28.4	4.31
Baseline(26M)	27.4	27.0	4.18
Marian-Score(5M)	26.7	26.1	xx

Table 2: Results: English to Japanese.

4 Results

In Table 2 and 3, we show the evaluation scores for our submissions based on BLEU metric (Papineni et al., 2002) and human evaluation (on 200 sentences selected by organizers) from ASPEC Corpus (official results). Our FDA based system is submitted for official human evaluation and is labeled as *sakura-fda* in the figures.

Figure 3 and 4 shows the detailed breakdown of adequacy scores from the organisers. No other team participated in the task, so top system summary is detailed in the Table 2 and 3.

We see that our best submission achieved +1.4 BLEU improvement over the system trained with the full JParaCrawl set (the baseline) in the English→Japanese direction and +2.4 points for Japanese→English. This is achieved by selecting 5M sentences, approximately 20% of the data. The second submission based on sum of normalised log-likelihood scores shows minor improvement of +0.5 BLEU on Japanese→English direction but

Submission	BLEU		Adequacy
	Dev	Test	Test
FDA(5M)	21.3	21.8	4.49
Marian-Score(5M)	19.5	19.9	xx
Baseline(26M)	20.6	19.4	4.35

Table 3: Results: Japanese to English.

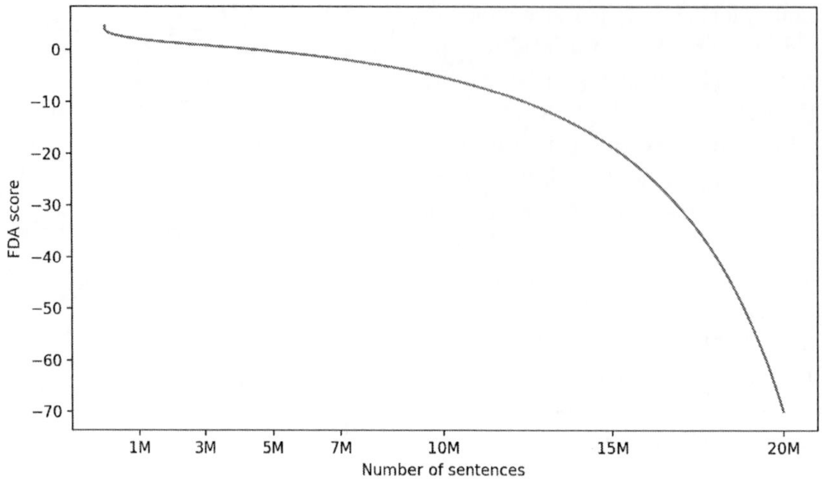

Figure 1: FDA scores of the top-20M sentences (in log scale).

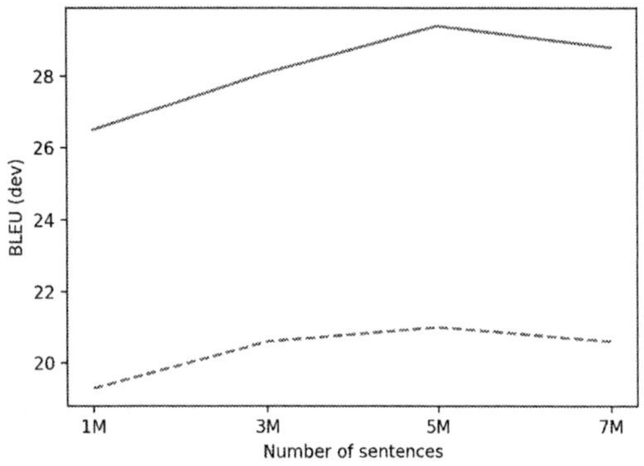

Figure 2: Evaluation of the NMT model (on dev set) built using different amount of sentences selected using FDA. The plot shows the BLEU scores for English→Japanese (blue line) and Japanese→English (dotted red line) models.

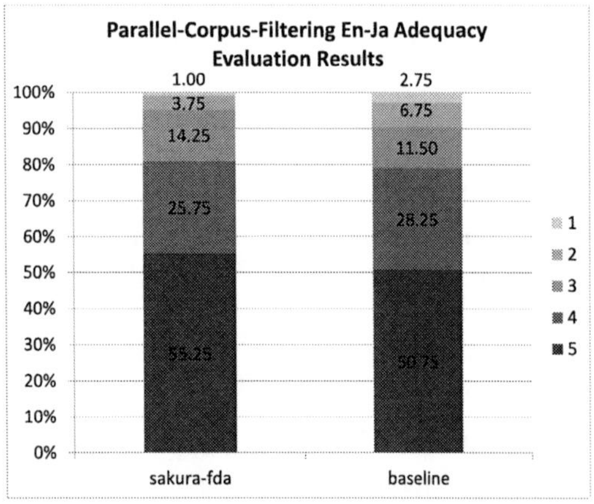

Figure 3: Adequacy evaluation results for English → Japanese.

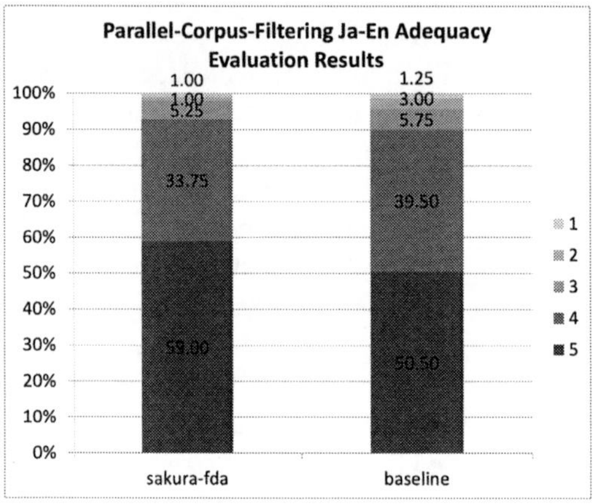

Figure 4: Adequacy evaluation results for Japanese → English.

underperforms in other direction as well as dev test.

5 Conclusion

We presented our submissions (team ID: *sakura*) to the WAT 2022 Parallel Data Filtering Task in this paper. We described our data selection system based on FDA and log-probability scores. FDA based filtering showed effectiveness in finding a subset of parallel sentences that were more useful to train a scientific-domain NMT model than using all the sentences. Our system was trained just on a 20% of the data and achieved +1.4 BLEU improvement over the baseline in the English→Japanese direction and +2.4 for Japanese→English.

As a future work, we want to use FDA in combination with the normalised log-probability scores. The work of Soto et al. (2020) demonstrated that the inclusion metrics such as lexical richness can boost the performance of FDA. More generally, we plan to explore how can we improve a scientific domain NMT model, by using limited amount of ASPEC data along with JParacrawl. The motivation is to gauge the efficacy of FDA based approach in data selection where very less in-domain data is available along with lot of noisy mixed domain data.

References

Ergun Biçici. 2013. Feature decay algorithms for fast deployment of accurate statistical machine translation systems. In *Proceedings of the Eighth Workshop on Statistical Machine Translation*, pages 78–84, Sofia, Bulgaria.

Ergun Biçici and Deniz Yuret. 2011. Instance selection for machine translation using feature decay algorithms. In *Proceedings of the Sixth Workshop on Statistical Machine Translation*, pages 272–283, Edinburgh, Scotland.

Ergun Biçici and Deniz Yuret. 2015. Optimizing instance selection for statistical machine translation with feature decay algorithms. *IEEE/ACM Transactions on Audio, Speech, and Language Processing*, 23(2):339–350.

Marcin Junczys-Dowmunt. 2018. Dual conditional cross-entropy filtering of noisy parallel corpora. In *Proceedings of the Third Conference on Machine Translation: Shared Task Papers*, pages 888–895, Belgium, Brussels. Association for Computational Linguistics.

Marcin Junczys-Dowmunt, Roman Grundkiewicz, Tomasz Dwojak, Hieu Hoang, Kenneth Heafield, Tom Neckermann, Frank Seide, Ulrich Germann, Alham Fikri Aji, Nikolay Bogoychev, André F. T. Martins, and Alexandra Birch. 2018. Marian: Fast neural machine translation in C++. In *Proceedings of ACL 2018, System Demonstrations*, pages 116–121, Melbourne, Australia. Association for Computational Linguistics.

Taku Kudo and John Richardson. 2018. SentencePiece: A simple and language independent subword tokenizer and detokenizer for neural text processing. In *Proceedings of the 2018 Conference on Empirical Methods in Natural Language Processing: System Demonstrations*, pages 66–71, Brussels, Belgium.

Makoto Morishita, Jun Suzuki, and Masaaki Nagata. 2020. JParaCrawl: A large scale web-based English-Japanese parallel corpus. In *Proceedings of The 12th Language Resources and Evaluation Conference*, pages 3603–3609, Marseille, France.

Toshiaki Nakazawa, Hideya Mino, Isao Goto, Raj Dabre, Shohei Higashiyama, Shantipriya Parida, Anoop Kunchukuttan, Makoto Morishita, Ondřej Bojar, Chenhui Chu, Akiko Eriguchi, Kaori Abe, Yusuke Oda, and Sadao Kurohashi. 2022. Overview of the 9th workshop on Asian translation. In *Proceedings of the 9th Workshop on Asian Translation (WAT2022)*, Gyeongju, Republic of Korea. Association for Computational Linguistics.

Toshiaki Nakazawa, Manabu Yaguchi, Kiyotaka Uchimoto, Masao Utiyama, Eiichiro Sumita, Sadao Kurohashi, and Hitoshi Isahara. 2016. Aspec: Asian scientific paper excerpt corpus. In *Proceedings of the Ninth International Conference on Language Resources and Evaluation (LREC 2016)*, pages 2204–2208, Portorož, Slovenia.

Myle Ott, Sergey Edunov, Alexei Baevski, Angela Fan, Sam Gross, Nathan Ng, David Grangier, and Michael Auli. 2019. fairseq: A fast, extensible toolkit for sequence modeling. In *Proceedings of the 2019 Conference of the North American Chapter of the Association for Computational Linguistics (Demonstrations)*, pages 48–53, Minneapolis, Minnesota.

Kishore Papineni, Salim Roukos, Todd Ward, and Wei-Jing Zhu. 2002. Bleu: a method for automatic evaluation of machine translation. In *Proceedings of the 40th annual meeting on association for computational linguistics*, pages 311–318, Philadelphia, Pennsylvania, USA.

Alberto Poncelas. 2019. *Improving transductive data selection algorithms for machine translation*. Ph.D. thesis, Dublin City University.

Alberto Poncelas, Gideon Maillette de Buy Wenniger, and Andy Way. 2017. Applying n-gram alignment entropy to improve feature decay algorithms. *The Prague Bulletin of Mathematical Linguistics*, 108(1):245–256.

Alberto Poncelas, Gideon Maillette de Buy Wenniger, and Andy Way. 2018. Feature decay algorithms for neural machine translation. In *21st Annual Conference of the European Association for Machine Translation*, pages 239–248, Alicante, Spain.

Alberto Poncelas, Gideon Maillette de Buy Wenniger, and Andy Way. 2019. Transductive data-selection algorithms for fine-tuning neural machine translation. In *Proceedings of The 8th Workshop on Patent and Scientific Literature Translation*, pages 13–23, Dublin, Ireland.

Alberto Poncelas, Gideon Maillette de Buy Wenniger, and Andy Way. 2022. Improved feature decay algorithms for statistical machine translation. *Natural Language Engineering*, 28:71–91.

Catarina Cruz Silva, Chao-Hong Liu, Alberto Poncelas, and Andy Way. 2018. Extracting in-domain training corpora for neural machine translation using data selection methods. In *Proceedings of the Third Conference on Machine Translation: Research Papers*, pages 224–231, Brussels, Belgium.

Xabier Soto, Dimitar Shterionov, Alberto Poncelas, and Andy Way. 2020. Selecting Backtranslated Data from Multiple Sources for Improved Neural Machine Translation. In *Proceedings of the 58th Annual Meeting of the Association for Computational Linguistics, ACL*, pages 3898–3908, Seattle, USA.

Ashish Vaswani, Noam Shazeer, Niki Parmar, Jakob Uszkoreit, Llion Jones, Aidan N Gomez, Łukasz Kaiser, and Illia Polosukhin. 2017. Attention is all you need. In *Advances in neural information processing systems*, pages 5998–6008, Long Beach, USA.

NIT Rourkela Machine Translation(MT) System Submission to WAT 2022 for MultiIndicMT: An Indic Language Multilingual Shared Task

Sudhansu Bala Das
NIT Rourkela
520cs6006@nitrkl.ac.in

Atharv Biradar
PICT Pune
atharvbiradar28@gmail.com

Tapas Kumar Mishra
NIT Rourkela
mishrat@nitrkl.ac.in

Bidyut Kumar Patra
IIT BHU
bidyut.cse@iitbhu.ac.in

Abstract

Multilingual Neural Machine Translation (MNMT) exhibits incredible performance with the development of a single translation model for many languages. Previous studies on multilingual translation reveal that multilingual training is effective for languages with limited corpus. This paper presents our submission (Team Id: NITR) in the WAT 2022 for "MultiIndicMT shared task" where the objective of the task is the translation between 5 Indic languages(which are newly added in WAT 2022 corpus) into English and vice versa using the corpus provided by the organizer of WAT. Our system is based on a transformer-based NMT using fairseq modelling toolkit with ensemble techniques. Heuristic pre-processing approaches are carried out before keeping the model under training. Our multilingual NMT systems are trained with shared encoder and decoder parameters followed by assigning language embeddings to each token in both encoder and decoder. Our final multilingual system was examined by using BLEU and RIBES metric scores.

1 Introduction

This paper illustrates the submission of the MultiIndicMT shared task at the 9th Workshop on Asian Translation (WAT 2022)(Nakazawa et al., 2022) by NIT Rourkela (Team Id: NITR). Building Machine Translation (MT) model for 5 Indic languages (Assamese(as), Sindhi(sd), Sinhala(si), Urdu(ur) and Nepali (ne)) to English and vice versa is the main goal of this shared task wherein NITR has taken part. These languages are newly added in WAT 2022 corpus. The method that is most often used in machine translation is neural machine translation (Vaswani et al., 2017), (Bahdanau et al., 2014). Language pairs with fewer parallel corpora are often subject to have poor NMT performance. This happens because of a lack of translation expertise as well as overfitting, which is unavoidable in a low-resource environment. Since many Indian languages suffer from limited resources on an individual basis, creating high-quality machine translation systems for Indian languages continues to be a difficult task. However, numerous methods, including back translation (Sennrich et al., 2015), transfer learning (Zoph et al., 2016), etc., are developed to enhance the quality of low resource language translations. Additionally, training is needed for the model in each translation direction using conventional methods. So, in order to enhance the performance of language pairs with low resources, it is standard procedure to develop Multilingual Neural Machine Translation(MNMT) models by sharing parameters with languages having high resources (Firat et al., 2016), (Johnson et al., 2017), (He et al., 2016). Hence, in this regard, the shared task for WAT 2022 MultiIndicMT's goal is to verify the usefulness of MT methods for Indian languages. We have provided two MNMT models: a) one for Indic to English and the other for b) English to Indic. NITR MT System is trained on two MNMT models (Many to One and One to Many) based on Transformer Architecture using WAT 2022 MulitIndic Corpus. Our MNMT systems are based on (Johnson et al., 2017)'s method, wherein a language-specific token is appended to the input phrase in both one-to-many and many-to-many models to identify the target language to which the model needs to convert. Our training corpus are cleaned up thoroughly by using a set of heuristics techniques because the transformer model is sensitive to training noise (Liu et al., 2018). Finally, the result are presented in terms of Bilingual Evaluation Understudy (BLEU)(Papineni et al., 2002) and Rank-based Intuitive Bilingual Evaluation Score (RIBES)(Isozaki et al., 2010). In this paper, Section 2 describes the related work which is followed by the the detail description of data set in Section 3. The experimental methodology being explained in Section 4. The findings with results are discussed

Proceedings of the 9th Workshop on Asian Translation, pages 73–77
October 17, 2022.

in Section 5, and the paper concludes in Section 6.

2 Related Work

NMT framework can naturally include numerous languages, despite the fact that the early study on NMT focused on developing translation systems between two languages. As a result, research work on MT systems, that involves more than two languages, keeps on increasing significantly. Recently, a lot of attention is paid to multilingual neural machine translation since it allows one single model to translate between different languages. A many-to-many paradigm for multi-way translation employing shared attention and language-specific encoders and decoders is presented by (Pan et al., 2021). While transfer learning occurs implicitly in multilingualism, more explicit use of fine-tuning is an approach to accomplish the same (Zoph et al., 2016). Transliteration across scripts of related languages, as discussed in (Haddow et al., 2018) (Goyal and Sharma, 2019), may enhance the quality of multilingual models. Likewise, different methods that can be utilized to implement MNMT systems are summarised by (Dabre et al., 2020). (Sun et al., 2020) employs a fixed cross-lingual embedding, a single shared encoder, and language-specific decoders. By permitting positive transfer from the high resource languages, multiple studies on Multilingual NMT emphasizes the benefits for language pairings with low resources, enhancing the quality of the low resource ones. In terms of the BLEU score, multilingual unsupervised model tends to fare better than the bilingual unsupervised baselines. Building on earlier research by (Siddhant et al., 2022), (Bapna et al., 2022) efforts are made to combine multilingual supervised MT, zero-resource MT (Firat et al., 2016), and self-supervised learning into a single model for 1000 languages. In the next section, we give detail about the dataset which we have used.

3 Dataset

We used the dataset given by the organisers for generating the parallel corpus for Assamese, Nepali, Sindhi, Sinhala and Urdu language. The organizer have shared the MultiIndicMT WAT 2022 corpora, which is made up of roughly 15 million parallel sentences for 15 language pairs. From that corpus, we have used the OPUS corpus (Tiedemann, 2012) for the language pairs of Assamese, Nepali, Sindhi, Urdu, Sinhala and English. No additional data is used from any other sources. Table 1 shows the data statistics of parallel corpus provided by WAT 2022 organizers. Urdu is having the largest number of sentences whereas Assamese and Nepali are relatively low in corpus size.

Table 1: Parallel corpora statistics

EN to Indic	Sentences
en-as	140000
en-ne	700000
en-ur	6100000
en-sd	1700000
en-si	3300000

4 Methodology

In this section, we give details about the system those are submitted to the WAT2022 for MultiIndicMT Shared Task (Nakazawa et al., 2022). We present findings for two categories of models: a) Many-En: Multilingual many-to-one system trained with all parallel data of five language pairs that are provided in WAT 2022, and b) En-Many: Multilingual many-to-one system trained with parallel data using the same corpus but in opposite direction. In this method, a shared encoder-decoder transformer architecture is employed to train our multilingual models.

4.1 Data Preprocessing

MultiIndicMT WAT 2022 corpora contains noisy sentences in many languages. So, filtering and pre-processing are carefully done to remove those. According to earlier research (Junczys-Dowmunt, 2018), a strict data filtering strategy is essential to keep quality of data. Out of many pre-processing techniques used by us, some of them are mentioned as inspired by (Li et al., 2019).

- Remove the sentence pair if either the source or the target sentence contains words longer than 35.

- If the source sentence has at least 10 characters in a different language, remove the sentence pair.

- Remove the sentence pair if the source sentence contains at least 60 % characters from a different language (UTF-8 ranges are utilised for this purpose).

- Remove sentences in which the language on the source and target sides is the same.
- Remove any sentences that have redundant translations or HTML elements.

Table 2: Filtered Parallel corpora statistics

EN to Indic	Filtered	Filtered Sentences
en-as	3.60%	134960
en-ne	5.80%	659400
en-ur	13.74%	5261860
en-sd	7.62%	1570460
en-si	11.65%	2915550

With implementation of the above techniques, We filtered the bilingual corpus accounting to approximate 8.48% sentence being filtered from the complete corpus as shown in Table 2. Then, we tokenize data for both Indian languages and English using the IndicNLP library and the Moses Tokenizer (Koehn et al., 2007) respectively.

4.2 Tokenization

Indic Languages do not share many terms at the non-root level despite having many cognates. Utilizing Indian languages at the sub-word level, which assures greater vocabulary overlap, is therefore the more effective strategy. As a result, we have used the widely accepted method of byte pair encoding (BPE) to break down each word into its sub-word parts (Sennrich et al., 2015). BPE units, which come in a variety of lengths, offer the proper context for translation systems involving related languages. Data sparsity is not an issue because their vocabularies are significantly smaller than those of the morpheme and word-level models. Learning BPE merging rules helps in a situation where numerous languages are involved. It not only helps in identifying common sub-words among them, but also ensures that each language pair is segmented properly.

5 Experimental Setup

This section describes the complete pipeline used to produce the translation systems for the WAT MultiIndic shared task submission.

5.1 Finetuning and Training

A multilingual model makes it possible to translate between several languages using a common word piece vocabulary. This is much easier than training separate models for each language pair. The Transformer(Vaswani et al., 2017) model (with 6 layers of encoder and decoder, 8 heads, 512 embedding size, and 2048 feed-forward size for each of them) is applied to implement our work. NITR MT System was trained on NVIDIA Quadro RTX 5000 machine having one GPU card. Further, for the implementation of the multilingual system, the advantage of Fairseq (Ott et al., 2019) library is considered. The method adopted by us is put forth by (Johnson et al., 2017) towards provisioning of a "language-specific token" driven technique that shares the attention mechanism and a single encoder-decoder network to create multilingual models. The input sequence includes a language token to indicate the direction of translation. Given this input, the decoder learns to produce the goal. This method, which is proven to be easy and efficient, compels the model to generalize across linguistic boundaries during training. To optimize model parameters, we have employed the Adam optimizer (Kingma and Ba, 2015).
Irrespective of time and resource constraints in order to experiment with several models, the last five checkpoints (360000–400000 iterations) are combined. Based on the correctness of the validation set, all our models are trained with early stopping criteria. After reassembling translated BPE segments during testing, the sentences translated are reverted to the previous language scripts. Lastly, the precision of our translation models is evaluated through BLEU and RIBES.

6 Results

The quality of our translation files are evaluated by the organisers using BLEU and RIBES, based on metrics on the official WAT 2022 MultiIndicMT test set (Nakazawa et al., 2022). To determine the BLEU scores of baseline models, multi-bleu.perl script is availed. When evaluating the MultiIndicMT task, organizers prefer to tokenized reference and hypothesis files to find out the BLEU score. Moses-tokenizer is used for tokenization. We present results provided by the organizers for English to Indic and Indic to English language pairs which are based on the translation files that we have submitted (Nakazawa et al., 2022). Table 3 and 4 displays the multilingual models official BLEU and RIBES scores. In terms of scores, we notice that Urdu is having more than 15 BLEU score for both

Table 3: Result of One to Many(EN -> Indic) languages considering the evaluation Metrics.

	Baseline		**Our System**	
en->Indic	**BLEU**	**RIBES**	**BLEU**	**RIBES**
en->as	-	-	10.20	0.634631
en->ur	-	-	19.60	0.718763
en->sd	-	-	6.30	0.579323
en->si	-	-	9.50	0.647028

Table 4: Result of Many to One (Indic->English) languages considering the evaluation Metrics.

	Baseline		**Our System**	
Indic->en	**BLEU**	**RIBES**	BLEU	RIBES
as->en	-	-	15.50	0.706743
ne->en	-	-	8.00	0.546125
ur->en	-	-	20.50	0.744934
sd->en	-	-	15.40	0.709039
si->en	-	-	8.20	0.632228

the directions (En->Indic and Indic->En). Because of the time and resource constraints, we were not able to work with other indic languages.

7 Conclusion

In this paper, we highlight the MultiIndicMT shared task as submitted by us to WAT 2022. Through provisioning of two multilingual NMT models, one-to-many (English to 5 Indic languages) and many-to-one (4 Indic languages to English) we get competitive outcomes. In our process, test-runs are executed combining with several pre-processing and training strategies sequentially. Although we have used sufficient data filtering techniques, still it is observed that the training data gets contaminated with noise. Therefore, investigating more efficient data filtering methods as well as their effects on MT performance is another promising future area. In future, we look forward to extend our research that will help in fine-tuning of both encoder and decoder during the monolingual unsupervised training in order to improve the quality of the synthetic data generated during the process.

References

Dzmitry Bahdanau, Kyunghyun Cho, and Yoshua Bengio. 2014. Neural machine translation by jointly learning to align and translate. *arXiv preprint arXiv:1409.0473*.

Ankur Bapna, Isaac Caswell, Julia Kreutzer, Orhan Firat, Daan van Esch, Aditya Siddhant, Mengmeng Niu, Pallavi Baljekar, Xavier Garcia, Wolfgang Macherey, et al. 2022. Building machine translation systems for the next thousand languages. *arXiv preprint arXiv:2205.03983*.

Raj Dabre, Chenhui Chu, and Anoop Kunchukuttan. 2020. A survey of multilingual neural machine translation. *ACM Computing Surveys*, pages 1–38.

Orhan Firat, Kyunghyun Cho, and Yoshua Bengio. 2016. Multi-way, multilingual neural machine translation with a shared attention mechanism. *arXiv preprint arXiv:1601.01073*.

Vikrant Goyal and Dipti Misra Sharma. 2019. The iiit-h gujarati-english machine translation system for wmt19. In *Proceedings of the Fourth Conference on Machine Translation*, pages 191–195.

Barry Haddow, Nikolay Bogoychev, Denis Emelin, Ulrich Germann, Roman Grundkiewicz, Kenneth Heafield, Antonio Valerio Miceli-Barone, and Rico Sennrich. 2018. The university of edinburgh's submissions to the wmt18 news translation task. In *Proceedings of the Third Conference on Machine Translation: Shared Task Papers*, pages 399–409.

Di He, Yingce Xia, Tao Qin, Liwei Wang, Nenghai Yu, Tie-Yan Liu, and Wei-Ying Ma. 2016. Dual learning for machine translation. *Advances in neural information processing systems*, pages 1–9.

Hideki Isozaki, Tsutomu Hirao, Kevin Duh, Katsuhito Sudoh, and Hajime Tsukada. 2010. Automatic evaluation of translation quality for distant language pairs. In *In Proceedings of conference on empirical methods in natural language processing*, pages 944–952.

Melvin Johnson, Mike Schuster, Quoc V Le, Maxim Krikun, Yonghui Wu, Zhifeng Chen, Nikhil Thorat, Fernanda Viégas, Martin Wattenberg, Greg Corrado, et al. 2017. Google's multilingual neural machine translation system: Enabling zero-shot translation.

Transactions of the Association for Computational Linguistics, pages 339–351.

Marcin Junczys-Dowmunt. 2018. Microsoft's submission to the wmt2018 news translation task: How i learned to stop worrying and love the data. *arXiv preprint arXiv:1809.00196*.

Diederik P. Kingma and Jimmy Ba. 2015. Adam: A method for stochastic optimization. *arXiv preprint arXiv:1412.6980*.

Philipp Koehn, Hieu Hoang, Alexandra Birch, Chris Callison-Burch, Marcello Federico, Nicola Bertoldi, Brooke Cowan, Wade Shen, Christine Moran, Richard Zens, Chris Dyer, Ondřej Bojar, Alexandra Constantin, and Evan Herbst. 2007. Moses: Open source toolkit for statistical machine translation. In *Proceedings of the Fourty fifth Annual Meeting of the Association for Computational Linguistics Companion Volume Proceedings of the Demo and Poster Sessions*, pages 177–180.

Bei Li, Yinqiao Li, Chen Xu, Ye Lin, Jiqiang Liu, Hui Liu, Ziyang Wang, Yuhao Zhang, Nuo Xu, and Zeyang Wang. 2019. The niutrans machine translation systems for wmt. In *Proceedings of the Fourth Conference on Machine Translation*, pages 257–266.

Hairong Liu, Mingbo Ma, Liang Huang, Hao Xiong, and Zhongjun He. 2018. Robust neural machine translation with joint textual and phonetic embedding. *arXiv preprint arXiv:1810.06729*.

Toshiaki Nakazawa, Hideya Mino, Isao Goto, Raj Dabre, Shohei Higashiyama, Shantipriya Parida, Anoop Kunchukuttan, Makoto Morishita, Ondřej Bojar, Chenhui Chu, Akiko Eriguchi, Kaori Abe, Yusuke Oda, and Sadao Kurohashi. 2022. Overview of the 9th workshop on Asian translation. In *Proceedings of the 9th Workshop on Asian Translation (WAT2022)*, Gyeongju, Republic of Korea. Association for Computational Linguistics.

Myle Ott, Sergey Edunov, Alexei Baevski, Angela Fan, Sam Gross, Nathan Ng, David Grangier, and Michael Auli. 2019. fairseq: A fast, extensible toolkit for sequence modeling. *arXiv preprint arXiv:1904.01038*.

Xiao Pan, Mingxuan Wang, Liwei Wu, and Lei Li. 2021. Contrastive learning for many-to-many multilingual neural machine translation. *arXiv preprint arXiv:2105.09501*.

Kishore Papineni, Salim Roukos, Todd Ward, and Wei-Jing Zhu. 2002. Bleu: a method for automatic evaluation of machine translation. In *Proceedings of the 40th annual meeting of the Association for Computational Linguistics*, pages 311–318.

Rico Sennrich, Barry Haddow, and Alexandra Birch. 2015. Improving neural machine translation models with monolingual data. *arXiv preprint arXiv:1511.06709*.

Aditya Siddhant, Ankur Bapna, Orhan Firat, Yuan Cao, Mia Xu Chen, Isaac Caswell, and Xavier Garcia. 2022. Towards the next 1000 languages in multilingual machine translation: Exploring the synergy between supervised and self-supervised learning. *arXiv preprint arXiv:2201.03110*.

Haipeng Sun, Rui Wang, Kehai Chen, Masao Utiyama, Eiichiro Sumita, and Tiejun Zhao. 2020. Unsupervised neural machine translation with cross-lingual language representation agreement. *ACM Transactions on Audio, Speech, and Language Processing*, pages 1170–1182.

Jörg Tiedemann. 2012. Parallel data, tools and interfaces in opus. In *Lrec*, volume 2012, pages 2214–2218. Citeseer.

Ashish Vaswani, Noam Shazeer, Niki Parmar, Jakob Uszkoreit, Llion Jones, Aidan N Gomez, Łukasz Kaiser, and Illia Polosukhin. 2017. Attention is all you need. *Advances in neural information processing systems*, 30.

Barret Zoph, Deniz Yuret, Jonathan May, and Kevin Knight. 2016. Transfer learning for low-resource neural machine translation. *arXiv preprint arXiv:1604.02201*.

Investigation of Multilingual Neural Machine Translation for Indian Languages

Sahinur Rahman Laskar[1], **Riyanka Manna**[2]
Partha Pakray[1], **Sivaji Bandyopadhyay**[1]
[1]Department of Computer Science and Engineering, National Institute of Technology, Silchar, India
[2]Department of Computer Science and Engineering, Adamas University, Kolkata, India
{sahinurlaskar.nits, riyankamanna16}@gmail.com
{parthapakray, sivaji.cse.ju}@gmail.com

Abstract

In the domain of natural language processing, machine translation is a well-defined task where one natural language is automatically translated to another natural language. The deep learning-based approach of machine translation, known as neural machine translation attains remarkable translational performance. However, it requires a sufficient amount of training data which is a critical issue for low-resource pair translation. To handle the data scarcity problem, the multilingual concept has been investigated in neural machine translation in different settings like many-to-one and one-to-many translation. WAT2022 (Workshop on Asian Translation 2022) organizes (hosted by the COLING 2022) Indic tasks: English-to-Indic and Indic-to-English translation tasks where we have participated as a team named CNLP-NITS-PP. Herein, we have investigated a transliteration-based approach, where Indic languages are transliterated into English script and shared sub-word level vocabulary during the training phase. We have attained BLEU scores of 2.0 (English-to-Bengali), 1.10 (English-to-Assamese), 4.50 (Bengali-to-English), and 3.50 (Assamese-to-English) translation, respectively.

1 Introduction

Due to the advancement of deep learning techniques, neural machine translation (NMT) attains remarkable progress for single pairs translation with a large amount of bilingual corpus (Bahdanau et al., 2015; Luong et al., 2015; Vaswani et al., 2017). Moreover, NMT shows good translational performance for low-resource Indian languages (Pathak and Pakray, 2018; Pathak et al., 2018; Laskar et al., 2019a,b, 2020, 2021b,a, 2022). Recent years, researchers have been investigating multilingual NMT from various aspects, zero-shot, pivot-based, and different settings, namely, many-to-one, one-to-many, many-to-many (Johnson et al., 2017; Tan et al., 2019). In (Ramesh et al., 2022), authors developed *Samanantar*, a parallel dataset for 11 Indian languages. They converted all Indic data into a common Devanagari script and took the advantage of lexical sharing at the sub-word level for transfer learning during the training process. They explored multilingual NMT models for English-to-Indic and vice-versa by considering language tags for indicating Indic languages on the source side (Johnson et al., 2017). Similarly, we have investigated multilingual NMT in the Indic tasks of WAT2022. The difference is that instead of converting all Indic data into a common Devanagari script, we have converted all Indic data into English script and attempted to take the benefits of lexical sharing at the sub-word level for both source and target languages.

The rest of the paper is organized as follows: Section 2 presents the review of related works. The system description is briefly discussed in Section 3. Section 4 reports the results and Section 5 concludes the paper with future scope.

2 Related Work

The literature survey finds out very limited work on multilingual NMT, specifically, for English-to-Indic and Indic-to-English translation (Ramesh et al., 2022). They contributed *Samanantar* dataset which comprises parallel corpora of 11 Indic languages with English side parallel sentences and explored the multilingual NMT model for English-to-Indic and Indic-to-English. They used Fairseq (Ott et al., 2019) toolkit for transformer-based model training via multilingual settings of many-to-one and one-to-many (Johnson et al., 2017).

3 System Description

We have employed the OpenNMT-py (Klein et al., 2017) toolkit to build multilingual transformer-based NMT models for English-to-Indic and Indic-to-English translation. We have used parallel corpora provided by the

Proceedings of the 9th Workshop on Asian Translation, pages 78–81
October 17, 2022.

WAT2022 organizers (Nakazawa et al., 2022). Additionally, we have used English-Assamese parallel corpus (Laskar et al., 2020). We have maintained the equal ratio (1 : 1) for Eng-Indic (Asm/Ben/Guj/Hin/Kan/Mal/Mar/Tel/Tam/Pan/Npi/ Ory) language pairs of the dataset in the multilingual NMT settings and data statistics are presented in Table 1. We have converted all Indic data into English script using the Indic-trans, transliteration script[1] (Bhat et al., 2014). We have performed jointly byte pair encoding (sub-word level) (Sennrich et al., 2016) on the transliterated Indic sentences and English sentences with $40k$ merge operations. The sub-word level source-target vocabulary is shared during the training process of the multilingual NMT model. We have used special tokens (language tags) for Indic side languages at the one-to-many (English-to-Indic) setting (Johnson et al., 2017). We have followed the default settings of the 6 layer transformer model (Vaswani et al., 2017) in the training process. The NMT model is trained on a single GPU with early stopping criteria i.e., the model training is halted if does not converge on the validation set for more than 10 epochs. The obtained trained model is used to translate the test data provided by the WAT2022 organizers. For English-to-Indic language translation, the predicted sentences are converted into the respective Indic languages using the Indic-trans script.

4 Results

The WAT2022 shared task organizer (Nakazawa et al., 2022) published the evaluation result[2] (INDIC22en-as/INDIC22as-en/INDIC22en-bn/INDIC22bn-en) at the Indic translation task for English-to-Indic and Indic-to-English and our team achieve the second position for English-to-Assamese and vice-versa translation. We have participated with a team name CNLP-NITS-PP in the English-Assamese and English-Bengali submission tracks of the same task where a total of two teams participated. The automatic evaluation metrics, BLEU (Papineni et al., 2002), RIBES (Isozaki et al., 2010) are used for evaluation of results. Table 2 presents the results of our system. The quantitative results show that our investigation of the transliteration Indic languages into English script does not provide a reasonable translation accuracy for the multilingual NMT model of English-Assamese and English-Bengali pairs translation.

[1]https://github.com/libindic/indic-trans

[2]http://lotus.kuee.kyoto-u.ac.jp/WAT/evaluation/index.html

Translation	BLEU	RIBES
Eng-to-Asm	1.10	0.359265
Asm-to-Eng	3.50	0.537859
Eng-to-Ben	2.00	0.503286
Ben-to-Eng	4.50	0.547407

Table 2: Our system's results (official) for Eng-Asm (English-Assamese) and Eng-Ben (English-Bengali) language pair at the Indic task.

5 Conclusion and Future Work

In this work, we have investigated multilingual NMT for Indic task of WAT2022 by taking the advantage of sub-word level source-target lexical sharing during the training. However, we need to do more experiments to improve the translational performance of low-resource pairs by utilizing pre-trained multilingual models.

Acknowledgements

We want to thank the Department of Computer Science and Engineering, Center for Natural Language Processing (CNLP), Artificial Intelligence (AI) Lab at the National Institute of Technology, Silchar for providing the requisite support and infrastructure to execute this work.

References

Dzmitry Bahdanau, Kyunghyun Cho, and Yoshua Bengio. 2015. Neural machine translation by jointly learning to align and translate. In *3rd International Conference on Learning Representations, ICLR 2015, San Diego, CA, USA, May 7-9, 2015, Conference Track Proceedings*.

Irshad Ahmad Bhat, Vandan Mujadia, Aniruddha Tammewar, Riyaz Ahmad Bhat, and Manish Shrivastava. 2014. Iiit-h system submission for fire2014 shared task on transliterated search. In *Proceedings of the Forum for Information Retrieval Evaluation*, FIRE '14, page 48–53, New York, NY, USA. Association for Computing Machinery.

Hideki Isozaki, Tsutomu Hirao, Kevin Duh, Katsuhito Sudoh, and Hajime Tsukada. 2010. Automatic evaluation of translation quality for distant language pairs. In *Proceedings of the 2010 Conference on Empirical Methods in Natural Language Processing*, pages 944–952, Cambridge, MA. Association for Computational Linguistics.

Language Pair	Type	Source	No. of Sentence
Eng-Asm	Train	Organizer	140172
		External	203315
		Total	343487
	Validation	Organizer	997
	Test	Organizer	1012
Eng-Ben/Guj/Hin/Kan/Mal/Mar/Tel/Tam/Pan/Npi/Ory	Train	Organizer	350000
	Validation	Organizer	997
	Test	Organizer	1012

Table 1: Data statistics of train, validation and test set. External: Taken permission from the organizer to use external parallel English-Assamese data (Laskar et al., 2020) (EnAsCorp1.0 has been updated and the updated version will be released at `https://github.com/cnlp-nits/EnAsCorp1.0`)

Melvin Johnson, Mike Schuster, Quoc V. Le, Maxim Krikun, Yonghui Wu, Zhifeng Chen, Nikhil Thorat, Fernanda Viégas, Martin Wattenberg, Greg Corrado, Macduff Hughes, and Jeffrey Dean. 2017. Google's multilingual neural machine translation system: Enabling zero-shot translation. *Transactions of the Association for Computational Linguistics*, 5:339–351.

Guillaume Klein, Yoon Kim, Yuntian Deng, Jean Senellart, and Alexander Rush. 2017. Opennmt: Open-source toolkit for neural machine translation. In *Proceedings of ACL 2017, System Demonstrations*, pages 67–72, Vancouver, Canada. Association for Computational Linguistics.

Sahinur Rahman Laskar, Abinash Dutta, Partha Pakray, and Sivaji Bandyopadhyay. 2019a. Neural machine translation: English to hindi. In *2019 IEEE Conference on Information and Communication Technology*, pages 1–6.

Sahinur Rahman Laskar, Abdullah Faiz Ur Rahman Khilji, Partha Pakray, and Sivaji Bandyopadhyay. 2020. EnAsCorp1.0: English-Assamese corpus. In *Proceedings of the 3rd Workshop on Technologies for MT of Low Resource Languages*, pages 62–68, Suzhou, China. Association for Computational Linguistics.

Sahinur Rahman Laskar, Partha Pakray, and Sivaji Bandyopadhyay. 2019b. Neural machine translation: Hindi-Nepali. In *Proceedings of the Fourth Conference on Machine Translation (Volume 3: Shared Task Papers, Day 2)*, pages 202–207, Florence, Italy. Association for Computational Linguistics.

Sahinur Rahman Laskar, Partha Pakray, and Sivaji Bandyopadhyay. 2021a. Neural machine translation: Assamese–bengali. In *Modeling, Simulation and Optimization: Proceedings of CoMSO 2020*, pages 571–579. Springer Singapore.

Sahinur Rahman Laskar, Partha Pakray, and Sivaji Bandyopadhyay. 2021b. Neural machine translation for low resource assamese–english. In *Proceedings of the International Conference on Computing and Communication Systems: I3CS 2020, NEHU, Shillong, India*, volume 170, page 35. Springer.

Sahinur Rahman Laskar, Abdullah Faiz Ur Rahman Khilji, Partha Pakray, and Sivaji Bandyopadhyay. 2022. Improved neural machine translation for low-resource english–assamese pair. *Journal of Intelligent and Fuzzy Systems*, 42(5):4727–4738.

Thang Luong, Hieu Pham, and Christopher D. Manning. 2015. Effective approaches to attention-based neural machine translation. In *Proceedings of the 2015 Conference on Empirical Methods in Natural Language Processing*, pages 1412–1421, Lisbon, Portugal. Association for Computational Linguistics.

Toshiaki Nakazawa, Hideya Mino, Isao Goto, Raj Dabre, Shohei Higashiyama, Shantipriya Parida, Anoop Kunchukuttan, Makoto Morishita, Ondřej Bojar, Chenhui Chu, Akiko Eriguchi, Kaori Abe, Yusuke Oda, and Sadao Kurohashi. 2022. Overview of the 9th workshop on Asian translation. In *Proceedings of the 9th Workshop on Asian Translation (WAT2022)*, Gyeongju, Republic of Korea. Association for Computational Linguistics.

Myle Ott, Sergey Edunov, Alexei Baevski, Angela Fan, Sam Gross, Nathan Ng, David Grangier, and Michael Auli. 2019. fairseq: A fast, extensible toolkit for sequence modeling. In *Proceedings of the 2019 Conference of the North American Chapter of the Association for Computational Linguistics (Demonstrations)*, pages 48–53, Minneapolis, Minnesota. Association for Computational Linguistics.

Kishore Papineni, Salim Roukos, Todd Ward, and Wei-Jing Zhu. 2002. Bleu: A method for automatic evaluation of machine translation. In *Proceedings of the 40th Annual Meeting on Association for Computational Linguistics*, ACL '02, pages 311–318, Stroudsburg, PA, USA. Association for Computational Linguistics.

Amarnath Pathak and Partha Pakray. 2018. Neural machine translation for indian languages. *Journal of Intelligent Systems*, pages 1–13.

Amarnath Pathak, Partha Pakray, and Jereemi Bentham. 2018. English–mizo machine translation using neural and statistical approaches. *Neural Computing and Applications*, 30:1–17.

Gowtham Ramesh, Sumanth Doddapaneni, Aravinth Bheemaraj, Mayank Jobanputra, Raghavan AK, Ajitesh Sharma, Sujit Sahoo, Harshita Diddee, Mahalakshmi J, Divyanshu Kakwani, Navneet Kumar, Aswin Pradeep, Srihari Nagaraj, Deepak Kumar, Vivek Raghavan, Anoop Kunchukuttan, Pratyush Kumar, and Mitesh Shantadevi Khapra. 2022. Samanantar: The largest publicly available parallel corpora collection for 11 indic languages. *Trans. Assoc. Comput. Linguistics*, 10:145–162.

Rico Sennrich, Barry Haddow, and Alexandra Birch. 2016. Neural machine translation of rare words with subword units. In *Proceedings of the 54th Annual Meeting of the Association for Computational Linguistics (Volume 1: Long Papers)*, pages 1715–1725, Berlin, Germany. Association for Computational Linguistics.

Xu Tan, Yi Ren, Di He, Tao Qin, Zhou Zhao, and Tie-Yan Liu. 2019. Multilingual neural machine translation with knowledge distillation. In *7th International Conference on Learning Representations, ICLR 2019, New Orleans, LA, USA, May 6-9, 2019*. OpenReview.net.

Ashish Vaswani, Noam Shazeer, Niki Parmar, Jakob Uszkoreit, Llion Jones, Aidan N Gomez, Ł ukasz Kaiser, and Illia Polosukhin. 2017. Attention is all you need. In I. Guyon, U. V. Luxburg, S. Bengio, H. Wallach, R. Fergus, S. Vishwanathan, and R. Garnett, editors, *Advances in Neural Information Processing Systems 30*, pages 5998–6008. Curran Associates, Inc.

Does partial pretranslation can improve low ressourced-languages pairs?

R.Blin, cnrs-crlao, blin@ehess.fr

Abstract

We study the effects of a local and punctual pretranslation of the source corpus on the performance of a Transformer translation model. The pretranslations are performed at the morphological (morpheme translation), lexical (word translation) and morphosyntactic (numeral groups and dates) levels. We focus on small and medium-sized training corpora (50K $\sim$ 2.5M bisegments) and on a linguistically distant language pair (Japanese and French). We find that this type of pretranslation does not lead to significant progress. We describe the motivations of the approach, the specific difficulties of Japanese-French translation. We discuss the possible reasons for the observed underperformance.

1 Introduction

There are many techniques to improve the performance of a neural translation system without changing the size of the training corpus, without increasing the computational power, and independently of the tuning of the translation system: enriching vocabulary embedding (e.g. Ding and Duh (2018)), injecting linguistic information (e.g. Sennrich and Haddow (2016)), reordering (e.g. Kawara et al. (2021)), etc. These techniques are absolutely crucial for language pairs with few corpora, and when computing power is limited.

We propose here to apply another technique, which to our knowledge has not been studied so far with neural translation. It consists in pretranslating short segments of the source corpus. We proceed with handmade rules and vocabulary translation lists. We will observe its effects on Japanese-French, with several corpus sizes (50K-2.5M bisegments). This is indeed a language pair that remains poorly endowed with large, freely accessible and good quality corpora.

The aim of pretranslation is to reduce the linguistic distance between the two languages and to facilitate learning. The advantage is that it can be applied even with limited knowledge about the translation rules between the two languages. In addition, building the pretranslation rule by hand does not necessitate annotated resources (that maybe do not exist).

In section 2 we present the difficulties specific to French-Japanese. In section 3 we describe the type of pretranslations we have carried out. In section 3, we describe an experimental setup used to evaluate the effects of those pretranslations. We will see in section 5 that it is difficult to correlate these results with the properties of the corpora.

2 Challenges of Japanese-French Translation

Japanese and French are known to be linguistically distant languages. We present here briefly the most notable points of divergence, which may impact their joint treatment.

Japanese and French use different writing systems. Japanese uses about 2300 characters. French uses about 50 (including capitals). The two systems share only Arabic numerals and some English words written in Latin characters in Japanese texts. The sharing of vocabulary is therefore of little interest when training a translation model.

Word formation in the two languages does not correspond. French is a richly inflected language. Flexion concerns almost all parts of speech. On the contrary, Japanese morphology varies only for a part of verbs and adjectives (native Japanese lexical stratum). Japanese is also considered an agglutinative language. With the same meaning, many expressions in Japanese and French are not formed at the same level: expressions formed at the morphological level in Japanese are formed at the syntactic level in French and vice versa (see example below "seem not to want to drink"; CONJ:conjugation suffix):

no- mita- kuna- katta- rou

Proceedings of the 9th Workshop on Asian Translation, pages 82–88
October 17, 2022.

RAD CONJ CONJ CONJ CONJ
drink want NEG PAST seem

sembl- ait ne pas vouloir boire
RAD CONJ AUX AUX V V
seem PAST NEG NEG want drink

Word order is different at several levels. In writing, Japanese is an SOV language where the order is semi-free, with possible pragmatic effects. French is a SVO language. Word order also diverges within phrases. In Japanese, in most cases, the complements (nominal, propositional) precede the head of the phrase. In French, they appear on either side of the head:

daidokoro[1] *no*[2] *ookii*[3] *teeburu*[4]
kitchen GEN large table
grande[3] *table*[4] *de*[2] *<la> cuisine*[1]
"large table of <the> kitchen"

A major source of difficulty in comparing or translating the two languages is the absence in Japanese of many components that are obligatory in French. Japanese uses few quantification marks (determiners etc.) and makes extensive use of bare nouns. A bare noun phrase will often have several possible translations in French (see also a discussion involving Japanese and English in (Bond, 2001). Many sentence components are elided in Japanese. Japanese is a pro-drop language. Unlike in French, the place of absent components is not occupied by a pronoun. In addition, titles and press headlines have a specific syntax in Japanese (Noguchi, 2002).

Constraints between distant structures exist in both languages but do not concern the same parts of speech. In French, distant words can share the same gender and number marks. This is the case of subject-verb agreement, for example. Japanese is known to use floating quantifiers consisting of a numeral and a classifier. The choice of the classifier depends on the quantified noun.

[kami/pen][1] *wo kitto san-[mai/bon]*[1] *kau.*
{paper/pen} O cert. 3 - CL/CL[1] buy
(He) certainly buy three papers/pens.

3 Pretranslation applied here

We study 5 levels of pretranslation. The pretranslations are applied recursively (the pretranslation of corpus i is added to that of corpus $i-1$). The idea is that a single modification cannot substantially improve the translation. We must therefore study an accumulation of pretranslations. An example of sentence pretranslation is given in the table 8. C0 is the baseline corpus.

3.1 C1: Compositional structures

We pretranslate two structures whose translation is in general independent of the context: numerals and dates. Japanese numerals come in two forms: Sino-Japanese system (百万) or anglophone "Arabic" system (1,000,000). The treatment of numerals may seem anecdotal, but we found that they were unexpectedly poorly translated by the models trained on small corpora. This can be explained, among other things, by the variants of notation. Pretranslation is therefore both a translation and a kind of normalisation:

The translation of dates requires a triple processing: reordering, pretranslation of the numerals, global translation.

$$1910年_{year}3月_{month}3日_{day}$$
$$\overset{reorder}{\rightarrow}\ 3日_{day}3月_{month}1910年_{year}$$
$$\overset{transl.}{\rightarrow}\ \text{3 mars 1910}$$

Ambiguous expressions are left as they are, such as 一日 which means «un jour» or «le premier (du mois)».

Choosing not to translate ambiguous expressions has disadvantages. Indeed, it is possible that some occurrences of an expression are not translated. We are not able to assess the number of cases involved, nor the effect on the performance of the translation model.

3.2 C2: Suffixes, punctuation, proper names

Affixes are translated if their translation is "relatively" regular: 主義 (*shugi*) → *isme*. In general, the linguistic segmentation of Japanese separates the suffix from the radical. But in order to get closer to the French form, which does not separate the suffix from its radical, we do not separate in Japanese either. It is left to the statistical segmentation (BPE) to separate or not. The form is systematically put in the singular.

$共産_{N}$ $主義_{SUFF}$ («*kyōsan shugi*»)
→ 共産 *isme* → 共産*isme*

Punctuation is simplified and brought closer to that of French. This concerns mainly interrogative marks: か? → ?; か。 → ? .

Most of the changes in C1 concern the translation of proper names. We used several resources: an existing dictionary (jalexgram 0.37), Wikipedia translations and translations available in unidic-cwj. Considering the possible segmentation errors and translation errors (in particular from the Wikipedia), we roughly filtered: the ratio <source word length / target word length> must not exceed 0.4 (in bytes). We do not translate one character-words because they are frequently ambiguous. We obtain a dictionary of 30,000 translated proper names.

It should be noted that the transcription (e.g. Hepburn: *Tōkyō*, Kunrei: *Toukyou*, other: *Tokyo*) is not unified within the corpora and within the dictionary. It is therefore possible that a translation in the dictionary does not correspond to a translation in the target corpus.

3.3 C3: Common nouns (CN)

In French, CNs are variable in number and are associated with a determiner, which does not exist in Japanese. We pretranslate using the singular and do not add a determiner. Most CNs have several translations, which depend on the context. For all occurrences of a noun, we will use a single translation, and always the same one. This is therefore a very rough pretranslation. 36,700 CNs have been translated (from Jalexgram).

3.4 C4:Verbal nouns (VN) in nominal position

Japanese VNs (e.g. *benkyō*) have two distributions. Followed by a support verb, they behave as verbal radicals (e.g. benkyō$_{vn}$ suru "litt. study do; to study"). Otherwise, they are used as CNs (e.g. "studies"). The corresponding forms in French occur with a determinant, but mostly at the singular form. We translate VNs in nominal position, in singular, without determiner. Here again, this is a rough pretranslation. 7,350 VNs were used.

4 Experiment

4.1 Corpus

We use the Cjafr-v3 (Blin and Cromières, 2022) corpus[1]. To our knowledge, this is the largest and freely available "ready to use" corpus currently available. The core contains 400K bisegments translated by humans. A majority of the bisegments are from TED (Reimers and Gurevych, 2020). We add a part of the extension of Cjafr ($\approx$2M of bisegments). It is made of various crawled corpora.

From this corpus of 2.5M bisegments, and after preprocessing, two training corpora of 50K and 500K bisegments are randomly extracted. For all experiments, the fine-tuning and evaluation corpora always remain the same (but the preprocessing is different).

The evaluation is carried out on two test corpora: PUD (1000 bisegments) [2] and ted.test (3000 bisegments from TED corpus).

The corpus are morphologically analysed and segmented using mecab (Kudo, 2006) and the Unidic-cwj (Oka, 2017) dictionary. Some segmentation errors are corrected with ad-hoc rules (the same for all the experiments, including the baseline corpus). We apply thus a BPE segmentation (12K words for Japanese, 8K words for French; with SentencePiece (Kudo and Richardson, 2018)). The segmentation model is trained with the pretranslated train corpus. A description of the corpora is provided in Tables 3, 6 and 7).In particular, we evaluate the proximity (with BLEU) between the pretranslated corpora and the target corpus, after BPE segmentation.

4.2 Training and results

The training is executed with Opennmt-py.2.0.0 (Klein et al., 2017) [3]. the `batch_size` is set to 2048 and the `word_vec_size` is set to 256.

In order to reduce the variance of the results due to the random nature of the training, we perform three trainings for each corpus and calculate the average. Table 1 and 2 provide the BLEU scores [4]. For the evaluation, punctuation is separated. The raw scores are of course very different depending on the size of the training corpus. To compare them, we propose the proportional difference between the baseline score (A) and the score after pretranslation (B): B-A/A.

Several additional settings have been experimented but no one provided a significant difference with those described above. For the sake of place, we do not present them here. Those settings are: segmentation with shared vocabulary (BPE segmentation set to 16K words; evaluation with TER (Snover et al., 2006) and Chrf (Popovic); best result instead of average; evaluation after re-tokenisation.

[1] Download from `http://crlao.ehess.fr/rblin/ tajafr.php`

[2] Test corpus used at CoNL 2017 shared task on parsing Universal Dependencies. lindat.mff.cuni.cz/ repository/ xmlui/ handle/11234/1-2184

[3] The hyperparameters are those suggested in `opennmt.net/OpenNMT-py/FAQ.html#how-do-i-use-the-transformer-model; 2021/06/01`

[4] Calculated using multi-BLEU `www.statmt.org/wmt06/shared-task/multi-bleu.perl`, default settings

	50	500	2M5
C0	4.20	14.27	15.75
C1	0.00%	2.22%	5.31%
C2	-18.08%	4.37%	-0.74%
C3	0.32%	4.13%	5.23%
C4	2.78%	3.62%	11.64%

Table 1: BLEU score; corpus PUD; proportional variation with respect to the baseline C0

	50	500	2M5
C0	3.05	9.53	15.64
C1	-1.97%	3.57%	-5.80%
C2	-10.18%	4.20%	-0.21%
C3	-0.55%	2.66%	-1.26%
C4	-2.84%	1.54%	-13.40%

Table 2: BLEU score; corpus ted.test; proportional variation with respect to the baseline

5 Discussion

As expected, pretranslation increases the proximity (measured in BLEU, on BPE segmented corpus) between the Japanese and French corpora (see Tab.5). For the smaller training corpora (50K bisegments), the progression is a little less than 1 point (knowing that in percentage, this represents 50%). The PUD corpus shows the most notable progress (+1.63 points). However, it should be noted that, whatever the corpus, the proximity is low, with or without pretranslation (<3.80 BLEU).

The results do not show significant progress. In some cases, there is even a deterioration. Nor is there a clear causal link between the (quantified) characteristics of the corpus and the results.

Compared to the size of the training corpus (50K, 500K or 2.5M bisegments), we observe a systematic but modest improvement for the 500K bisegment corpus. This behaviour is correlated with a very slight superiority of the vocabulary variety (tab.4). In other words, for this size of corpus and type of corpus, the greater variety of the corpus could improve the translation.

Concerning the test corpora, we observe better results for PUD. Again, in parallel, we note that the variety of vocabulary is slightly higher for PUD (tab.4). Moreover, if we observe the proportional difference of the number of words in Japanese and French (# words ja - # words fr/ # words ja) we see that PUD is close to train.2M5 (tab.7). We also observe a (very slightly) higher proximity between ja and fr (BLEU) for PUD (Tab.5).

We also repeated the C2 and C4 experiment with vocabulary sharing (word number for BPE segmentation is set at 16K). The results are slightly lower than with the separated vocabularies. This can be explained by the low number of common word strings, even after pre-translation. Vocabulary sharing does not improve the results after pre-translation.

It is difficult to establish a causal relationship between the (quantifiable) characteristics of the corpora and the results. Indeed, it can be observed that corpus features such as proximity (BLEU) or vocabulary variety are present in the base corpus CO. The pre-translation does not change anything, and even reduces these features.

6 Conclusion

Based on the assumption that proximity between languages could facilitate learning by a neural translation model, we locally pre-translated words and morphosyntactic structures in the source language. No significant results were observed. Some results have deteriorated. We tried to correlate these results with quantifiable features of the corpora but no clear causal relationships appeared. Several hypotheses are possible. Either the pre-translation is not thorough enough and more components need to be pre-translated to see a notable positive effect. In this case, a more massive intervention should be considered, or even coordinated with an intervention on the target. Or the linguistic characteristics of the two languages do not allow any progress through pre-translation. This could be confirmed by carrying out the same work on another language, for example SOV language (e.g. Basque) and/or with a poorer morphology SVO language (English). We have observed three corpus sizes. There is a slight improvement for the corpus of 500K words (*vs* 50K and 2.5M). To better understand the reasons for this behaviour, we propose to repeat the experiments with intermediate corpus sizes .

Acknowledgements

I sincerely thank Fabien Cromières for his valuable advice and comments.

References

Raoul Blin and Fabien Cromières. 2022. Cjafr-v3 : A freely available filtered japanese-french aligned corpus.

Francis Bond. 2001. *Determiners and Number in English contrasted with Japanese, as exemplified in Machine Translation*. Ph.D. thesis, University of Queensland.

Shuoyang Ding and Kevin Duh. 2018. How do source-side monolingual word embeddings impact neural machine translation? *arXiv preprint arXiv:1806.01515*.

Yuki Kawara, Chenhui Chu, and Yuki Arase. 2021. Preordering encoding on transformer for translation. *IEEE/ACM Transactions on Audio, Speech, and Language Processing*, 29:644–655.

Guillaume Klein, Yoon Kim, Yuntian Deng, Jean Senellart, and Alexander Rush. 2017. OpenNMT: Open-Source Toolkit for Neural Machine Translation. In *Proceedings of ACL 2017, System Demonstrations*, pages 67–72, Vancouver, Canada. Association for Computational Linguistics.

Taku Kudo. 2006. Mecab: yet another part-of-speech and morphological analyzer.

Taku Kudo and John Richardson. 2018. Sentencepiece: A simple and language independent subword tokenizer and detokenizer for neural text processing. In *Proceedings of the 2018 Conference on Empirical Methods in Natural Language Processing, EMNLP 2018: System Demonstrations, Brussels, Belgium, October 31 - November 4, 2018*, pages 66–71. Association for Computational Linguistics.

Takako Noguchi. 2002. "midashi" no 'bunpo' - kaidoku heno tebiki to shomondai- ['Syntax' of the "headlines" - Problems and guidance to the reading]. *kouza nihongo kyouiku*, 38:94–124.

Teruaki Oka. 2017. Unidic for morphological analysis with reduced model size by review of crf feature templates. In *Proceedings of Language Resource Workshop*, volume 2, pages 144–153. NINJAL.

Maja Popovic. chrf:character n-gram f-score for automatic mt evaluation. In *Proceedings of the Tenth Workshop on Statistical Machine Translation*.

Nils Reimers and Iryna Gurevych. 2020. Making monolingual sentence embeddings multilingual using knowledge distillation. In *Proceedings of the 2020 Conference on Empirical Methods in Natural Language Processing*. Association for Computational Linguistics.

Rico Sennrich and Barry Haddow. 2016. Linguistic input features improve neural machine translation. *arXiv preprint arXiv:1606.02892*.

Matthew Snover, Bonnie Dorr, Rich Schwartz, Linnea Micciulla, and John Makhoul. 2006. A study of translation edit rate with targeted human annotation. In *Proceedings of the 7th Conference of the Association for Machine Translation in the Americas: Technical Papers*, pages 223–231, Cambridge, Massachusetts, USA. Association for Machine Translation in the Americas.

A Description of the corpus and example of pre-translation

	train.2M5	val	PUD	ted.test
C0	2,527,216	2,964	1,000	2,929

Table 3: # bisegments

	train.50	train.500	train.2M5	val	PUD	ted.test
fr	30.44	31.33	30.88	21.24	27.49	24.93
C0	31.74	32.27	30.80	18.81	25.83	24.95
C1	31.11	32.48	31.01	19.20	25.93	25.07
C2	32.30	32.48	30.95	19.34	26.54	25.37
C3	31.42	32.13	31.14	20.25	26.90	25.06
C4	31.78	32.25	31.03	20.21	27.19	26.13

Table 4: Vocabulary variety (# of original words in a sample of 10K words/10K).

	train.50	train.500	train.2M5	val	PUD	ted.test
C0	2.84	2.60	2.17	0.07	0.49	0.12
C1	2.82	2.60	2.18	0.12	0.70	0.18
C2	3.13	2.87	2.46	0.42	1.43	0.44
C3	3.61	3.40	2.92	0.64	1.95	0.67
C4	3.79	3.57	3.07	0.65	2.12	0.74

Table 5: Proximity of the ja src corpora and the fr corpus; BLEU scores

	train.2M5	val	PUD	ted.test
C0	19.36	25.12	33.10	25.91
C1	19.32	25.08	33.00	25.93
C2	19.37	25.13	33.40	25.96
C3	20.04	25.93	34.51	26.84
C4	20.19	26.09	34.84	27.00

Table 6: Average length of the japanese segments, after BPE segmentation

	train.2M5	val	PUD	ted.test
	48,970,553	71,855	33,673	79,270
C0	-0.11%	3.61%	-1.70%	-4.27%
C1	-0.28%	3.47%	-1.99%	-4.20%
C2	-0.05%	3.66%	-0.82%	-4.08%
C3	3.43%	6.94%	2.49%	-0.84%
C4	4.19%	7.61%	3.45%	-0.24%

Table 7: # words; proportional variation with respect to the French target corpus

C0	_196 9 _年 _8 _月 _, _パウロ _6 _世 _法 王 _が _バ チ カン _の _法律 _から _死刑 _を _廃止 _し _, _すべて _の _犯 行 _に _対し _て _死刑 _判決 _は _取り除 か _れ _た _。
C1	_août _196 9 _, _パウロ _6 _世 _法 王 _が _バ チ カン _の _法律 _から _死刑 _を _廃止 _し _, _すべて _の _犯 行 _に _対し _て _死刑 _判決 _は _取り除 か _れ _た _。
C2	_août _196 9 _, _Paul os _6 _世 _法 王 _が _V at ican _の _法律 _から _死刑 _を _廃止 _し _, _すべて _の _犯 行 _に _対し _て _死刑 _判決 _は _取り除 か _れ _た _。
C3	_août _196 9 _, _Paul os _6 _世 _pape _が _V a tic an _の _loi _から _peine _de _mort _を _廃止 _し _, _すべて _の _crime _に _対し _て _peine _de _mort _判決 _は _取り除 か _れ _た _。
C4	_août _196 9 _, _Paul os _6 _世 _pa pe _が _V a tic an _の _loi _から _peine _de _mort _を _廃止 _し _, _すべて _の _crime _に _対し _て _peine _de _mort _jugement _は _取り除 か _れ _た _。
C4’	_août _196 9 _, _Paul os _6 _世 _pa pe _が _V a tic an _の _loi _から _peine _de _mort _を _廃止 _し _, _すべて _の _crime _に _対し _て _peine _de _mort _jugement _は _取り除 か _れ _た _。
fr	_en _août _196 9 _, _le _p ape _Paul _VI _a _reti ré _la _peine _de _mort _de _la _loi _du _V ati can _et _l _’ _a _reti rée _de _toutes _les _infra ctions _.

Table 8: Example of pretranslations and BPE segmentation; C4’ is obtained sharing the vocabulary; “In August 1969 , Pope Paul VI removed the death penalty from the Vatican law and revoked it from all offences . ”

Multimodal Neural Machine Translation with Search Engine Based Image Retrieval

Zhenhao Tang **Xiaobing Zhang**
College of Application and Technology,
Shenzhen University,
Shenzhen, China

Zi Long* **Xianghua Fu**
College of Big Data and Internet,
Shenzhen Technology University,
Shenzhen, China

Abstract

Recently, numbers of works shows that the performance of neural machine translation (NMT) can be improved to a certain extent with using visual information. However, most of these conclusions are drawn from the analysis of experimental results based on a limited set of bilingual sentence-image pairs, such as *Multi30K*. In these kinds of datasets, the content of one bilingual parallel sentence pair must be well represented by a manually annotated image, which is different with the actual translation situation. Some previous works are proposed to addressed the problem by retrieving images from exiting sentence-image pairs with topic model. However, because of the limited collection of sentence-image pairs they used, their image retrieval method is difficult to deal with the out-of-vocabulary words, and can hardly prove that visual information enhance NMT rather than the co-occurrence of images and sentences. In this paper, we propose an open-vocabulary image retrieval methods to collect descriptive images for bilingual parallel corpus using image search engine. Next, we propose text-aware attentive visual encoder to filter incorrectly collected noise images. Experiment results on *Multi30K* and other two translation datasets show that our proposed method achieves significant improvements over strong baselines.

1 Introduction

With the development of NMT, the role of visual information in machine translation has attracted researchers' attention(Elliott et al., 2017; Barrault et al., 2018; Specia et al., 2016). Although we are still not clear about the specific role of visual information in NMT(Caglayan et al., 2019; Elliott, 2018), visual information can assist NMT model to achieve better translation performance (Calixto and Liu, 2017; Calixto et al., 2017; Su et al., 2021). Different with those text-only NMT(Bahdanau et al., 2014; Gehring et al., 2016), a bilingual parallel corpora with manual image annotations are used to train a multimodal NMT model by an end-to-end framework, and therefore, most of the previous conclusions are drawn from the analysis of experimental results based on a limited set of manually annotated bilingual sentence-image pairs, specifically, *Multi30K*(Elliott et al., 2016).

Data source	Image	Sentence
Multi30K		**EN:** A dog is running in the snow. **DE:** Ein Hund rennt im Schnee.
UN News		**EN:** Marine plastic debris has impacted over 600 marine species. **DE:** Plastik aus dem meer betroffen mehr als 600 meerestiere.

Table 1: Comparison of example from *Multi30K* dataset and United Nations News.

In *Multi30K*, as shown in 1, the sentences consists mostly of common and simple words, and the content of each bilingual parallel sentence pair is well represented by a single image. Table 1 also shows an example of bilingual sentence-image pair from an actual news report of United Nations News[1]. It is obviously that there is a dramatic difference between the data of *Multi30K* and the real-world multimodal translation situations. Therefore, results and evidences based on *Multi30K* can hardly proved the effectiveness of multimodal NMT model in an actual translation situation, in which sentences contain rare and uncommon words and are partially described by images.

To address the problem, Zhang et al. (2019) proposed to transform the existing sentence-image pairs into a topic-image lookup table, and a group

*Corresponding author

[1]https://news.un.org/en/

Proceedings of the 9th Workshop on Asian Translation, pages 89–98
October 17, 2022.

of images with similar topics to the source sentence is retrieved from the topic-image lookup table. However, the topic-image lookup table is made from a limited collection of sentence-image pairs, such as *Multi30K* and MS COCO image caption dataset (Lin et al., 2014), their image retrieval method is difficult to deal with the out-of-vocabulary words. Besides, results from Zhang et al. (2019) can hardly prove that the performance of NMT is improved by visual information rather than the co-occurrence of images and sentences. Their model may suffer problems in translating sentences with images that are not contained in the topic-image lookup table.

In this paper, we propose an open-vocabulary image retrieval methods to collect images for bilingual parallel corpus using image search engine, thus addressing the problems caused by limited collection of sentence-image pairs in Zhang et al. (2019). In detail, to focus on the major part of the sentence, we apply the term frequency-inverse document frequency (TF-IDF). Instead of a single keyword, we use multiple words as search query for image retrieval to ensure that the contents of collected images are partially consistent with the given sentences. Since the quality of images from search engine may be varied, we propose to apply a simple but effective attention layer, and introduce a text-aware attentive visual encoder to filter incorrectly collected noise images. The proposed method is then evaluated on three translation datasets, including the *Multi30K* English-to-German, WMT'16 English-to-German, Global Voices (Tiedemann, 2012) English-to-German. Experiment results show that our proposed method achieves significant improvements over strong baselines. To summarize, out contributions are primarily three-fold:

(1) We present an open-vocabulary image retrieval methods with image search engine that overcomes the shortcomings of Zhang et al. (2019) caused by limited image collection.

(2) The proposed method enables the text-only NMT to use visual information from the collected images that are partially consistent with input sentences, which is more close to the actual translation situations.

(3) We further discuss the influence of visual information in the proposed multimodal NMT model , which verified the effectiveness and generality of the proposed approach.

2 Related Work

Recently, multimodal NMT models have gradually become a hot topic in machine translation research. They use image information to improve the translation effect of NMT models through different methods.

In some cases, visual features are directly used as supplementary information to the text presentation. For example, Huang et al. (2016) takes global visual features and local visual features as additional information for sentences. Calixto and Liu (2017) initializes the encoder hidden states or decoder hidden states through global visual features. (Calixto et al., 2017) uses an independent attention mechanism to capture visual representations. (Caglayan et al., 2016) incorporates spatial visual features into the multimodal NMT model via an independent attention mechanism. On this basis, Delbrouck and Dupont (2017) employs Compact Bilinear Pooling to fuse two modalities. Su et al. (2021) introduces image-text mutual interactions to refine their semantic representations. Lin et al. (2020) attempts to introduce the capsule network into multimodal NMT, they use the timestep-specific source-side context vector to guide the routing procedure.

All the above work is performed on the *Multi30K* dataset. However, some recent studies indicate that the visual features may play a less important role in the NMT model than previously thought. (Ive et al., 2019; Zhang et al., 2017; Grönroos et al., 2018). Such problems are mainly caused by the limitations of the *Multi30K* dataset. Zhang et al. (2019) presents a universal visual representation method that overcomes the shortcomings of *Multi30K* dataset. However, all their image information still comes from *Multi30K*, which is obviously not enough to represent complex machine translation corpus.

3 Background

In this section, we give a simple description of the multimodal NMT model proposed by Calixto et al. (2017). The multimodal NMT model is composed of one text encoder, one visual encoder and one decoder with two attention mechanisms. The multimodal NMT aims to construct an end-to-end neural network to model $P = (Y|X, I)$ as follows:

$$\log p(Y|X, I) = \sum_{i=1}^{M} \log p(y_t|y_{<t}, C, A)$$

where I represents visual features, $X = (x_1, x_2, \dots, x_L)$ is the source sentence, and $Y = (y_1, y_2, \dots, y_M)$ is the target sentence. The text encoder is a Bi-directional Recurrent Neural Network (RNN) with Gated Unit(GRU)(Cho et al., 2014) and learn a time-dependent text hidden states $C = (h_1, h_2, \dots, h_N)$ for the source sentence. The visual encoder is a pretrained convolutional neural network (CNN) and a visual representation A for the given image.

The decoder is a conditional GRU (cGRU)[2] with two separate attention mechanisms. The text attention mechanism generates a time-dependent context vector c_t based on the text hidden states C and the hidden state proposal $s_t^{'}$ as follows:

$$c_t = f_{att\_text}(C, s_t^{'}) \tag{1}$$

Meanwhile, the visual attention computes a time-dependent context vector i_t based on the visual feature maps A and the hidden state proposal $s_t^{'}$ as follows:

$$i_t = f_{att\_img}(A, s_t^{'}) \tag{2}$$

Where $s_t^{'}$ is calculated by the previous hidden state s_{t-1} and the previously generated target word y_{t-1}.

4 Our Proposed Method

Figure 1 shows the 4 components of our proposed method, consisting of image retrieval, text-aware attentive visual encoder, RNN text encoder and translation decoder with co-attention & bi-attention.

4.1 Image Retrieval

In this section, we will introduce the proposed open-vocabulary image retrieval methods using image search engine.

Similar with Zhang et al. (2019), to focus on the major part of the sentence and suppress the noise such as stopwords and low-frequency words, we apply the term frequency-inverse document frequency (TF-IDF) (Witten et al., 2005) to create search queries for image search engines. Specifically, given the ith ($i = 1, 2, \dots, N$, N represents the number of samples in the training set) source language sentence $X_i = \{x_i^1, x_i^2, \dots, x_i^L\}$ of length L, X_i is first filtered by as stopword list[3], and the filtered input sentence X_i^f is obtained. We then regard X_i^f as a document d_i, and compute the TF-IDF score $TI_{i,j}$ for each word x_i^j ($j = 1, 2, \dots, L$) in d_i. The formula is as follows:

$$TI_{i,j} = \frac{n_{i,j}}{\sum_k n_{i,k}} \times \log \frac{|D|}{1 + |\{k|x_i^j \in d_k]\}|}$$

where $n_{i,j}$ is the number of occurrences of the word x_i^j in document d_i, $\sum_k n_{i,k}$ represents the total number of words in document d_i. $|D| = N$ represents the total number of source language sentences in the training data, and $|\{k|x_i^j \in d_k]\}|$ represents the number of sentences including x_i^j in the dataset. For input sentence X_i, words are then listed in descending order by $TI_{i,j}$ score, represented as $Q_i = (x_i^{t_1}, x_i^{t_2}, \dots, x_i^{t_L})$ $(TI_{i,t_1} \geq TI_{i,t_2} \geq \dots \geq TI_{i,t_L})$.

Instead of using the top-k high TF-IDF words separately, we concatenate several words from the top-k high TF-IDF words as search query. Specifically, for the sorted words list Q_i, the mth search query q_m is defined as following:

$$q_m = \text{concat}(x_i^{t_1}, x_i^{t_2}, \dots, x_i^{t_m})$$

Where $\text{concat}(\cdot)$ means that words are concatenated with blanks as separator. search query q_m is then applied in image search engine and the first available image is collected as the mth image for input sentence X_i, represented as A_i^m. According to the results of preliminary experiment, we build 5 search queries and collect 5 images for each sentence[4].

4.2 Text-Aware Attentive Visual Encoder

For each collected image, we employ a 50-layer Residual Network (ResNet-50) (He et al., 2016) to represent the visual semantic information as a 196×1024 feature vector.

As described in Section 4.1, for source language sentence X_i, we collect 5 images $A_i^1, A_i^2, \dots, A_i^5$ using image search engine. In order to filter the incorrectly collected noise images, we apply a simple but effective scaled dot-product attention in visual encoder, where the visual representation A_i of input sentence X_i is defined as the following formula:

$$A_i = \sum_{m=1}^{5} \alpha_{i,m} A_i^m$$

[2] https://github.com/nyu-dl/dl4mt-tutorial/blob/master/docs/cgru.pdf

[3] `https://github.com/stopwords-iso/stopwords-en`

[4] In the preliminary experiments, we find that the proposed image retrieval method collect less noise and achieves a slightly better translation performance than the method that uses a single word as search query.

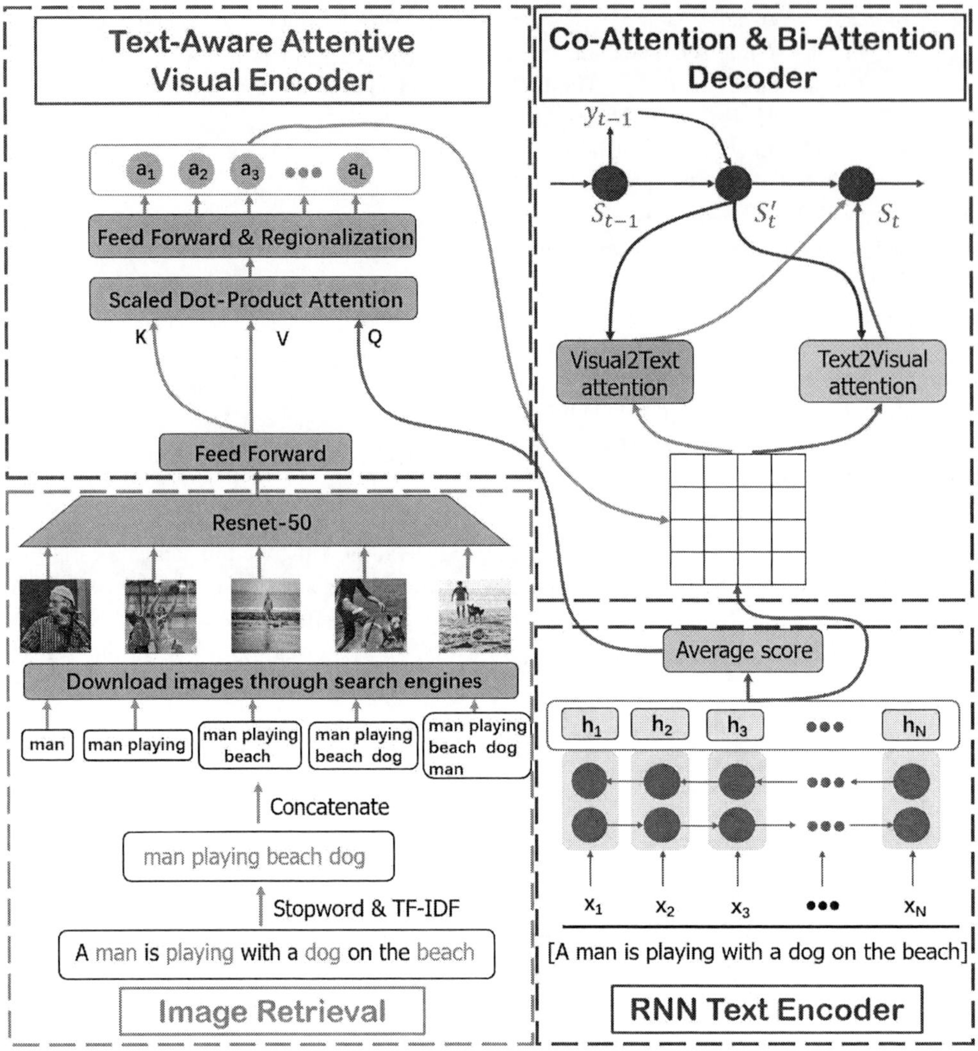

Figure 1: The overview of the framework of our proposed method

where $\alpha_{i,m}$ represents the weight of mth images for input sentence X_i. The $\alpha_{i,m}$ is then computed as follows:

$$\alpha_{i,m} = \mathrm{softmax}(W(A_i^m) \cdot C_i^{'})$$
$$C_i^{'} = \frac{1}{N}\sum_{t=1}^{N} h_i^t$$

where $\mathrm{softmax}(\cdot)$ stands for softmax activation function, and $C_i^{'}$ represents an average pool of the hidden states $C_i = (h_i^1, h_i^2, \ldots, h_i^N)$ for input sentence X_i.

Finally, the obtained 196×1024D visual representation is considered as a matrix $A_i = (\boldsymbol{a}_i^1, \boldsymbol{a}_i^2, \ldots, \boldsymbol{a}_i^L)$, $\boldsymbol{a}_i^l \in R^{1024}$. Each of the $L = 196$ rows consists of a 1024D feature vector that represents a specific image region. Visual representation $A_i = (a_i^1, a_i^2, \ldots, a_i^L)$ and text representation $C_i = (h_i^1, h_i^2, \ldots, h_i^N)$ are then used as the inputs of tanslation decoder .

4.3 Translation Decoder

As shown in figure 2, we apply a bi-directional attention network[5] and a co-attention network (Su et al., 2021) to model underlying semantic interactions between text and image.

The bi-directional attention network is used

[5]According to the result of the preliminary experiment, we found that Transformer-based model can hardly produce an advantage in performance on such small dataset as *Multi30K*. Therefore, we chosed LSTM as our basic model. As a future work, we are going to integrate Transformer into our proposed method and evaluate it on some larger datasets.

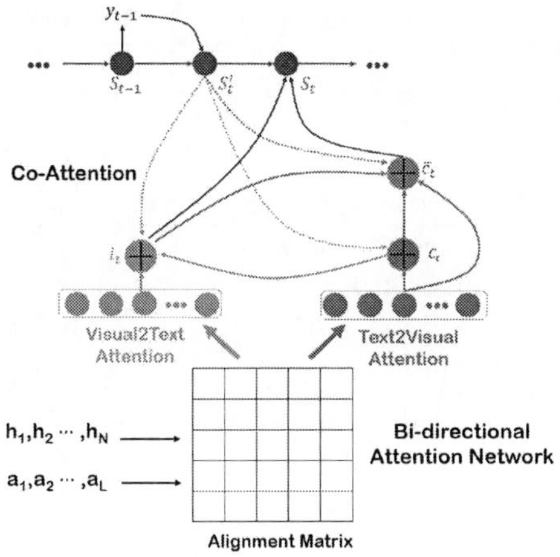

Figure 2: multimodel NMT model with deep semantic interactions

to enhance text and image representations. Specifically, we use text representation $C_i = (h_i^1, h_i^2, \ldots, h_i^N)$ and visual representation $A_i = (a_i^1, a_i^2, \ldots, a_i^L)$ for bi-direction attention network to obtain a shared alignment matrix $S \in R^{N \times L}$.The alignment matrix is computed as follows:

$$S_{n,l} \;=\; g(h_i^n \cdot a_i^l)$$

where $g(\cdot)$ is a scalar function.The $S_{n,l} \in R^{N \times L}$ measures how well the n-th row vector in C_i semantically matches the l-th row vector in A_i. After that, *Text-to-Visual Attention* $\overline{h_i^n}$ and *Visual-to-Text Attention* $\overline{a_i^l}$ will be calculated respectively according to the alignment matrix S. The $\overline{h_i^n}$ calculation formula is as follows:

$$\begin{aligned} w_n^{t2v} &= \mathrm{softmax}(S_{n:}) \\ \overline{h_i^n} &= h_i^n + \sum_l w_{nl}^{t2v} a_i^n \end{aligned}$$

The $\overline{a_i^l}$ calculation formula is as follows:

$$\begin{aligned} w_l^{v2t} &= \mathrm{softmax}(S_{:l}) \\ \overline{a_i^l} &= a_i^l + \sum_i w_{ln}^{v2t} h_i^n \end{aligned}$$

Among them, w_n^{t2v} signifies which image regions are most relevant to each source word. w_l^{v2t} signifies which source words semantically match each visual region mostly. Thus, we can get the final visual feature maps $\overline{A_i}$=$(\overline{a}_i^1, \overline{a}_i^2, \ldots, \overline{a}_i^L)$, and the vectors for the whole source sentence $\overline{C_i}$=$(\overline{h}_i^1, \overline{h}_i^2, \ldots, \overline{h}_i^N)$. Finally, we substituted $\overline{C_i}$ and $\overline{A_i}$ into formulas (1) and (2) in Section 3 to obtain the time-dependent context vector c_t and the time-dependent visual vector i_t.

5 Experiments

5.1 Data

To evaluate our approach, we experimented with three commonly used machine translation dataset, including multimodal machine translation dataset *Multi30K* (Elliott et al., 2016) English-to-German (EN-DE), Global Voices English-to-German (EN-DE)(Tiedemann, 2012), and WMT' 16 (100k) English-to-German (EN-DE).

Multi30K *Multi30K* dataset consists of about 31k bilingual sentence-images pairs, . In this paper, we use 29K English to German parallel sentence pairs with visual annotations as the training set. The 1,014 English to German sentence pairs visual annotations are used as dev set. Finally, the test2016 test dataset is used for evaluation.

Global Voices Global Voices (EN-DE) dataset consists of more than 70k bilingual sentence pairs from summaries of news articles. We randomly sample 2000 data as dev set, 2000 as test set, and use the remained as training set.

WMT'16 (100k) WMT dataset (EN-DE) consists of more than 4.5M bilingual sentence pairs mainly from the proceedings of the European Parliament. In order to focus on evaluating the effectiveness of the retrieved visual information, we attempt to exclude the influence of data size, and randomly sampled 100k sentence pairs as our training set instead of the total 4.5M sentence pairs, which is similar to the number of sentences in the *Multi30K* dataset and Global Voices. We used Newstest2016 as the test set.

5.2 System Setting

Image Retrieval Implementation We used the Microsoft Bing[6] as image search engine. As described in Section 4.1, for each source language sentence, we build 5 search queries and collect 5 images for each sentence. Specifically, if the number of words is less than 5 after stopword filtering, we simpley repeat the keyword list several times

[6] https://global.bing.com/images

to ensure that the number of remained words is enough for creating 5 search queries.

Model Implementation: We implemented our proposed model on the top of Su et al. (2021), which was developed based on OpenNMT (Klein et al., 2017). We used *MOSES*[7] scripts to tokenize, normalize, and lowercase both source and target sentences. For text encoder, we used bi-directional RNN with GRU to extract text features. One 256D single-layer RNN was used for both forward and backward. For visual encoder, we used the res4f layer of pre-trained ResNet-50 (He et al., 2016) to extract visual features. We used Adam optimizer with mini-batches size of 32 to train all models, and set the learning rate as 0.001.

We trained the model up to 15 epochs, and the training was early-stopped if BLEU (Papineni et al., 2002) score of dev set did not improve for 3 epochs. The model with highest BLEU score of the dev set was selected to evaluate the test set. In order to reduce the influence of random seeds on the experimental results and ensure the stability of the final experimental results, we repeated the experiment 5 times with fixed 5 random seeds and used the macro average of BLEU scores as the final result.

Baseline For each dataset, we used the text-only LSTM (Graves, 2012) as a baseline.

For *Multi30K* dataset, we quantitatively compared the proposed method with the following models:

- Zhang et al. (2019) used a text-only Transformer and proposed a universal visual representation method by retrieving images from a topic-image lookup table.
- Su et al. (2021) used a bi-direction attention network and a co-attention mechanism to enhance semantic interaction of text and images.
- Zhao et al. (2021) proposed a novel integration strategy Word-Region Alignment(WRA) of the MNMT model that leverages the WRA to guide the model to translate certain source words into target words while attending to semantically relevant image regions.

We trained these models by employing the same training set and the same training parameters as the proposed model, and report the 4-gram BLEU score (Papineni et al., 2002) for all baselines as well as the proposed method.

[7]http://www.statmt.org/moses/

Method	BLEU Score
Text-only NMT	
Bi-LSTM (Calixto et al., 2017)	33.7
Transformer (Zhang et al., 2019)	36.86
Multimodal NMT with Original Images	
Zhang et al. (2019)	36.86
Zhao et al. (2021)	38.40
Su et al. (2021)	39.20
The proposed method	38.14
Multimodal NMT with Retrieved Images	
Zhang et al. (2019)	36.94
The proposed method	**38.43**

Table 2: Results on Multi30K

System	BLEU Score	
	Global Voices	WMT'16 (100k)
Text-only LSTM	9.22	7.99
The proposed Method	**9.81**	**8.41**

Table 3: Results on Global Voices and WMT'16 (100k)

5.3 Experimental Results

Table 2 shows the experimental results on *Multi30K* dataset. The proposed method obtains a BLEU score of 38.43. Compared with the text-only NMT (Calixto et al., 2017; Vaswani et al., 2017), the proposed method obtains a significantly higher BLEU score. Compared with the multimodal NMT methods with original images (Zhang et al., 2019; Zhao et al., 2021; Su et al., 2021), our proposed method obtains a comparable BLEU score[8]. Compared with the multimodal NMT method with retrieved images (Zhang et al., 2019), the performance gain of the proposed method is approximately 1.5 BLEU.

Futhermore, we quantitiatively compared our study with text-only NMT (Calixto et al., 2017) on two dataset, i.e., Global Voices and WMT'16 (100k), which consist of bilingual sentence pairs without visual annotation. As shown in Table 3, the proposed method achieved a higher BLUE score, demonstrating the effectiveness of the proposed search engine based image retrieval. More experi-

[8]For Su et al. (2021), we trained the multimodal NMT model using the same parameters with our proposed method, and got a comprable BLEU score of 38.1 with our proposed method.

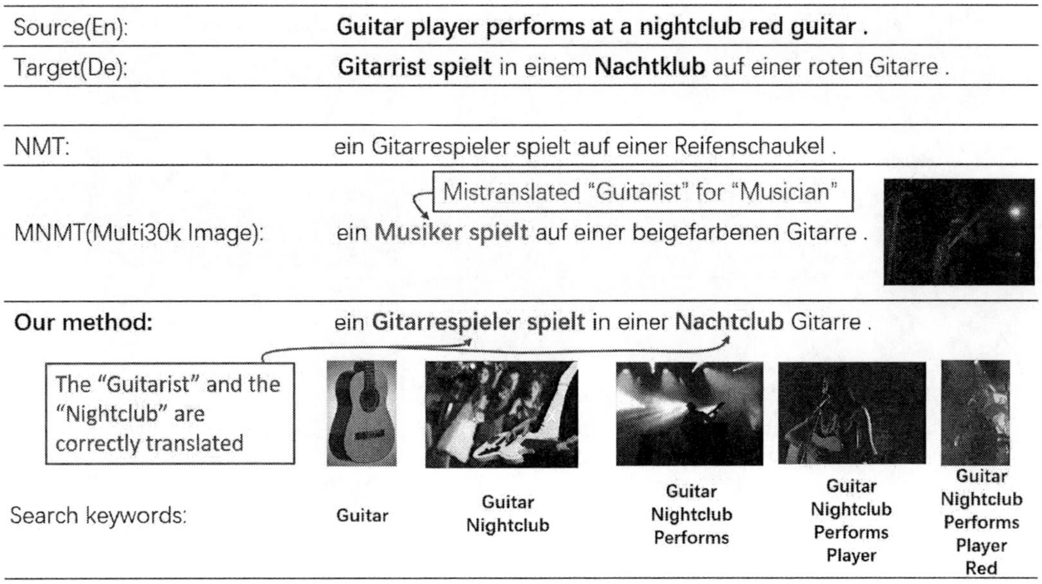

Figure 3: Example of correct translation by the proposed method

mental results and discussions for the influence of collected images are described in Section 6.

Figure 3 shows an example of correct translation by the proposed method. In this example, English words "nightclub" is failed to be translated by the model of Su et al. (2021), as well as the text-only NMT. It is mainly because that the text infomation is not enough for translating while the original image from *Multi30K* is ambiguous and misleading. In the proposed method, we collected 5 images with image search engine according to the method described in Section 4.1, among which 3 images provide effective visual information about "nightclub", and therefore, the proposed method correctly translate "nightclub" into "Nachtclub". Besides, benefit from visual information about "guitar player", the proposed method generates a partially correct translation "Gitarrespieler spielt", while is the model of Su et al. (2021) incorrectly translate "guitar player" into "Musiker spielt" (musician).

6 Analysis and Discussion

6.1 Influence of the Number of Images

For each sentence, several images can be obtained by following the image retrieval method in section 4.1. To evaluate the influence of the number of paired images m, we constrained m in $\{1, 2, 3, 4, 5, 6, 7, 8\}$ for experiments on the *Multi30K* dataset. As shown in figure 4, for different m, we used the images retrieved by search engine and the original images in *Multi30K* dataset respectively for experiments. For images retrieved based on search engines, as the number of images increases, the BLEU score also increased at the beginning(from 37.96 to 38.43) and then decreased when m exceeds 5. The reason might be that retrieving too many images through search engines will lead to an increase in the number of noise images. Therefore, we set $m = 5$ in our models, and drawn a same conclusion as Zhang et al. (2019).

Dataset	images	BLEU
Multi30K	Text-only	37.77
	Random Images	37.65
	Blank Images	37.79
	Retrieved Images	**38.43**
Global Voices	Text-only	9.22
	Random Images	9.29
	Blank Images	9.46
	Retrieved Images	**9.81**
WMT'16 (100k)	Text-only	7.99
	Random Images	8.11
	Blank Images	8.31
	Retrieved Images	**8.41**

Table 4: Translation effect of different data sets under different image conditions

For the original *Multi30K* image, it only has the visual features of an image, so as the number of

Dataset	Sentence	Retrieved image
Multi30K	The person in the striped shirt is mountain climbing.	
Global Voices	Now the city is under a siege from the security forces.	
WMT'16	In the future, integration will be a topic for the whole of society even more than it is today.	

Table 5: Examples of retrieved image from different datasets

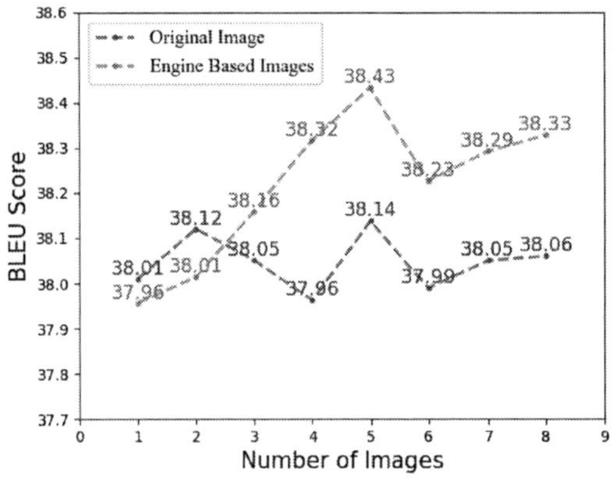

Figure 4: Influence of number of images on the BLEU score.

images increases, the BLEU score has no obvious upward trend. In addition, when m is less than 3, the BLEU score of the image using the original *Multi30K* is higher than that of the retrieved image.

6.2 Influence of the Quality of Images

To evaluate the influence of the quality of collected images, we train the proposed model with randomly retrieved unrelated images, blank images, and retrieved images from image search engine, respectively. The evaluation results are shown in table 4. It is obvious that proposed method achieves the highest BLEU score on all *Multi30K* and Global Voices, demonstrating the effectiveness of visual information from collected images.

Dataset	Number of noise images
Multi30K	61
Global Voices	228
WMT'16	685

Table 6: Number of noise images in 1000 collected images for each dataset

Compared with the model with random images and blank images, the performance gain of collected images is approximately 0.7 & 0.6 BLEU score on *Multi30K*, and 0.5 & 0.3 BLUE score on Global Voices. However, on the WMT'16 (100k) dataset, model with collected images obtains almost the same BLUE score as the model with blank images.

One of the possible reason is that sentences from WMT dataset contains fewer entity words that can be represented by images, and therefore, the proposed search engine based image retrieval method collects numbers of noise images. Sentences from

WMT'16 (100k) describe abstract concepts and complex events, while sentences from *Multi30K* and Global Voices describe real objects and people, which is more reliable for image retrieval. Examples of retrieved images of each dataset are shown in Table 5. For the sentence from *Multi30K* dataset, our method easily retrieves an image that represents "A man is rock climbing". For the sentence from Global Voice dataset, the retrieved image is partially consistent with the source sentence, containing contents of "city","siege" and"forces". However, for the sentence from WMT'16 dataset, it is obvious that the retrieved image contains little effective visual information and can hardly provide assistance to translation.

To verify the hypotheses, we randomly sampled 1,000 images from the collected image set of each dataset, and manually classify the collected images into 2 classes, i.e., class of images that can provide visual information of the search query, and class of images that can not. Images in second class are defined as noise images. As shown in Table 6, for *Multi30K* dataset, only 61 out of 1000 collected images sampled are noise images, and the proportion is 6.1%. However, in the WMT'16 dataset, the number of noise images obtained through retrieval is 685, accounting for more than half of the total number of images.Therefore, our method performs poorly on the WMT'16 dataset. For the Global Voices dataset, the number of noise images is 228, which is between the *Multi30K* and WMT'16 dataset, and the retrieved images also show better performance than the NMT model. It is insteresting to find that collected image set for *Multi30K* has smallest proportion of noise image and achieves the biggest gain of translation performance, while the collected image set has the largest proportion of noise image and achieves the smallest gain of translation performance.

7 Conclusions

In this paper, inspired by problem of Zhang et al. (2019) caused by applying limited collections of sentence-image pairs, we propose an open-vocabulary image retrieval methods to collect descriptive images for bilingual parallel corpus using image search engine, and introduce text-aware attentive visual encoder to filter incorrectly collected noise images. Experiment results show that our proposed method achieves significant improvements over strong baselines, especially on *Multi30K* and Global Voices. Further analysis shows that the effectiveness of the proposed methods in translating sentences that describe real objects and people.

As one of our future work, we are going to evaluate our proposed method on some larger datasets, such as the entire WMT'16 dataset, and analyze the influence of the number of texts for the task of multimodal NMT.

Acknowledgements

This research is supported by the Stable Support Project for Shenzhen Higher Education Institutions (SZWD2021011).

References

Dzmitry Bahdanau, Kyunghyun Cho, and Yoshua Bengio. 2014. Neural machine translation by jointly learning to align and translate. *arXiv preprint arXiv:1409.0473*.

Loïc Barrault, Fethi Bougares, Lucia Specia, Chiraag Lala, Desmond Elliott, and Stella Frank. 2018. Findings of the third shared task on multimodal machine translation. In *Proceedings of the Third Conference on Machine Translation: Shared Task Papers*, volume 2, pages 308–327.

Ozan Caglayan, Loïc Barrault, and Fethi Bougares. 2016. Multimodal attention for neural machine translation. *arXiv preprint arXiv:1609.03976*.

Ozan Caglayan, Pranava Madhyastha, Lucia Specia, and Loïc Barrault. 2019. Probing the need for visual context in multimodal machine translation. In *Proceedings of the 2019 Conference of the North*, pages 4159–4170. Association for Computational Linguistics.

Iacer Calixto and Qun Liu. 2017. Incorporating global visual features into attention-based neural machine translation. In *Proceedings of the 2017 Conference on Empirical Methods in Natural Language Processing*, pages 992–1003.

Iacer Calixto, Qun Liu, and Nick Campbell. 2017. Doubly-attentive decoder for multi-modal neural machine translation. In *Proceedings of the 55th Annual Meeting of the Association for Computational Linguistics (Volume 1: Long Papers)*, pages 1913–1924.

Kyunghyun Cho, Bart Van Merriënboer, Dzmitry Bahdanau, and Yoshua Bengio. 2014. On the properties of neural machine translation: Encoder-decoder approaches. *arXiv preprint arXiv:1409.1259*.

Jean-Benoit Delbrouck and Stephane Dupont. 2017. Multimodal compact bilinear pooling for multimodal neural machine translation. *arXiv preprint arXiv:1703.08084*.

Desmond Elliott. 2018. Adversarial evaluation of multimodal machine translation. In *Proceedings of the 2018 Conference on Empirical Methods in Natural Language Processing*, pages 2974–2978.

Desmond Elliott, Stella Frank, Loïc Barrault, Fethi Bougares, and Lucia Specia. 2017. Findings of the second shared task on multimodal machine translation and multilingual image description. In *Proceedings of the Second Conference on Machine Translation*, pages 215–233.

Desmond Elliott, Stella Frank, Khalil Sima'an, and Lucia Specia. 2016. Multi30k: Multilingual english-german image descriptions. *arXiv preprint arXiv:1605.00459*.

Jonas Gehring, Michael Auli, David Grangier, and Yann N Dauphin. 2016. A convolutional encoder model for neural machine translation. *arXiv preprint arXiv:1611.02344*.

Alex Graves. 2012. Long short-term memory. *Supervised sequence labelling with recurrent neural networks*, pages 37–45.

Stig-Arne Grönroos, Benoit Huet, Mikko Kurimo, Jorma Laaksonen, Bernard Merialdo, Phu Pham, Mats Sjöberg, Umut Sulubacak, Jörg Tiedemann, Raphael Troncy, et al. 2018. The memad submission to the wmt18 multimodal translation task. *arXiv preprint arXiv:1808.10802*.

Kaiming He, Xiangyu Zhang, Shaoqing Ren, and Jian Sun. 2016. Deep residual learning for image recognition. In *Proceedings of the IEEE conference on computer vision and pattern recognition*, pages 770–778.

Po-Yao Huang, Frederick Liu, Sz-Rung Shiang, Jean Oh, and Chris Dyer. 2016. Attention-based multimodal neural machine translation. In *Proceedings of the First Conference on Machine Translation: Volume 2, Shared Task Papers*, pages 639–645.

Julia Ive, Pranava Madhyastha, and Lucia Specia. 2019. Distilling translations with visual awareness. *arXiv preprint arXiv:1906.07701*.

Guillaume Klein, Yoon Kim, Yuntian Deng, Jean Senellart, and Alexander M Rush. 2017. Opennmt: Open-source toolkit for neural machine translation. In *Proceedings of ACL 2017, System Demonstrations*, pages 67–72.

Huan Lin, Fandong Meng, Jinsong Su, Yongjing Yin, Zhengyuan Yang, Yubin Ge, Jie Zhou, and Jiebo Luo. 2020. Dynamic context-guided capsule network for multimodal machine translation. In *Proceedings of the 28th ACM International Conference on Multimedia*, pages 1320–1329.

Tsung-Yi Lin, Michael Maire, Serge Belongie, James Hays, Pietro Perona, Deva Ramanan, Piotr Dollár, and C Lawrence Zitnick. 2014. Microsoft coco: Common objects in context. In *European conference on computer vision*, pages 740–755. Springer.

Kishore Papineni, Salim Roukos, Todd Ward, and Wei-Jing Zhu. 2002. Bleu: a method for automatic evaluation of machine translation. In *Proceedings of the 40th annual meeting of the Association for Computational Linguistics*, pages 311–318.

Lucia Specia, Stella Frank, Khalil Sima'An, and Desmond Elliott. 2016. A shared task on multimodal machine translation and crosslingual image description. In *Proceedings of the First Conference on Machine Translation: Volume 2, Shared Task Papers*, pages 543–553.

Jinsong Su, Jinchang Chen, Hui Jiang, Chulun Zhou, Huan Lin, Yubin Ge, Qingqiang Wu, and Yongxuan Lai. 2021. Multi-modal neural machine translation with deep semantic interactions. *Information Sciences*, 554:47–60.

Jörg Tiedemann. 2012. Parallel data, tools and interfaces in opus. In *Proceedings of the Eight International Conference on Language Resources and Evaluation (LREC'12)*, Istanbul, Turkey. European Language Resources Association (ELRA).

Ashish Vaswani, Noam Shazeer, Niki Parmar, Jakob Uszkoreit, Llion Jones, Aidan N Gomez, Łukasz Kaiser, and Illia Polosukhin. 2017. Attention is all you need. *Advances in neural information processing systems*, 30.

Ian H Witten, Gordon W Paynter, Eibe Frank, Carl Gutwin, and Craig G Nevill-Manning. 2005. Kea: Practical automated keyphrase extraction. In *Design and Usability of Digital Libraries: Case Studies in the Asia Pacific*, pages 129–152. IGI global.

Jingyi Zhang, Masao Utiyama, Eiichiro Sumita, Graham Neubig, and Satoshi Nakamura. 2017. Nict-naist system for wmt17 multimodal translation task. In *Proceedings of the Second Conference on Machine Translation*, pages 477–482.

Zhuosheng Zhang, Kehai Chen, Rui Wang, Masao Utiyama, Eiichiro Sumita, Zuchao Li, and Hai Zhao. 2019. Neural machine translation with universal visual representation. In *International Conference on Learning Representations*.

Yuting Zhao, Mamoru Komachi, Tomoyuki Kajiwara, and Chenhui Chu. 2021. Word-region alignment-guided multimodal neural machine translation. *IEEE/ACM Transactions on Audio, Speech, and Language Processing*, 30:244–259.

Silo NLP's Participation at WAT2022

Shantipriya Parida[*], Subhadarshi Panda[†], Stig-Arne Grönroos [*‡], Mark Granroth-Wilding [*], Mika Koistinen [*]
[*]Silo AI, Helsinki, Finland
{firstname.lastname}@silo.ai
[†]Graduate Center, City University of New York, USA
spanda@gradcenter.cuny.edu
[‡]University of Helsinki, Finland

Abstract

This paper provides the system description of "Silo NLP's" submission to the Workshop on Asian Translation (WAT2022). We have participated in the Indic Multimodal tasks (English→Hindi, English→Malayalam, and English→Bengali, Multimodal Translation). For text-only translation, we trained Transformers from scratch and fine-tuned mBART-50 models. For multimodal translation, we used the same mBART architecture and extracted object tags from the images to use as visual features concatenated with the text sequence.

Our submission tops many tasks including English→Hindi multimodal translation (evaluation test), English→Malayalam text-only and multimodal translation (evaluation test), English→Bengali multimodal translation (challenge test), and English→Bengali text-only translation (evaluation test).

1 Introduction

Machine translation (MT) is a classic sub-field in NLP which investigates the usage of computer software to translate text or speech from one language to another without human involvement (Yang et al., 2020). Although MT performance has reached near the level of human translators for many high-resource languages, it remains challenging for many low-resource languages (Popel et al., 2020; Costa-jussà et al., 2022). Also, effective usage of other modalities (e.g. image) in MT is an important research area in the past few years (Sulubacak et al., 2020; Parida et al., 2021b,a).

The WAT is an open evaluation campaign focusing on Asian languages since 2013 (Nakazawa et al., 2020, 2022). In the WAT2022 Multimodal track, a new Indian language *Bengali* was introduced for English→Bengali text, multimodal translation, and Bengali image captioning task.[1]

The multimodal translation tasks in WAT2022 consist of image caption translation, in which the input is a descriptive source language caption together with the image it describes, while the output is a target language caption. The multimodal input enables the use of image context to disambiguate source words with multiple senses.

In this system description paper, we explain our approach for the tasks (including the sub-tasks) we participated in:

Task 1: English→Hindi (EN-HI) Multimodal Translation

- EN-HI text-only translation
- EN-HI multimodal translation

Task 2: English→Malayalam (EN-ML) Multimodal Translation

- EN-ML text-only translation
- EN-ML multimodal translation

Task 3: English→Bengali (EN-BN) Multimodal Translation

- EN-BN text-only translation
- EN-BN multimodal translation

2 Data sets

We used the data sets specified by the organizer for the related tasks along with additional synthetic data for performance improvement. The use of additional data places some[2] of our submissions in the unconstrained track.

Task 1: English→Hindi Multimodal Translation For this task, the organizers provided HindiVisualGenome 1.1 (Parida et al., 2019)[3] dataset (HVG for short). The training part consists of 29k English and Hindi short captions of rectangular areas in photos of various scenes and it is complemented

[1] https://ufal.mff.cuni.cz/bengali-visual-genome/wat-2022-english-bengali-multim

[2] All except the EN–HI and EN–ML text-only systems.

[3] https://lindat.mff.cuni.cz/repository/xmlui/handle/11234/1-3267

Proceedings of the 9th Workshop on Asian Translation, pages 99–105
October 17, 2022.

by three test sets: development (D-Test), evaluation (E-Test) and challenge test set (C-Test). Our WAT submissions were for E-Test (denoted "EV" in WAT official tables) and C-Test (denoted "CH" in WAT tables).

For the synthetic image features, we use the Flickr8k data set (Hodosh et al., 2013). Even though it is an image captioning data set, we discard the images, treating the data set as in-domain monolingual data. We use a machine translation into Hindi (Rathi, 2020) as the target side, and generate image features using the procedure described in Section 3.4.

The statistics of the datasets are shown in Table 1.

Task 2: English→Malayalam Multimodal Translation For this task, the organizers provided MalayalamVisualGenome 1.0 dataset[4] (MVG for short). MVG is an extension of the HVG dataset for supporting Malayalam, which belongs to the Dravidian language family (Kumar et al., 2017). The dataset size and images are the same as HVG. While HVG contains bilingual English–Hindi segments, MVG contains bilingual English–Malayalam segments, with the English, shared across HVG and MVG, see Table 1.

Task 3: English→Bengali Multimodal Translation For this task, the organizers provided BengaliVisualGenome 1.0 dataset[5] (BVG for short). BVG is an extension of the HVG dataset for supporting Bengali. The dataset size and images are the same as HVG, and MVG, see Table 1.

3 Experimental Details

This section describes the experimental details of the tasks we participated in.

3.1 EN-HI, EN-ML, EN-BN text-only translation

For EN–HI and EN–ML text-only (E-Test and C-Test) translation, we fine-tuned a pre-trained mBART-50 model (Tang et al., 2020) without using any additional resources.

For EN-BN text-only (E-Test) translation, we used the Transformer base model as implemented in Open-NMT-Py[6] using Bangla Natural Language

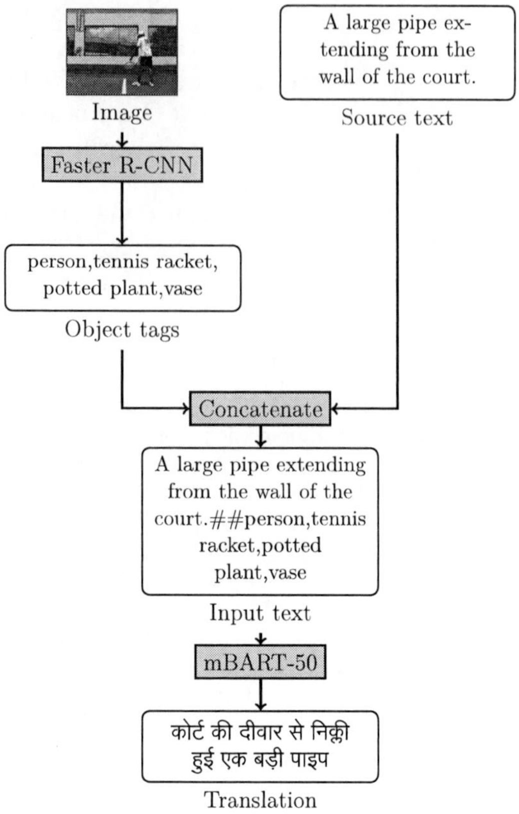

Figure 1: Multimodal translation pipeline.

Image to Text (BNLIT) (Jishan et al., 2019) as an additional dataset. The BNLIT is an image-to-text dataset containing 8743 images and their corresponding text in Bengali. For our experiment, we used Bengali text and translated it into English.

Subword units were constructed using the word pieces algorithm (Johnson et al., 2017). Tokenization is handled automatically as part of the preprocessing pipeline of word pieces. We generated the vocabulary of 32k sub-word types jointly for both the source and target languages. The training steps are defined for 300K with 5K as validation steps and checkpoint steps. For translation, we decoded using beam search with beam size 5.

For C-Test we fine-tuned a pre-trained m-BART-50 model without any additional resources.

3.2 EN-HI, EN-ML, EN-BN Multimodal translation

Our multimodal translation pipeline is shown in Figure 1. For EN-HI multimodal (E-Test and C-Test) translation, we used the object tags extracted from the HVG dataset images (see Section 3.3) for image features and concatenated them with the text.

[4] https://lindat.mff.cuni.cz/repository/xmlui/handle/11234/1-3533

[5] http://hdl.handle.net/11234/1-3722

[6] https://opennmt.net/OpenNMT-py/

Set	Sentences	Tokens			
		English	Hindi	Malayalam	Bengali
Train	28930	143164	145448	107126	113978
D-Test	998	4922	4978	3619	3936
E-Test	1595	7853	7852	5689	6408
C-Test	1400	8186	8639	6044	6657

Table 1: Statistics of our data used in the English→Hindi, English→Malayalam, and English→Bengali Multimodal task: the number of sentences and tokens.

Additionally, we used synthetic image features (see Section 3.4. The combined data set was used to fine-tune a pre-trained mBART-50 model.

For EN-ML multimodal (E-Test and C-Test) translation, we used object tags extracted from the MVG dataset images and concatenated with the text, and fine-tuned on the mBART-50 model.

For EN-BN (E-Test and C-Test) translation, we used object tags extracted from the BVG dataset images and concatenated with the text, and fine-tuned on the mBART-50 model.

For all the multimodal translation experiments using mBART, the decoding beam size was set to 5. Since we used the pre-trained mBART model and fine-tuned it on the visual genome datasets, we did not build our own vocabulary but rather used the pre-trained mBART vocabulary without any modifications.

3.3 Extracted image features

We derive the list of object tags for a given image using the pre-trained Faster R-CNN with ResNet-101-C4 backbone. It can recognize 80 object types from the COCO data set (Lin et al., 2014). Based on their confidence scores, we pick the top 10 object tags. In cases where less than 10 object tags are detected, we consider all the detected tags. Figure 2 shows examples of object tags detected for images from the challenge test set. The detected object tags are then concatenated to the English sentence which needs to be translated to Hindi, Malayalam, and Bengali. The concatenation is done using the special token '##' as the separator. The separator is followed by comma-separated object tags. Adding objects enables the model to utilize visual concepts which may not be readily available in the original sentence. The English sentences along with the object tags are fed to the encoder of the mBART model.

3.4 Synthetic image features

We generate synthetic training data for the multimodal translation task by enriching text-only data using synthetic image features (Grönroos et al., 2018). Grönroos et al. (2018) use continuous image features and generate the synthetic dummy features by taking the average vector of the features in the training data. We improve on this procedure by generating discrete features individually for each enriched training example by decoding from a sequence-to-sequence (s2s) model. The s2s model is trained using the multimodal training data (HVG), but instead of training the normal way, we use both source language and target language text as input (with a separator token between), and our object tags as the output. The model is a Transformer-base (Vaswani et al., 2017) model trained using the Marian-NMT (Junczys-Dowmunt et al., 2018) framework. The trained model is then used to enrich text-only parallel data with synthetic features.

Our method applies to any text-only parallel data, even though in this experiment we use it to enrich the text from an image captioning data set. Due to the relatively small size of the multimodal training data sets, domain match of additional training data has great importance for multimodal translation (Grönroos et al., 2018). It is therefore important to apply domain adaptation techniques when using general-domain text-only parallel data.

4 Results

We report the official automatic evaluation results of our models for all the participating tasks in Table 2.

On the E-Test sets, our multimodal systems receive the highest BLEU scores for English→Hindi and English→Malayalam, and our text-only systems outperform other text-only systems for English→Malayalam and English→Bengali. Our multimodal systems consistently outperform our text-only systems, with increases between +1.1 and +10.2 BLEU.

On the C-Test challenge sets, we have the highest BLEU score for English→Bengali multimodal translation. Again, our multimodal systems outper-

English input: Red dragon fruit on a fruit stand.
Object tags: person, banana, apple, broccoli
Text-only translation: एक स्वाद के फल पर लाल नारंगी फल
Gloss: Red orange fruit on a flavored fruit
Multimodal translation: एक फल स्टैंड पर लाल ड्रैगन फल।
Gloss: Red dragon fruit on a fruit stand.
Reference: फल स्टैंड पर लाल ड्रैगन फल।
Gloss: Red dragon fruit on a fruit stand.

English input: A metal and stone column holding a bell and cross.
Object tags: clock
Text-only translation: एक धातु और घड़ी पकड़े हुए
Gloss: Holding a metal and a watch
Multimodal translation: एक धातु और पत्थर के स्तंभ एक घंटी और क्रॉस पकड़े हुए।
Gloss: A metal and stone pillar holding a bell and a cross.
Reference: एक धातु और पत्थर के स्तंभ एक घंटी और क्रॉस के आधार बनें हुए।
Gloss: A metal and stone pillar forming the basis of a bell and cross.

English input: date the photo was taken
Object tags: teddy bear, cat
Text-only translation: ছবি ছবি চিত্র করা হয়
Gloss: Picture is picture picture
Multimodal translation: ছবি তোলা হয়েছিল
Gloss: The picture was taken
Reference: তারিখটি ছবি তোলা হয়েছিল
Gloss: The date it was photographed

English input: open door of a second bus
Object tags: suitcase, person, bus, backpack, truck, traffic light
Text-only translation: একটি দুটি বাসের খোলা দরজা
Gloss: An open door of two buses
Multimodal translation: একটি দ্বিতীয় বাসের দরজা
Gloss: A second bus door
Reference: দ্বিতীয় বাসের দরজা খোলা
Gloss: The door of the second bus is open

English input: the two male players are after the ball
Object tags: person, sports ball, motorcycle, umbrella, tennis racket, backpack
Text-only translation: ഒരു ജിറാഫ് പുല്ല് തിന്നുന്നു
Gloss: A giraffe eats grass
Multimodal translation: രണ്ട് പുരുഷ കളിക്കാർ പന്തിന് ശേഷം
Gloss: Two male players after the ball
Reference: രണ്ട് പുരുഷ കളിക്കാർ പന്തിന് പുറകേയാണ്
Gloss: Two male players are behind the ball

English input: Grass growing on the grass tennis court.
Object tags: person, tennis racket, sports ball
Text-only translation: പുല്ല് ടെന്നീസ് കോർട്ടിൽ വളരുന്ന പുല്ല്.
Gloss: Grass is the grass that grows on a tennis court.
Multimodal translation: പുല്ല് ടെന്നീസ് കോർട്ടിൽ പുല്ല് വളരുന്നു.
Gloss: Grass grows on a grass tennis court.
Reference: ഗ്രാസ് ടെന്നീസ് കോർട്ടിൽ പുല്ല് വളരുന്നു.
Gloss: Grass grows on a grass tennis court.

Figure 2: Sample translations for the challenge test set. Both the text-only and multimodal translations are shown. The object tags detected and used in the multimodal translation setup are also shown. Hindi translations are shown for the top two images, Bengali translations are shown for the middle two images, and Malayalam translations are shown for the bottom two images.

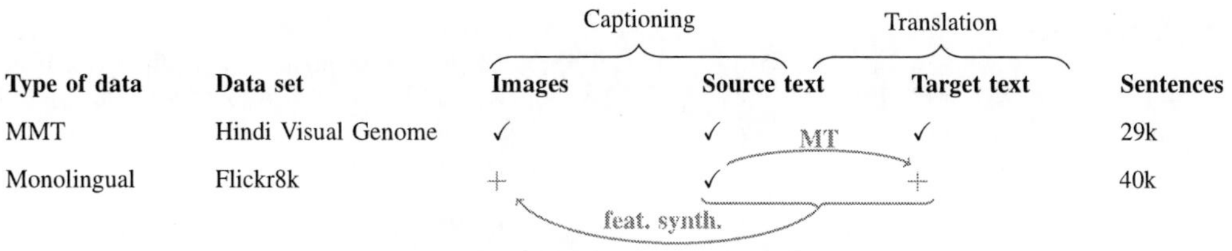

Figure 3: Process for generating synthetic image features. Green arrows indicate processes to synthesize data, and green plus signs indicate the resulting synthetic data. MT is short for machine translation, feat. synth. for image feature synthesis.

System and WAT Task Label	WAT BLEU Silo NLP	WAT BLEU Best Comp	HUMAN Silo NLP	HUMAN Best Comp	NOTE
English→Hindi MM Task					
MMEVTEXT21en-hi	36.2	**42.9**			
MMEVMM22en-hi	**42.0**	39.4			
MMCHTEXT22en-hi	29.6	**41.8**	2.715	**3.078**	
MMCHMM22en-hi	39.1	**39.3**			
English→Malayalam MM Task					
MMEVTEXT21en-ml	**30.8**	30.6			
MMEVMM22en-ml	**41.0**	–			
MMCHTEXT22en-ml	14.6	**19.5**	2.013	Not Available	
MMCHMM22en-ml	**20.4**	–			
English→Bengali MM Task					
MMEVTEXT22en-bn	**41.0**	**41.0**			
MMEVMM22en-bn	42.1	**43.9**			
MMCHTEXT22en-bn	22.6	32.9	2.658	**3.525**	Competitor used external data
MMCHMM22en-bn	**28.7**	**28.7**			

Table 2: WAT2022 Automatic and Manual Evaluation Results for English→Hindi, English→Malayalam, and English→Bengali. Rows containing "TEXT" in the task label name denote text-only translation track, and the rows representing "MM" denote multimodal translation including text and images. "–" indicates single submission for the task. For each task, we show the score of our system (Silo NLP) and the score of the best competitor in the respective task.

form our text-only systems, with increases between +5.7 and +9.5 BLEU.

It should be noted that our English→Hindi multimodal system and English→Bengali text-only system are unconstrained, making use of substantial additions of in-domain data. For these language pairs, the increase in translation quality can not be attributed entirely to multimodality. However, for English→Malayalam both systems use the same training sentences, making these systems comparable. The English→Malayalam multimodal system outperforms the text-only system by +10.2 BLEU for E-test and +5.7 BLEU for C-test. As the C-test challenge set is constructed to contain translational ambiguity, the improvement is an indication that the image features are useful for disambiguation. The human evaluation scores from the WAT organizers for the available sub-tasks are updated in Table 2.

We demonstrate examples of translations obtained for the challenge test set in Figure 2. The extracted image features in the form of object tags are also shown for each image in the figure. We observe that the multimodal translations are notably better than the text-only translations. This is consistent with the pattern of the BLEU scores in Table 2.

5 Conclusions

In this system description paper, we presented our system for three tasks in WAT2022: (a) English→Hindi, (b) English→Malayalam, and (c) English→Bengali Multimodal Translation. We released the code through Github for research[7].

In the next step, we will explore the usage of synthetic features in multimodal translation for the Malayalam and Bengali languages, to make use of available text-only corpora for these language pairs.

[7]https://github.com/shantipriyap/SiloNLP_WAT2022

Acknowledgements

We are thankful to Silo AI[8], Helsinki, Finland for the computation resources and the necessary support for participating in WAT2022.

References

Marta R Costa-jussà, James Cross, Onur Çelebi, Maha Elbayad, Kenneth Heafield, Kevin Heffernan, Elahe Kalbassi, Janice Lam, Daniel Licht, Jean Maillard, et al. 2022. No language left behind: Scaling human-centered machine translation. *arXiv e-prints*, pages arXiv–2207.

Stig-Arne Grönroos, Benoit Huet, Mikko Kurimo, Jorma Laaksonen, Bernard Merialdo, Phu Pham, Mats Sjöberg, Umut Sulubacak, Jörg Tiedemann, Raphaël Troncy, and Raúl Vázquez. 2018. The MeMAD submission to the WMT18 multimodal translation task. In *Proceedings of the Third Conference on Machine Translation (WMT)*. The Association for Computational Linguistics.

Micah Hodosh, Peter Young, and Julia Hockenmaier. 2013. Framing image description as a ranking task: Data, models and evaluation metrics. *Journal of Artificial Intelligence Research*, 47:853–899.

Md. Asifuzzaman Jishan, Khan Raqib Mahmud, and Abul Kalam Al Azad. 2019. Bangla natural language image to text (bnlit).

Melvin Johnson, Mike Schuster, Quoc V. Le, Maxim Krikun, Yonghui Wu, Zhifeng Chen, Nikhil Thorat, Fernanda Viégas, Martin Wattenberg, Greg Corrado, Macduff Hughes, and Jeffrey Dean. 2017. Google's multilingual neural machine translation system: Enabling zero-shot translation. *Transactions of the Association for Computational Linguistics*, 5:339–351.

Marcin Junczys-Dowmunt, Roman Grundkiewicz, Tomasz Dwojak, Hieu Hoang, Kenneth Heafield, Tom Neckermann, Frank Seide, Ulrich Germann, Alham Fikri Aji, Nikolay Bogoychev, André F. T. Martins, and Alexandra Birch. 2018. Marian: Fast neural machine translation in C++. In *Proceedings of ACL 2018, System Demonstrations*, pages 116–121, Melbourne, Australia. Association for Computational Linguistics.

Arun Kumar, Ryan Cotterell, Lluís Padró, and Antoni Oliver. 2017. Morphological analysis of the Dravidian language family. In *Proceedings of the 15th Conference of the European Chapter of the Association for Computational Linguistics: Volume 2, Short Papers*, pages 217–222.

Tsung-Yi Lin, Michael Maire, Serge Belongie, James Hays, Pietro Perona, Deva Ramanan, Piotr Dollár, and C Lawrence Zitnick. 2014. Microsoft COCO: Common objects in context. In *European conference on computer vision*, pages 740–755. Springer.

Toshiaki Nakazawa, Hideya Mino, Isao Goto, Raj Dabre, Shohei Higashiyama, Shantipriya Parida, Anoop Kunchukuttan, Makoto Morishita, Ondřej Bojar, Chenhui Chu, Akiko Eriguchi, Kaori Abe, Yusuke Oda, and Sadao Kurohashi. 2022. Overview of the 9th workshop on Asian translation. In *Proceedings of the 9th Workshop on Asian Translation (WAT2022)*, Gyeongju, Republic of Korea. Association for Computational Linguistics.

Toshiaki Nakazawa, Hideki Nakayama, Chenchen Ding, Raj Dabre, Shohei Higashiyama, Hideya Mino, Isao Goto, Win Pa Pa, Anoop Kunchukuttan, Shantipriya Parida, et al. 2020. Overview of the 7th workshop on Asian translation. In *Proceedings of the 7th Workshop on Asian Translation*, pages 1–44.

Shantipriya Parida, Ondřej Bojar, and Satya Ranjan Dash. 2019. Hindi visual genome: A dataset for multi-modal English to Hindi machine translation. *Computación y Sistemas*, 23(4).

Shantipriya Parida, Subhadarshi Panda, Satya Prakash Biswal, Ketan Kotwal, Arghyadeep Sen, Satya Ranjan Dash, and Petr Motlicek. 2021a. Multimodal neural machine translation system for English to Bengali. In *Proceedings of the First Workshop on Multimodal Machine Translation for Low Resource Languages (MMTLRL 2021)*, pages 31–39, Online (Virtual Mode). INCOMA Ltd.

Shantipriya Parida, Subhadarshi Panda, Ketan Kotwal, Amulya Ratna Dash, Satya Ranjan Dash, Yashvardhan Sharma, Petr Motlicek, and Ondřej Bojar. 2021b. Nlphut's participation at wat2021. In *Proceedings of the 8th Workshop on Asian Translation (WAT2021)*, pages 146–154.

Martin Popel, Marketa Tomkova, Jakub Tomek, Łukasz Kaiser, Jakob Uszkoreit, Ondřej Bojar, and Zdeněk Žabokrtský. 2020. Transforming machine translation: a deep learning system reaches news translation quality comparable to human professionals. *Nature communications*, 11(1):1–15.

Ankit Rathi. 2020. Deep learning apporach for image captioning in Hindi language. In *2020 International Conference on Computer, Electrical & Communication Engineering (ICCECE)*, pages 1–8. IEEE.

Umut Sulubacak, Ozan Caglayan, Stig-Arne Grönroos, Aku Rouhe, Desmond Elliott, Lucia Specia, and Jörg Tiedemann. 2020. Multimodal machine translation through visuals and speech. *Machine Translation*, 34(2):97–147.

Yuqing Tang, Chau Tran, Xian Li, Peng-Jen Chen, Naman Goyal, Vishrav Chaudhary, Jiatao Gu, and Angela Fan. 2020. Multilingual translation with extensible multilingual pretraining and finetuning. *arXiv preprint arXiv:2008.00401*.

Ashish Vaswani, Noam Shazeer, Niki Parmar, Jakob Uszkoreit, Llion Jones, Aidan N. Gomez, Lukasz Kaiser, and Illia Polosukhin. 2017. Attention is all

[8]https://silo.ai

you need. In *Advances in Neural Information Processing Systems*, pages 6000–6010.

Shuoheng Yang, Yuxin Wang, and Xiaowen Chu. 2020. A survey of deep learning techniques for neural machine translation. *arXiv preprint arXiv:2002.07526*.

PICT@WAT 2022: Neural Machine Translation Systems for Indic Languages

Anupam Patil
anupampatil44@gmail.com

Isha Joshi
joshiishaa@gmail.com

Dipali Kadam
ddk@pict.edu

SCTR's Pune Institute of Computer Technology, India

(Team ID: 5592)

Abstract

Translation entails more than simply translating words from one language to another. It is vitally essential for effective cross-cultural communication, thus making good translation systems an important requirement. We describe our systems in this paper, which were submitted to the WAT 2022 translation shared tasks. As part of the Multi-modal translation tasks' text-only translation sub-tasks, we submitted three Neural Machine Translation systems based on Transformer models for English to Malayalam, English to Bengali, and English to Hindi text translation. We found significant results on the leaderboard for English-Indic (en-xx) systems utilizing BLEU and RIBES scores as comparative metrics in our studies. For the respective translations of English to Malayalam, Bengali, and Hindi, we obtained BLEU scores of 19.50, 32.90, and 41.80 for the challenge subset and 30.60, 39.80, and 42.90 on the benchmark evaluation subset data.

1 Introduction

The initial approach used in machine translation was rule-based. RBMT (Rule-Based Machine Translation) models use linguistic information about both the source and the target language to generate the translation. Platforms such as Apertium [1] use this approach. Eventually, SMT (Statistical Machine Translation) models came about, which did not use a predefined set of rules but inferred the rules by analyzing the given text (Koehn and Senellart, 2010). While SMT-based models provide more natural translations, RBMT systems provide translations that are truer to the original text (Forcada et al., 2011).

Machine translation (MT) systems have struggled with ambiguity in the source language while translating text, among other challenges. With the advent of deep learning techniques, neural networks are being used for machine translation tasks. Neural machine translation (NMT) models use massive amounts of training data and computational power to correctly identify the importance of the portion of the text data to generate the output text (Popel et al., 2020).

Recent advances in neural machine translation have focused on translating a source language into a specific target language. For this job, several approaches have been offered. Early NMT architectures used a fixed length approach to generate variable length outputs. The source text's length was fixed, irrespective of the length of the text. Models such as RCTM (Kalchbrenner and Blunsom, 2013) and RNNEncdec (Cho et al., 2014) use this approach. Eventually, newer architectures began using a variable length representation for the input text. GNMT (Wu et al., 2016) and ByteNet (Kalchbrenner et al., 2016) are architectures that use layered neural networks for translation (Tan et al., 2020).

In this paper, we describe our NMT systems, which were submitted to the translation shared tasks at WAT 2022 (Nakazawa et al., 2022) .

2 Related Work

The majority of NMT research has focused on using monolingual data or parallel data that includes other language pairs. NMT systems have consistently outperformed conventional machine translation methods such as rule-based and statistical-based approaches. NMT models typically operate with a fixed vocabulary; however, the translation is an open-vocabulary problem. Several approaches have been proposed to resolve this issue. Byte-Pair-Encoding (BPE) (Sennrich et al., 2015) enables NMT model translation on open vocabulary by en-

[1] https://github.com/apertium

Proceedings of the 9th Workshop on Asian Translation, pages 106–110
October 17, 2022.

English Sentence	Malayalam Translation	Bengali Translation	Hindi Translation
Little gray metal scissors	ചാരനിറത്തിലുള്ള മെറ്റൽ കത്രിക	ছোট ধূসর ধাতব কাঁচি	छोटे ग्रे धातु के कैंची
Dog has black nose	നായയ്ക്ക് കറുത്ത മൂക്ക് ഉണ്ട്	কুকুরের নাক কালো	कुत्ते की नाक काली होती है
A person is holding a kite	ഒരു വ്യക്തി ഒരു കൈറ്റ് പിടിക്കുന്നു	একজন ব্যক্তি একটি ঘুড়ি ধরে আছেন	एक व्यक्ति पतंग पकड़ा हुआ है

Table 1: Sample translations generated by our systems for the given English inputs.

coding rare and unknown words as a sequence of subword units.

NMT models typically employ the conventional sequence-to-sequence learning architecture, made up of an encoder and a decoder. In encoder-decoder mechanisms, words are translated into word embeddings in the encoder and then transferred to the decoder, which generates the following word in the translation using an attention mechanism, encoder representations, and preceding words. Several methodologies based on deep neural networks have been proposed, such as Recurrent Neural Networks (Cho et al., 2014), LSTM (Sutskever et al., 2014), Convolutional Neural Networks (Gehring et al., 2017), and Transformers (Vaswani et al., 2017), which can serve as encoders and decoders. Several approaches have been explored for machine translation in Malayalam, Bengali and Hindi.

2.1 Malayalam

Malayalam is a Dravidian language primarily spoken in southern India. It is a low resource language with very few usable resources for the purpose of training NMT models (Premjith et al., 2019). A rule-based approach for English to Malayalam translations has been proposed by Rajan et al. (2009). A modified rule-based approach using an SMT system was introduced by Rahul et al. (2009). There is little work in English to Malayalam translation systems that are based on deep neural networks, an example being the Google NMT system (Johnson et al., 2017).

2.2 Bengali

Bengali is the world's seventh most widely spoken language, however, it has received less focus in NMT work due to a lack of resources and poor corpus quality. Attempts to bridge this gap, specifically with regard to machine translation have been made by proposing new corpora (Hasan et al., 2020) and the use of attention-based techniques (Dabre et al. (2021), Abujar et al. (2021)) for improving upon existing systems.

2.3 Hindi

There has been a lot of focus given to the Hindi language in NMT literature in recent years, with the availability of good quality corpora (Kunchukuttan et al. (2017), Bojar et al. (2014)) thus enabling the development of effective NMT systems.

The recent development of Multilingual Models ((Dabre et al. (2021), Kakwani et al. (2020)) primarily focused on Indic languages has helped gain traction in the research community for MT.

3 Methodology

3.1 Data Description and Preprocessing

We use the datasets provided in the WAT 2022 shared tasks for our experiments. The datasets of all the three languages comprise 28,929, 997, and 1,595 English-Indic language sentence pairs for the training, dev, and eval subsets respectively, along with their corresponding images. We train and fine-tune the models using this data. The challenge subset additionally comprises 1,400 similar instances. The Malayalam and Bengali datasets are an extension to the HindiVisualGenome dataset, thus all three sets have the same set of sentence pairs while supporting their respective language. The language pair (English-Bengali) is running for the first time as a shared task.

We perform Normalisation, which minimizes the number of unique tokens in the text, and use the SentencePiece [2] tokenizer while utilizing the Byte-Pair-Encoding (BPE) (Sennrich et al., 2015) technique on the words present in a sentence.

3.2 Models and Training

We trained models using cutting-edge transformer-based neural machine translation (NMT). The architecture is based on a standard transformer architecture with 6 self-attentive layers in both the encoder and decoder networks, each with 8 attention

[2] `https://github.com/google/sentencepiece`

Team	en–ml		en–bn		en–hi	
	BLEU	RIBES	BLEU	RIBES	BLEU	RIBES
nlp_novices (ours)	19.50	0.536689	32.90	0.706596	41.80	0.812483
Team 1	14.60	0.392158	22.60	0.605676	29.60	0.728801
Team 2	12.98	0.378045	22.50	0.614267	30.72	0.736262
Team 3	–	–	26.70	0.680655	37.20	0.770640

Table 2: Details of official submission results on the challenge subset of data for en–ml, en–bn and en–hi translation systems.

Team	en–ml		en–bn		en–hi	
	BLEU	RIBES	BLEU	RIBES	BLEU	RIBES
nlp_novices (ours)	30.60	0.643987	39.80	0.745190	42.90	0.816564
Team 1	30.80	0.589471	41.00	0.767212	36.20	0.785673
Team 2	30.49	0.580807	40.90	0.758246	39.78	0.776892
Team 3	–	–	40.90	0.752543	37.01	0.795302

Table 3: Details of official submission results on the evaluation subset of data for en–ml, en–bn and en–hi translation systems.

heads per layer. For all our experiments, we use transformer models that follow the strategy implemented in OPUS MT (Tiedemann and Thottingal, 2020), which utilizes the Marian-NMT (Junczys-Dowmunt et al., 2018) toolkit and finetune them on the data provided for the shared tasks.

We obtained optimal performance on the English-Malayalam and English-Hindi translation tasks using en-ml [3] and en-hi [4] bilingual NMT models respectively. For the English-Bengali translation task, we achieved competent results using a multilingual NMT model [5].

The experiments were conducted in a Linux environment using an NVIDIA Tesla P100 GPU accelerator with 16 GB RAM and CUDA 11.2 installed. We train three separate MT models for the three indic languages in our experiments. The models utilize the AdamW (Loshchilov and Hutter, 2017) optimizer for optimization of model parameters with 0.00002 as the initial learning rate.

We observed varied results based on the number of epochs of training for each Indic language we translate to. We train the English to Hindi, English to Malayalam, and English to Bengali NMT models for 30, 20, and 25 epochs respectively after observing optimal performance for the respective systems.

4 Results

The metrics used to evaluate the translations were the Bilingual Evaluation Understudy (BLEU) (Papineni et al., 2002) and Rank-based Intuitive Bilingual Evaluation Score (RIBES) (Isozaki et al., 2010) metrics. Table 2 and 3 contain the BLEU and RIBES scores[6] obtained in each translation task, i.e. English to Malayalam, English to Bengali and English to Hindi on the challenge subset and the evaluation subset. For the English to Malayalam, English to Bengali and English to Hindi translation tasks, we were able to achieve BLEU scores of 19.50, 32.90 and 41.80 respectively (on the challenge subset), as reported in Table 2. As seen in Table 3, for the evaluation set, BLEU scores of 30.60, 39.80 and 42.90 were achieved for each translation task.

We have provided a comparative analysis between the effects of using fine-tuned pre-trained models and models trained from scratch. The optimal results on the leaderboard were obtained using the fine-tuned models. Table 4 depicts the difference in performance of the models with and without pre-training under similar training methods. To obtain comparable results using non pre-trained models, additional training and data resources would be required.

[3] https://github.com/Helsinki-NLP/OPUS-MT-train/tree/master/models/en-ml

[4] https://github.com/Helsinki-NLP/Tatoeba-Challenge/tree/master/models/eng-hin

[5] https://github.com/Helsinki-NLP/Tatoeba-Challenge/tree/master/models/eng-mul

[6] http://lotus.kuee.kyoto-u.ac.jp/WAT/evaluation/index.html

Language Pair	With pre-training		Without pre-training	
	Test	Challenge	Test	Challenge
en-ml	30.60	19.50	0.65342	0.21455
en-bn	39.80	32.90	0.00057	0.14980
en-hi	42.90	41.80	2.03818	0.92631

Table 4: Effect of using pre-trained models on the performance by comparative analysis using BLEU scores.

The disparity between the performance with respect to the challenge set and the evaluation set (reported in Table 2 and 3) can be attributed to the following reasons:

- Firstly, the challenge set had 1232 unique English words (ignoring stopwords), while the evaluation set had 1256; the number of common words between the two of them being only 552.
- Additionally, the number of intersecting terms (ignoring stopwords) between the train set + the challenge set and the train set + the evaluation set is 976 and 1109 respectively.

The above reasons may explain the ambiguity that arises when it comes to the translation of some unique words.

Table 1 illustrates sample translations of three common English sentences taken from the shared task data. The table reports translations of the given English inputs in Malayalam, Bengali, and Hindi.

5 Conclusion

In this paper, we discuss the submissions made to three tasks at WAT 2022: Neural Machine Translation Systems for Indic Languages. We participated in the text-only subtask of the multimodal translation tasks of English to Malayalam, English to Bengali, and English to Hindi translations. In the future, we would like to experiment with multimodal MT models and incorporate multimodal aspects for the facilitation of better translation systems.

References

Sheikh Abujar, Abu Kaisar Mohammad Masum, Abhishek Bhattacharya, Soumi Dutta, and Syed Akhter Hossain. 2021. English to bengali neural machine translation using global attention mechanism. In *Emerging Technologies in Data Mining and Information Security*, pages 359–369. Springer.

Ondřej Bojar, Vojtěch Diatka, Pavel Rychlý, Pavel Straňák, Vít Suchomel, Aleš Tamchyna, and Daniel Zeman. 2014. Hindencorp-hindi-english and hindi-only corpus for machine translation. In *Proceedings of the Ninth International Conference on Language Resources and Evaluation (LREC'14)*, pages 3550–3555.

Kyunghyun Cho, Bart Van Merriënboer, Caglar Gulcehre, Dzmitry Bahdanau, Fethi Bougares, Holger Schwenk, and Yoshua Bengio. 2014. Learning phrase representations using rnn encoder-decoder for statistical machine translation. *arXiv preprint arXiv:1406.1078*.

Raj Dabre, Himani Shrotriya, Anoop Kunchukuttan, Ratish Puduppully, Mitesh M Khapra, and Pratyush Kumar. 2021. Indicbart: A pre-trained model for natural language generation of indic languages. *arXiv preprint arXiv:2109.02903*.

Mikel L Forcada, Mireia Ginestí-Rosell, Jacob Nordfalk, Jim O'Regan, Sergio Ortiz-Rojas, Juan Antonio Pérez-Ortiz, Felipe Sánchez-Martínez, Gema Ramírez-Sánchez, and Francis M Tyers. 2011. Apertium: a free/open-source platform for rule-based machine translation. *Machine translation*, 25(2):127–144.

Jonas Gehring, Michael Auli, David Grangier, Denis Yarats, and Yann N Dauphin. 2017. Convolutional sequence to sequence learning. In *International conference on machine learning*, pages 1243–1252. PMLR.

Tahmid Hasan, Abhik Bhattacharjee, Kazi Samin, Masum Hasan, Madhusudan Basak, M Sohel Rahman, and Rifat Shahriyar. 2020. Not low-resource anymore: Aligner ensembling, batch filtering, and new datasets for bengali-english machine translation. *arXiv preprint arXiv:2009.09359*.

Hideki Isozaki, Tsutomu Hirao, Kevin Duh, Katsuhito Sudoh, and Hajime Tsukada. 2010. Automatic evaluation of translation quality for distant language pairs. In *Proceedings of the 2010 conference on empirical methods in natural language processing*, pages 944–952.

Melvin Johnson, Mike Schuster, Quoc V Le, Maxim Krikun, Yonghui Wu, Zhifeng Chen, Nikhil Thorat, Fernanda Viégas, Martin Wattenberg, Greg Corrado, et al. 2017. Google's multilingual neural machine translation system: Enabling zero-shot translation. *Transactions of the Association for Computational Linguistics*, 5:339–351.

Marcin Junczys-Dowmunt, Roman Grundkiewicz, Tomasz Dwojak, Hieu Hoang, Kenneth Heafield, Tom Neckermann, Frank Seide, Ulrich Germann, Alham Fikri Aji, Nikolay Bogoychev, et al. 2018. Marian: Fast neural machine translation in c++. *arXiv preprint arXiv:1804.00344*.

Divyanshu Kakwani, Anoop Kunchukuttan, Satish Golla, NC Gokul, Avik Bhattacharyya, Mitesh M Khapra, and Pratyush Kumar. 2020. Indicnlpsuite: Monolingual corpora, evaluation benchmarks and pre-trained multilingual language models for indian languages. In *Findings of the Association for Computational Linguistics: EMNLP 2020*, pages 4948–4961.

Nal Kalchbrenner and Phil Blunsom. 2013. Recurrent continuous translation models. In *Proceedings of the 2013 conference on empirical methods in natural language processing*, pages 1700–1709.

Nal Kalchbrenner, Lasse Espeholt, Karen Simonyan, Aaron van den Oord, Alex Graves, and Koray Kavukcuoglu. 2016. Neural machine translation in linear time. *arXiv preprint arXiv:1610.10099*.

Philipp Koehn and Jean Senellart. 2010. Convergence of translation memory and statistical machine translation. In *Proceedings of AMTA Workshop on MT Research and the Translation Industry*, pages 21–31.

Anoop Kunchukuttan, Pratik Mehta, and Pushpak Bhattacharyya. 2017. The iit bombay english-hindi parallel corpus. *arXiv preprint arXiv:1710.02855*.

Ilya Loshchilov and Frank Hutter. 2017. Decoupled weight decay regularization. *arXiv preprint arXiv:1711.05101*.

Toshiaki Nakazawa, Hideya Mino, Isao Goto, Raj Dabre, Shohei Higashiyama, Shantipriya Parida, Anoop Kunchukuttan, Makoto Morishita, Ondřej Bojar, Chenhui Chu, Akiko Eriguchi, Kaori Abe, Yusuke Oda, and Sadao Kurohashi. 2022. Overview of the 9th workshop on Asian translation. In *Proceedings of the 9th Workshop on Asian Translation (WAT2022)*, Gyeongju, Republic of Korea. Association for Computational Linguistics.

Kishore Papineni, Salim Roukos, Todd Ward, and Wei-Jing Zhu. 2002. Bleu: a method for automatic evaluation of machine translation. In *Proceedings of the 40th annual meeting of the Association for Computational Linguistics*, pages 311–318.

Martin Popel, Marketa Tomkova, Jakub Tomek, Łukasz Kaiser, Jakob Uszkoreit, Ondřej Bojar, and Zdeněk Žabokrtský. 2020. Transforming machine translation: a deep learning system reaches news translation quality comparable to human professionals. *Nature communications*, 11(1):1–15.

B Premjith, M Anand Kumar, and KP Soman. 2019. Neural machine translation system for english to indian language translation using mtil parallel corpus. *Journal of Intelligent Systems*, 28(3):387–398.

C Rahul, K Dinunath, Remya Ravindran, Soman, and KP. 2009. Rule based reordering and morphological processing for english-malayalam statistical machine translation. In *2009 International Conference on Advances in Computing, Control, and Telecommunication Technologies*, pages 458–460. IEEE.

Remya Rajan, Remya Sivan, Remya Ravindran, and KP Soman. 2009. Rule based machine translation from english to malayalam. In *2009 International Conference on Advances in Computing, Control, and Telecommunication Technologies*, pages 439–441. IEEE.

Rico Sennrich, Barry Haddow, and Alexandra Birch. 2015. Neural machine translation of rare words with subword units. *arXiv preprint arXiv:1508.07909*.

Ilya Sutskever, Oriol Vinyals, and Quoc V Le. 2014. Sequence to sequence learning with neural networks. *Advances in neural information processing systems*, 27.

Zhixing Tan, Shuo Wang, Zonghan Yang, Gang Chen, Xuancheng Huang, Maosong Sun, and Yang Liu. 2020. Neural machine translation: A review of methods, resources, and tools. *AI Open*, 1:5–21.

Jörg Tiedemann and Santhosh Thottingal. 2020. Opus-mt–building open translation services for the world. In *Proceedings of the 22nd Annual Conference of the European Association for Machine Translation*. European Association for Machine Translation.

Ashish Vaswani, Noam Shazeer, Niki Parmar, Jakob Uszkoreit, Llion Jones, Aidan N Gomez, Łukasz Kaiser, and Illia Polosukhin. 2017. Attention is all you need. *Advances in neural information processing systems*, 30.

Yonghui Wu, Mike Schuster, Zhifeng Chen, Quoc V Le, Mohammad Norouzi, Wolfgang Macherey, Maxim Krikun, Yuan Cao, Qin Gao, Klaus Macherey, et al. 2016. Google's neural machine translation system: Bridging the gap between human and machine translation. *arXiv preprint arXiv:1609.08144*.

English to Bengali Multimodal Neural Machine Translation using Transliteration-based Phrase Pairs Augmentation

Sahinur Rahman Laskar[1], **Pankaj Dadure**[2],
Riyanka Manna[3], **Partha Pakray**[1], **Sivaji Bandyopadhyay**[1]
[1]Department of Computer Science and Engineering, National Institute of Technology, Silchar, India
[2]School of Computer Science, University of Petroleum & Energy Studies, Dehradun, India
[3]Department of Computer Science and Engineering, Adamas University, Kolkata, India
{sahinurlaskar.nits, krdadure, riyankamanna16}@gmail.com
{parthapakray, sivaji.cse.ju}@gmail.com

Abstract

Automatic translation of one natural language to another is a popular task of natural language processing. Although the deep learning-based technique known as neural machine translation (NMT) is a widely accepted machine translation approach, it needs an adequate amount of training data, which is a challenging issue for low-resource pair translation. Moreover, the multimodal concept utilizes text and visual features to improve low-resource pair translation. WAT2022 (Workshop on Asian Translation 2022) organizes (hosted by the COLING 2022) English to Bengali multimodal translation task where we have participated as a team named CNLP-NITS-PP in two tracks: 1) text-only and 2) multimodal translation. Herein, we have proposed a transliteration-based phrase pairs augmentation approach which shows improvement in the multimodal translation task and achieved benchmark results on Bengali Visual Genome 1.0 dataset. We have attained the best results on the challenge and evaluation test set for English to Bengali multimodal translation with BLEU scores of 28.70, 43.90 and RIBES scores of 0.688931, 0.780669, respectively.

1 Introduction

In recent years, multimodel approaches have shown remarkable contributions in various NLP applications such as machine translation, caption generation, etc. Especially in machine translation, multiple input modalities, like text, image, or audio/speech, integrate with NMT, known as multimodal NMT (MNMT), attempts to improve low-resource pair translation by merging visual features in addition to textual features (Shah et al., 2016). The attention-based encoder-decoder architecture of NMT handles various issues of long-term dependency and variable-length phrases via sequence-to-sequence learning and attains a state-of-the-art technique of machine translation (MT) (Bahdanau et al., 2015; Luong et al., 2015). Also, NMT shows remarkable performance for low-resource Indian languages (Pathak and Pakray, 2018; Pathak et al., 2018; Laskar et al., 2019a,b, 2020a, 2021b, 2022b). Further, to handle the data scarcity problem, the authors (Sen et al., 2020) augmenting phrase pairs and the source language transliteration-based (Laskar et al., 2022a) approach to enhance text-only based for low-resource pair translation. This paper aims to investigate English to Bengali multimodal translation task in WAT2022 with a proposed transliteration-based phrase pairs augmentation approach.

The rest of the paper is organized as follows: Section 2 presents the review of related works. The system description is briefly discussed in Section 3. Section 4 reports the results and Section 5 concludes the paper with future scope.

2 Related Work

In the literature survey, there is minimal existing work, particularly on the English to Bengali multimodal translation task (Parida et al., 2021). In (Parida et al., 2021), they used Bengali Visual Genome 1.0 (Sen et al., 2022b) adopted ViTA (Gupta et al., 2021) approach where they extracted object tags from the image and utilized mBART model (Liu et al., 2020) for encoding English sentences with the object tags and decoding to generate the Bengali translation. The obtained BLEU scores were 43.5 and 26.8 on the evaluation and challenge test sets, respectively. Moreover, the related existing works are available on English to Hindi multimodal translation task (Dutta Chowdhury et al., 2018; Sanayai Meetei et al., 2019; Laskar et al., 2019c, 2020b, 2021a). The authors (Laskar et al., 2020b, 2021a) used Hindi Visual Genome 1.1 and adopts RNN-based MNMT model (Calixto and Liu, 2017; Calixto et al., 2017) with advantages pre-trained word embeddings on monolingual corpus, achieved BLEU scores of 39.28, 39.46 on

Proceedings of the 9th Workshop on Asian Translation, pages 111–116
October 17, 2022.

challenge and evaluation test set respectively. This work investigates transliteration-based phrase pairs augmentation to improve the multimodal translation task of English to Bengali.

3 System Description

We have carried out four operations: transliteration-based phrase pairs augmentation, data preprocessing, model training, and testing. The OpenNMT-py (Klein et al., 2017) tool is utilized to build multimodal and text-only models separately.

3.1 Dataset Description

The dataset namely, Bengali Visual Genome 1.0[1] (Sen et al., 2022b,a) is used in this task, which is provided by WAT2022 organizer (Nakazawa et al., 2022). In this dataset, the duplicates (text and image) are present in the train set, which have image ID numbers 2328549, 2391240, and 2385507. Therefore, we have removed those duplicates, and thus train set contains 28,927 images and the same number of corresponding English-Bengali parallel sentences. The validation and test (evaluation and challenge) set contains 998, 1,595, and 1,400 images and parallel text data.

3.2 Transliteration-based Phrase Pairs Augmentation

In this phase, firstly, we have expanded the training amount of data via augmentation of phrase pairs to the train set. To improve low-resource pair translation, (Sen et al., 2020) utilized SMT-based phrase pairs to increase training data via augmentation strategy. We have also followed same (Sen et al., 2020) and utilized Giza++ (Och and Ney, 2003) to extract phrase pairs(Laskar et al., 2021a) from the English-Bengali parallel train set. Before augmentation to the parallel train set, duplicates and blank lines are removed. The statistics of extracted phrase pairs are shown in Table 1.

Secondly, English source sentences are transliterated using indic-trans[2] (Bhat et al., 2014)in to Bengali script following (Laskar et al., 2022a). The goal of the transliteration approach is to allow subword-level lexical sharing between source and target sentences that will be shared during the training process.

[1]https://lindat.mff.cuni.cz/repository/xmlui/handle/11234/1-3722

[2]https://github.com/libindic/indic-trans

3.3 Data Preprocessing, Model Training, and Testing

The image/visual features are independently extracted from the image data using pre-trained CNN-VGG19[3] for train, validation, and test data. During feature extraction, the coordinate or bounded box region information (X, Y, width, height) of the images is considered, which is available in the Bengali Visual Genome 1.0 (Sen et al., 2022b). Moreover, we have augmented image features of extracted phrase pairs. To select relevant images of the corresponding phrase pairs, we have searched each phrase in the original parallel corpus (train set), if it is found, then the corresponding image and its coordinate information are considered. But there is a problem if multiple sentences contain the same phrase subset. To tackle this issue, a filtering step solution is considered.

- First, for every phrase pair extracted from the corpus, we found the matching English segments from the corpus which have the English phrase of the En-Bn phrase pair as a sub-string (filter-1).
- If the length of the resulting data frame, i.e., the number of matching English segments for the English part of the phrase is 0, then the phrase is skipped and considered invalid. If the length is 1, since only one English segment matches it, that segment is directly selected.
- On the other hand, if the length is more than 1, i.e., more than 1 English segments have the English phrase as a sub-string, the resulting English segments are again filtered (filter-2) to check if the corresponding Bengali phrase of the phrase pairs also has subset in the Bengali segments.
  - If after filter-2, the result is 0, i.e., there are no matching Bengali segments that have the Bengali phrase as a sub-string, then from the filter-1 data-frame, i.e., the final segment from matching English segments is randomly selected.
  - If the number of matches after Bengali segment matching is 1, then that single segment is selected.

[3]https://github.com/iacercalixto/MultimodalNMT

Number of Phrase Pairs	Tokens	
	En	Bn
127,897	442,657	364,644

Table 1: Statistics of extracted phrase pairs.

- If the number of Bengali phrase matches is more than 1, then a matching segment is randomly selected with a seed value.

For tokenization and preprocessing of text data, the OpenNMT-py toolkit is utilized. We have trained separately for multimodal and text-only NMT using the OpenNMT-py toolkit. During multimodal NMT training, the bidirectional RNN (BRNN) at the encoder and doubly-attentive RNN at the decoder are used by following default settings of (Calixto and Liu, 2017; Calixto et al., 2017). We have trained on a single GPU with early stopping criteria i.e., the model training is halted if does not converge on the validation set for more than 10 epochs. We have used a batch size of 32 during the training process. The optimum trained models of multimodal and text-only NMT are applied to the evaluation and challenge test set. The primary difference in the testing phase is that multimodal NMT uses visual features of image test data. The source English sentences of test data are transliterated and then applied to the trained model to generate the predicted target Bengali sentences.

4 Result and Analysis

The WAT2022 shared task organizer (Nakazawa et al., 2022) published the evaluation result[4] of the multimodal translation task for English to Bengali, where our team achieves the first position in multimodal submission for both challenge and evaluation test set. Herein, we have participated with a team named CNLP-NITS-PP in the multimodal and text-only submission tracks, where a total of three teams participated. The automatic evaluation metrics, BLEU (Papineni et al., 2002), RIBES (Isozaki et al., 2010) are used for evaluation of results. Table 2 presents the results of our system. The quantitative results show that the multimodal NMT outperforms text-only NMT due to the use of visual and textual features. Furthermore, we have attained benchmark results on the evaluation and challenge test set, which is higher compared to (Parida et al., 2021). It shows +0.40 and +1.9 increment in terms of BLEU score, which realized that our approach i.e., transliteration-based phrase pairs augmentation improves the translational performance of multimodal NMT. Moreover, Figure 1 and 2 present best and worst outputs along with transliteration of Bengali words and Google translation. In Figure 1, the predicted sentences for both multimodal and text-only represent the same contextual meaning. Here, the only difference is that *prachir* ("wall") word in the case of the multimodal predicted sentence whereas *dewal* word in the case of the text-only predicted sentence and Google translation. These two words represent the same meaning corresponding to the reference sentence. However, both multimodal and text-only predicted wrong translations.

[4]http://lotus.kuee.kyoto-u.ac.jp/WAT/evaluation/index.html

5 Conclusion and Future Work

In this work, we have proposed a transliteration-based phrase pairs augmentation approach which has been introduced in the WAT2022 multimodal translation task of English to Bengali. The multimodal NMT attains a higher score than the text-only NMT model and other existing works. Furthermore, the designed multilingual-based approach will be investigated to improve the translational performance of low-resource multimodal NMT.

Acknowledgements

We want to thank the Department of Computer Science and Engineering, Center for Natural Language Processing (CNLP), Artificial Intelligence (AI) Lab at the National Institute of Technology, Silchar for providing the requisite support and infrastructure to execute this work.

References

Dzmitry Bahdanau, Kyunghyun Cho, and Yoshua Bengio. 2015. Neural machine translation by jointly learning to align and translate. In *3rd International Conference on Learning Representations, ICLR 2015, San Diego, CA, USA, May 7-9, 2015, Conference Track Proceedings*.

Our System	Test Set	BLEU	RIBES
Text-only NMT	Challenge	26.70	0.680655
	Evaluation	40.90	0.752543
Multi-modal NMT	Challenge	28.70	0.688931
	Evaluation	43.90	0.780669

Table 2: Our system's results (official) on English to Bengali multimodal translation task.

Image id: 2373836

Multi-modal Translation Track
Source Language: English
Target Language: Bengali

Source	a blue wall beside tennis court
Predicted	টেনিস কোর্টের পাশে একটি নীল প্রাচীর *(tenis courter pashey ekti nil prachir)*
Reference	টেনিস কোর্টের পাশে একটি নীল প্রাচীর *(tenis courter pashey ekti nil prachir)*
Google Translation	টেনিস কোর্টের পাশে একটি নীল দেয়াল *(tenis courter pashey ekti nil dewal)*

Text-only Translation Track
Predicted: টেনিস কোর্ট পাশে একটি নীল দেয়াল
(tenis courter pashey ekti nil dewal)

Figure 1: Sample output of best predicted on challenge test data.

Image id: 2417756

Multi-modal Translation Track
Source Language: English
Target Language: Bengali

Source	March 7th is the date on the calendar
Predicted	টাটকা ঝুড়ি ট্রেনে তারিখ রয়েছে (tatka juri traine tarikh royeche)
Reference	৭ই মার্চ ক্যালেন্ডারে তারিখ (7e march kelendare tarikh)
Google Translation	7 ই মার্চ ক্যালেন্ডারে তারিখ (7e march kelendare tarikh)

Text-only Translation Track
Predicted: টেমস টেবিলটি স্নানের তারিখ তারিখ
(tems tableti snaner tarikh tarikh)

Figure 2: Sample output of worst predicted on challenge test data.

Irshad Ahmad Bhat, Vandan Mujadia, Aniruddha Tammewar, Riyaz Ahmad Bhat, and Manish Shrivastava. 2014. Iiit-h system submission for fire2014 shared task on transliterated search. In *Proceedings of the Forum for Information Retrieval Evaluation*, FIRE '14, page 48–53, New York, NY, USA. Association for Computing Machinery.

Iacer Calixto and Qun Liu. 2017. Incorporating global visual features into attention-based neural machine translation. In *Proceedings of the 2017 Conference on Empirical Methods in Natural Language Processing*, pages 992–1003, Copenhagen, Denmark. Association for Computational Linguistics.

Iacer Calixto, Qun Liu, and Nick Campbell. 2017. Doubly-attentive decoder for multi-modal neural machine translation. In *Proceedings of the 55th Annual Meeting of the Association for Computational Linguistics, ACL 2017, Vancouver, Canada, July 30 - August 4, Volume 1: Long Papers*, pages 1913–1924. Association for Computational Linguistics.

Koel Dutta Chowdhury, Mohammed Hasanuzzaman, and Qun Liu. 2018. Multimodal neural machine translation for low-resource language pairs using synthetic data. In *"."*, pages 33–42.

Kshitij Gupta, Devansh Gautam, and Radhika Mamidi. 2021. ViTA: Visual-linguistic translation by aligning object tags. In *Proceedings of the 8th Workshop on Asian Translation (WAT2021)*, pages 166–173, Online. Association for Computational Linguistics.

Hideki Isozaki, Tsutomu Hirao, Kevin Duh, Katsuhito Sudoh, and Hajime Tsukada. 2010. Automatic evaluation of translation quality for distant language pairs. In *Proceedings of the 2010 Conference on Empirical Methods in Natural Language Processing*, pages 944–952, Cambridge, MA. Association for Computational Linguistics.

Guillaume Klein, Yoon Kim, Yuntian Deng, Jean Senellart, and Alexander Rush. 2017. Opennmt: Open-source toolkit for neural machine translation. In *Proceedings of ACL 2017, System Demonstrations*, pages 67–72, Vancouver, Canada. Association for Computational Linguistics.

Sahinur Rahman Laskar, Abinash Dutta, Partha Pakray, and Sivaji Bandyopadhyay. 2019a. Neural machine translation: English to hindi. In *2019 IEEE Conference on Information and Communication Technology*, pages 1–6.

Sahinur Rahman Laskar, Abdullah Faiz Ur Rahman Khilji, Darsh Kaushik, Partha Pakray, and Sivaji Bandyopadhyay. 2021a. Improved English to Hindi multimodal neural machine translation. In *Proceedings of the 8th Workshop on Asian Translation (WAT2021)*, pages 155–160, Online. Association for Computational Linguistics.

Sahinur Rahman Laskar, Abdullah Faiz Ur Rahman Khilji, Partha Pakray, and Sivaji Bandyopadhyay. 2020a. EnAsCorp1.0: English-Assamese corpus. In *Proceedings of the 3rd Workshop on Technologies for MT of Low Resource Languages*, pages 62–68, Suzhou, China. Association for Computational Linguistics.

Sahinur Rahman Laskar, Abdullah Faiz Ur Rahman Khilji, Partha Pakray, and Sivaji Bandyopadhyay. 2020b. Multimodal neural machine translation for English to Hindi. In *Proceedings of the 7th Workshop on Asian Translation*, pages 109–113, Suzhou, China. Association for Computational Linguistics.

Sahinur Rahman Laskar, Partha Pakray, and Sivaji Bandyopadhyay. 2019b. Neural machine translation: Hindi-Nepali. In *Proceedings of the Fourth Conference on Machine Translation (Volume 3: Shared Task Papers, Day 2)*, pages 202–207, Florence, Italy. Association for Computational Linguistics.

Sahinur Rahman Laskar, Partha Pakray, and Sivaji Bandyopadhyay. 2021b. Neural machine translation for low resource assamese–english. In *Proceedings of the International Conference on Computing and Communication Systems: I3CS 2020, NEHU, Shillong, India*, volume 170, page 35. Springer.

Sahinur Rahman Laskar, Bishwaraj Paul, Partha Pakray, and Sivaji Bandyopadhyay. 2022a. Improving english-assamese neural machine translation using transliteration-based approach. In *Proceedings of the International Conference on Frontiers of Intelligent Computing: Theory and Applications, FICTA 2022*. In press.

Sahinur Rahman Laskar, Rohit Pratap Singh, Partha Pakray, and Sivaji Bandyopadhyay. 2019c. English to Hindi multi-modal neural machine translation and Hindi image captioning. In *Proceedings of the 6th Workshop on Asian Translation*, pages 62–67, Hong Kong, China. Association for Computational Linguistics.

Sahinur Rahman Laskar, Abdullah Faiz Ur Rahman Khilji, Partha Pakray, and Sivaji Bandyopadhyay. 2022b. Improved neural machine translation for low-resource english–assamese pair. *Journal of Intelligent and Fuzzy Systems*, 42(5):4727–4738.

Yinhan Liu, Jiatao Gu, Naman Goyal, Xian Li, Sergey Edunov, Marjan Ghazvininejad, Mike Lewis, and Luke Zettlemoyer. 2020. Multilingual denoising pre-training for neural machine translation. *Transactions of the Association for Computational Linguistics*, 8:726–742.

Thang Luong, Hieu Pham, and Christopher D. Manning. 2015. Effective approaches to attention-based neural machine translation. In *Proceedings of the 2015 Conference on Empirical Methods in Natural Language Processing*, pages 1412–1421, Lisbon, Portugal. Association for Computational Linguistics.

Toshiaki Nakazawa, Hideya Mino, Isao Goto, Raj Dabre, Shohei Higashiyama, Shantipriya Parida,

Anoop Kunchukuttan, Makoto Morishita, Ondřej Bojar, Chenhui Chu, Akiko Eriguchi, Kaori Abe, Yusuke Oda, and Sadao Kurohashi. 2022. Overview of the 9th workshop on Asian translation. In *Proceedings of the 9th Workshop on Asian Translation (WAT2022)*, Gyeongju, Republic of Korea. Association for Computational Linguistics.

Franz Josef Och and Hermann Ney. 2003. A systematic comparison of various statistical alignment models. *Computational Linguistics*, 29(1):19–51.

Kishore Papineni, Salim Roukos, Todd Ward, and Wei-Jing Zhu. 2002. Bleu: A method for automatic evaluation of machine translation. In *Proceedings of the 40th Annual Meeting on Association for Computational Linguistics*, ACL '02, pages 311–318, Stroudsburg, PA, USA. Association for Computational Linguistics.

Shantipriya Parida, Subhadarshi Panda, Satya Prakash Biswal, Ketan Kotwal, Arghyadeep Sen, Satya Ranjan Dash, and Petr Motlicek. 2021. Multimodal neural machine translation system for English to Bengali. In *Proceedings of the First Workshop on Multimodal Machine Translation for Low Resource Languages (MMTLRL 2021)*, pages 31–39, Online (Virtual Mode). INCOMA Ltd.

Amarnath Pathak and Partha Pakray. 2018. Neural machine translation for indian languages. *Journal of Intelligent Systems*, pages 1–13.

Amarnath Pathak, Partha Pakray, and Jereemi Bentham. 2018. English–mizo machine translation using neural and statistical approaches. *Neural Computing and Applications*, 30:1–17.

Loitongbam Sanayai Meetei, Thoudam Doren Singh, and Sivaji Bandyopadhyay. 2019. WAT2019: English-Hindi translation on Hindi visual genome dataset. In *Proceedings of the 6th Workshop on Asian Translation*, pages 181–188, Hong Kong, China. Association for Computational Linguistics.

Arghyadeep Sen, Shantipriya Parida, Ketan Kotwal, Subhadarshi Panda, Ondřej Bojar, and Satya Ranjan Dash. 2022a. Bengali visual genome: A multimodal dataset for machine translation and image captioning. In *Intelligent Data Engineering and Analytics*, pages 63–70. Springer.

Arghyadeep Sen, Shantipriya Parida, Ketan Kotwal, Subhadarshi Panda, Ondřej Bojar, and Satya Ranjan Dash. 2022b. Bengali visual genome: A multimodal dataset for machine translation and image captioning. In *Intelligent Data Engineering and Analytics*, pages 63–70, Singapore. Springer Nature Singapore.

Sukanta Sen, Mohammed Hasanuzzaman, Asif Ekbal, Pushpak Bhattacharyya, and Andy Way. 2020. Neural machine translation of low-resource languages using smt phrase pair injection. *Natural Language Engineering*, page 1–22.

Kashif Shah, Josiah Wang, and Lucia Specia. 2016. SHEF-multimodal: Grounding machine translation on images. In *Proceedings of the First Conference on Machine Translation: Volume 2, Shared Task Papers*, pages 660–665, Berlin, Germany. Association for Computational Linguistics.

Investigation of English to Hindi Multimodal Neural Machine Translation using Transliteration-based Phrase Pairs Augmentation

Sahinur Rahman Laskar[1], **Rahul Singh**[1], **Md Faizal Karim**[1]
Riyanka Manna[2], **Partha Pakray**[1], **Sivaji Bandyopadhyay**[1]
[1]Department of Computer Science and Engineering, National Institute of Technology, Silchar, India
[2]Department of Computer Science and Engineering, Adamas University, Kolkata, India
{sahinurlaskar.nits, rahuljan, faizal.karim.metro}@gmail.com
{riyankamanna16, parthapakray, sivaji.cse.ju}@gmail.com

Abstract

Machine translation translates one natural language to another, a well-defined natural language processing task. Neural machine translation (NMT) is a widely accepted machine translation approach, but it requires a sufficient amount of training data, which is a challenging issue for low-resource pair translation. Moreover, the multimodal concept utilizes text and visual features to improve low-resource pair translation. WAT2022 (Workshop on Asian Translation 2022) organizes (hosted by the COLING 2022) English to Hindi multimodal translation task where we have participated as a team named CNLP-NITS-PP in two tracks: 1) text-only and 2) multimodal translation. Herein, we have proposed a transliteration-based phrase pairs augmentation approach, which shows improvement in the multimodal translation task. We have attained the second best results on the challenge test set for English to Hindi multimodal translation with BLEU score of 39.30, and a RIBES score of 0.791468.

1 Introduction

The multimodal NMT (MNMT) concept aims to include different input modalities, such as images in addition to text and attempts to improve low-resource pair translation by merging visual features in addition to textual features (Shah et al., 2016). The attention-based encoder-decoder architecture for NMT handles various issues of long-term dependency and variable-length phrases via sequence-to-sequence learning and attains a state-of-the-art technique of machine translation (MT) (Bahdanau et al., 2015; Luong et al., 2015). Also, NMT shows remarkable performance for low-resource Indian languages (Pathak and Pakray, 2018; Pathak et al., 2018; Laskar et al., 2019a,b, 2020a, 2021c,b). Further, to handle the data scarcity problem, the authors (Sen et al., 2020) augmenting phrase pairs and the source language transliteration-based (Laskar et al., 2022) approach to enhance text-only based for low-resource pair translation. This paper aims to investigate the English to Hindi multimodal translation task in WAT2022 with a proposed transliteration-based phrase pairs augmentation approach (as discussed in 3.2).

The rest of the paper is organized as follows: Section 2 presents the review of related works. The system description is briefly discussed in Section 3. Section 4 reports the results and Section 5 concludes the paper with future scope.

2 Related Works

The literature survey explores existing works on MNMT for English-Hindi language pair (Dutta Chowdhury et al., 2018; Sanayai Meetei et al., 2019; Laskar et al., 2019c, 2021a). We participated in WAT2020 on multimodal translation task for English to Hindi translation and attained the best results with a BLEU score of 33.57 on the challenge test set(Laskar et al., 2020b) using RNN-based MNMT model (Calixto and Liu, 2017; Calixto et al., 2017) and taking advantage of pretrained word embeddings of the monolingual corpus. Later, we improved the results in WAT2021 (Laskar et al., 2021a) using phrase pairs augmentation. In this work, we have investigated a proposed transliteration-based phrase pairs augmentation approach to enhance the multimodal translational performance of English to Hindi.

3 System Description

The experiments are carried out in four operations, namely, transliteration-based phrase pairs augmentation, data preprocessing, model training, and testing. The OpenNMT-py (Klein et al., 2017) tool is utilized to build multimodal and text-only models independently. The difference between our previous work (Laskar et al., 2020b) and this work is that the current work uses transliteration-based phrase pairs augmentation.

Proceedings of the 9th Workshop on Asian Translation, pages 117–122
October 17, 2022.

3.1 Dataset Description

The dataset namely, Hindi Visual Genome 1.1[1] (Parida and Bojar, 2020) is used in the multimodal translation task of English-to-Hindi, which is provided by WAT2022 organizer (Nakazawa et al., 2022). In this dataset, duplicates (text and image) are present in the train set (Laskar et al., 2020b), which have image ID numbers 2328549, 2391240, and 2385507. Therefore, we have removed those duplicates and thus train set contains 28,927 images and the same number of corresponding English-Hindi parallel sentences. The validation, test (evaluation and challenge) set contains 998, 1,595, and 1,400 images and parallel sentences.

3.2 Transliteration-based Phrase Pairs Augmentation

In this operation, the English-Hindi parallel train set is first used to extract source-target phrase pairs, which are then added to the train set. (Sen et al., 2020) used SMT-based phrase pairs to enrich training data in order to enhance low-resource pair translation. To extract phrase pairs (Laskar et al., 2021a), we have used Giza++ (Och and Ney, 2003) following (Sen et al., 2020). Duplicates and blank lines are eliminated before adding to the parallel train set. Table 1 presents the statistics for the phrase pairs that were extracted. Table 2 presents the data statistics for the train set (before and after augmentation). Afterwards, the sentences from English sources are transliterated into Hindi script using indic-trans [2] (Bhat et al., 2014). The transliteration strategy aims to enable lexical sharing at the sub-word level between source and target sentences that will take place during training. The sample overlaps words (bold marks) of transliterated En and Hi tokens of the training set, are presented in Figure 1.

Image ID	En	En Transliterated Hi	Hi
17	**Computer** screens turned on	**कंप्यूटर** स्क्रीन्स टर्न्ड ऑन	**कंप्यूटर** स्क्रीन चालू
21	**photo album** open on an adult's lap	**फोटो एल्बम** ओपन ऑन अन अदुल्ट'स लैप	एक वयस्क की गोद में **फोटो एल्बम** खुला
23	there is a group of girls beside the black **car**	तेरे इस आ ग्रुप ऑफ गर्ल्स बेसाइड थे ब्लैक **कार**	काली **कार** के पास लड़कियों का एक समूह है
80	the **cabinet** is wood	थे **कैबिनेट** इस वुड	**कैबिनेट** लकड़ी है

Figure 1: Sample overlap words (bold marks) in the transliterated source (En) and target (Hi) sentence (train set).

3.3 Data Preprocessing, System Training, and Testing

The pre-trained CNN-VGG19[3] is used to extract the image/visual features from the image data. Unlike (Laskar et al., 2020b, 2021a), we have considered the co-ordinate or bounded box region information (X, Y, width, height) of the images as the visual features, which are available in the Hindi Visual Genome 1.1 (Parida and Bojar, 2020). Moreover, we have augmented image features of extracted phrase pairs. To select relevant images of the corresponding phrase pairs, we have searched each phrase in the original parallel corpus, if it is found then the corresponding image and its co-ordinate information are considered. But there is a problem if multiple sentences contain the same phrase subset. To handle this issue, a filtering step solution is considered.

- First, for every En-Hi phrase pair extracted from the corpus, we found the matching English segments from the corpus which have the English part of the phrase pair as a sub-string (filter-1).
- If the length of the resulting data-frame i.e., the number of matching English segments for the English part of the phrase is 0, then the phrase is skipped as it is invalid. If the length is 1, since only one English segment matches it, that segment is directly selected.
- On the other hand, if the length is more than 1 i.e. more than 1 English segments have the English phrase as sub-string, the resulting English segments are again filtered (filter-2) to check if the corresponding Hindi phrase of the phrase pairs also has subset in the Hindi segments.
  - If after filter-2, the result is 0, i.e., there are no matching Hindi segments that have the Hindi phrase as sub-string, then from the filter-1 data-frame, i.e. the final segment from matching English segments is randomly selected.

[1] https://lindat.mff.cuni.cz/repository/xmlui/handle/11234/1-3267

[2] https://github.com/libindic/indic-trans

[3] https://github.com/iacercalixto/MultimodalNMT

Number of Phrase Pairs	Tokens	
	En	Hi
158,131	392,966	410,696

Table 1: Data Statistics of extracted phrase pairs.

Train Set	Number of Parallel Sentence/Segments
Before Augmentation	28,927
After Augmentation	187058

Table 2: Data Statistics of train set (before and after augmentation).

  - If the number of matches after Hindi segment matching is 1, then that single segment is selected.
  - If the number of Hindi phrase matches is more than 1, then a matching segment is randomly selected with a seed value.

The OpenNMT-py toolkit has been used for text data tokenization, preprocessing, and conducting independent training sessions for text-only and multimodal NMT. We have followed the default settings of (Calixto and Liu, 2017; Calixto et al., 2017) and employed the bidirectional RNN (BRNN) at the encoder and doubly-attentive RNN at decoder during the training process of multimodal NMT. We have used a batch size of 32, a dropout value of 0.3, and an Adam optimizer with 0.002 learning rate during the training process. We have trained on a single GPU with early stopping criteria i.e., the model training is halted if does not converge on the validation set for more than 10 epochs. The obtained optimum trained models of multimodal and text-only NMT were applied to the evaluation and challenge test set. The basic difference in the testing phase is that multimodal NMT uses visual features of image test data. The source English sentences of test data are transliterated and then applied to the trained model to generate the predicted target Hindi sentences.

Image id: 2358957

Multi-modal Translation Track Source Language: English Target Language: Hindi	
Source	Candle on glass candle stand
Predicted	कांच मोमबत्ती स्टैंड पर मोमबत्ती *(kaach mombati stand par mombati)*
Reference	कांच के मोमबत्ती स्टैंड पर मोमबत्ती *(kaach ke mombati stand par mombati)*
Google Translation	कांच मोमबत्ती स्टैंड पर मोमबत्ती *(kaach mombati stand par mombati)*
Text-only Translation Track	
Predicted:	कांच मोमबत्ती स्टैंड पर मोमबत्ती *(kaach mombati stand par mombati)*

Figure 2: Sample predicted output on challenge test data.

4 Result and Analysis

The WAT2022 shared task organizer (Nakazawa et al., 2022) published the evaluation result[5] of the multimodal translation task for English to Hindi. We participated with the team name CNLP-NITS-PP in the multimodal and text-only submission tracks of the same task where four teams participated. The automatic evaluation metrics, BLEU

[5] `http://lotus.kuee.kyoto-u.ac.jp/WAT/evaluation/index.html`

Our System	Test Set	BLEU	RIBES
Text-only NMT	Challenge	37.20	0.770640
	Evaluation	37.00	0.795302
Multi-modal NMT	Challenge	39.30	0.791468
	Evaluation	39.40	0.802635

Table 3: Our system's results (official) on English to Hindi multimodal translation Task.

Other System	Test Set	BLEU	RIBES
Multi-modal NMT (Team: Volta (First Position))	Challenge	51.60	0.859645
Multi-modal NMT (Team: Organizer)	Challenge	20.34	0.644230

Table 4: Other system's results (official)[4] on English to Hindi multimodal translation Task.

Image ID	MNMT Output (Without Transliterated)	MNMT Output (With Transliterated)	Source	Reference
2407547	अदालत में दो खिलाड़ी हैं	कोर्ट में दो खिलाड़ी हैं	there are two players in the **court**	क़ोर्ट में दो खिलाड़ी हैं
2368444	पेड़ों का एक <unk>	पुस्तकों का एक **स्टैंड**	A **stand** of trees	पेड़ों का एक **झाड़**
2402752	गहरे लकड़ी की <unk> **स्टैंड**	गहरे लकड़ी के **अंडे स्टैंड**	dark wooden wash **stand**	गाढ़े रंग की लकड़ी का वाश **स्टैंड**

Figure 3: Manual comparison of MNMT output (without transliteration and with transliteration).

(Papineni et al., 2002), RIBES (Isozaki et al., 2010) were used for evaluation of results. Table 3 and 4 reported the official results of our and other systems (Team: Volta (first position) and Organizer). Our team and another team (Volta) achieved the second and first position in multimodal submission for the challenge test set. The quantitative results show that the MNMT outperforms text-only NMT due to the use of visual and textual features. Furthermore, our system's results have improved compared to our previous work on the same task (Laskar et al., 2020b). The BLEU, RIBES scores of the present work show (+5.73, +0.037327), increments on the challenge test set for MNMT, where it is realized that transliteration-based phrase pairs augmentation improves translational performance. The sample examples of outputs, along with Google translation and transliteration of Hindi words, are presented in Figure 2. Moreover, Figure 3 presents a manual comparison of MNMT predicted outputs where we have considered with or without transliteration in the phrase pairs augmentation model.

5 Conclusion and Future Work

In this work, we have proposed the use of transliteration-based phrase pairs augmentation in the WAT2022 multimodal translation task for English to Hindi translation. Our multimodal NMT attained a higher score than that of the text-only NMT model and existing work of (Laskar et al., 2020b). A multilingual-based approach will be investigated to improve the translational performance of low-resource multimodal NMT.

Acknowledgements

We want to thank the Department of Computer Science and Engineering, Center for Natural Language Processing (CNLP), Artificial Intelligence (AI) Lab at the National Institute of Technology, Silchar for providing the requisite support and infrastructure to execute this work.

References

Dzmitry Bahdanau, Kyunghyun Cho, and Yoshua Bengio. 2015. Neural machine translation by jointly learning to align and translate. In *3rd International Conference on Learning Representations, ICLR 2015, San Diego, CA, USA, May 7-9, 2015, Conference Track Proceedings*.

Irshad Ahmad Bhat, Vandan Mujadia, Aniruddha Tammewar, Riyaz Ahmad Bhat, and Manish Shrivastava. 2014. Iiit-h system submission for fire2014 shared task on transliterated search. In *Proceedings of the Forum for Information Retrieval Evaluation*, FIRE '14, page 48–53, New York, NY, USA. Association for Computing Machinery.

Iacer Calixto and Qun Liu. 2017. Incorporating global visual features into attention-based neural machine translation. In *Proceedings of the 2017 Conference on Empirical Methods in Natural Language Processing*, pages 992–1003, Copenhagen, Denmark. Association for Computational Linguistics.

Iacer Calixto, Qun Liu, and Nick Campbell. 2017. Doubly-attentive decoder for multi-modal neural machine translation. In *Proceedings of the 55th Annual*

Meeting of the Association for Computational Linguistics, ACL 2017, Vancouver, Canada, July 30 - August 4, Volume 1: Long Papers, pages 1913–1924. Association for Computational Linguistics.

Koel Dutta Chowdhury, Mohammed Hasanuzzaman, and Qun Liu. 2018. Multimodal neural machine translation for low-resource language pairs using synthetic data. In *"."*, pages 33–42.

Hideki Isozaki, Tsutomu Hirao, Kevin Duh, Katsuhito Sudoh, and Hajime Tsukada. 2010. Automatic evaluation of translation quality for distant language pairs. In *Proceedings of the 2010 Conference on Empirical Methods in Natural Language Processing*, pages 944–952, Cambridge, MA. Association for Computational Linguistics.

Guillaume Klein, Yoon Kim, Yuntian Deng, Jean Senellart, and Alexander Rush. 2017. Opennmt: Open-source toolkit for neural machine translation. In *Proceedings of ACL 2017, System Demonstrations*, pages 67–72, Vancouver, Canada. Association for Computational Linguistics.

Sahinur Rahman Laskar, Abinash Dutta, Partha Pakray, and Sivaji Bandyopadhyay. 2019a. Neural machine translation: English to hindi. In *2019 IEEE Conference on Information and Communication Technology*, pages 1–6.

Sahinur Rahman Laskar, Abdullah Faiz Ur Rahman Khilji, Darsh Kaushik, Partha Pakray, and Sivaji Bandyopadhyay. 2021a. Improved English to Hindi multimodal neural machine translation. In *Proceedings of the 8th Workshop on Asian Translation (WAT2021)*, pages 155–160, Online. Association for Computational Linguistics.

Sahinur Rahman Laskar, Abdullah Faiz Ur Rahman Khilji, Partha Pakray, and Sivaji Bandyopadhyay. 2020a. EnAsCorp1.0: English-Assamese corpus. In *Proceedings of the 3rd Workshop on Technologies for MT of Low Resource Languages*, pages 62–68, Suzhou, China. Association for Computational Linguistics.

Sahinur Rahman Laskar, Abdullah Faiz Ur Rahman Khilji, Partha Pakray, and Sivaji Bandyopadhyay. 2020b. Multimodal neural machine translation for English to Hindi. In *Proceedings of the 7th Workshop on Asian Translation*, pages 109–113, Suzhou, China. Association for Computational Linguistics.

Sahinur Rahman Laskar, Partha Pakray, and Sivaji Bandyopadhyay. 2019b. Neural machine translation: Hindi-Nepali. In *Proceedings of the Fourth Conference on Machine Translation (Volume 3: Shared Task Papers, Day 2)*, pages 202–207, Florence, Italy. Association for Computational Linguistics.

Sahinur Rahman Laskar, Partha Pakray, and Sivaji Bandyopadhyay. 2021b. Neural machine translation: Assamese–bengali. In *Modeling, Simulation and Optimization: Proceedings of CoMSO 2020*, pages 571–579. Springer Singapore.

Sahinur Rahman Laskar, Partha Pakray, and Sivaji Bandyopadhyay. 2021c. Neural machine translation for low resource assamese–english. In *Proceedings of the International Conference on Computing and Communication Systems: I3CS 2020, NEHU, Shillong, India*, volume 170, page 35. Springer.

Sahinur Rahman Laskar, Bishwaraj Paul, Partha Pakray, and Sivaji Bandyopadhyay. 2022. Improving english-assamese neural machine translation using transliteration-based approach. In *Proceedings of the International Conference on Frontiers of Intelligent Computing: Theory and Applications, FICTA 2022*. In press.

Sahinur Rahman Laskar, Rohit Pratap Singh, Partha Pakray, and Sivaji Bandyopadhyay. 2019c. English to Hindi multi-modal neural machine translation and Hindi image captioning. In *Proceedings of the 6th Workshop on Asian Translation*, pages 62–67, Hong Kong, China. Association for Computational Linguistics.

Thang Luong, Hieu Pham, and Christopher D. Manning. 2015. Effective approaches to attention-based neural machine translation. In *Proceedings of the 2015 Conference on Empirical Methods in Natural Language Processing*, pages 1412–1421, Lisbon, Portugal. Association for Computational Linguistics.

Toshiaki Nakazawa, Hideya Mino, Isao Goto, Raj Dabre, Shohei Higashiyama, Shantipriya Parida, Anoop Kunchukuttan, Makoto Morishita, Ondřej Bojar, Chenhui Chu, Akiko Eriguchi, Kaori Abe, Yusuke Oda, and Sadao Kurohashi. 2022. Overview of the 9th workshop on Asian translation. In *Proceedings of the 9th Workshop on Asian Translation (WAT2022)*, Gyeongju, Republic of Korea. Association for Computational Linguistics.

Franz Josef Och and Hermann Ney. 2003. A systematic comparison of various statistical alignment models. *Computational Linguistics*, 29(1):19–51.

Kishore Papineni, Salim Roukos, Todd Ward, and Wei-Jing Zhu. 2002. Bleu: A method for automatic evaluation of machine translation. In *Proceedings of the 40th Annual Meeting on Association for Computational Linguistics*, ACL '02, pages 311–318, Stroudsburg, PA, USA. Association for Computational Linguistics.

Shantipriya Parida and Ondřej Bojar. 2020. Hindi visual genome 1.1. LINDAT/CLARIAH-CZ digital library at the Institute of Formal and Applied Linguistics (ÚFAL), Faculty of Mathematics and Physics, Charles University.

Amarnath Pathak and Partha Pakray. 2018. Neural machine translation for indian languages. *Journal of Intelligent Systems*, pages 1–13.

Amarnath Pathak, Partha Pakray, and Jereemi Bentham. 2018. English–mizo machine translation using neural and statistical approaches. *Neural Computing and Applications*, 30:1–17.

Loitongbam Sanayai Meetei, Thoudam Doren Singh, and Sivaji Bandyopadhyay. 2019. WAT2019: English-Hindi translation on Hindi visual genome dataset. In *Proceedings of the 6th Workshop on Asian Translation*, pages 181–188, Hong Kong, China. Association for Computational Linguistics.

Sukanta Sen, Mohammed Hasanuzzaman, Asif Ekbal, Pushpak Bhattacharyya, and Andy Way. 2020. Neural machine translation of low-resource languages using smt phrase pair injection. *Natural Language Engineering*, page 1–22.

Kashif Shah, Josiah Wang, and Lucia Specia. 2016. SHEF-multimodal: Grounding machine translation on images. In *Proceedings of the First Conference on Machine Translation: Volume 2, Shared Task Papers*, pages 660–665, Berlin, Germany. Association for Computational Linguistics.

Author Index

Association for Computational Linguistics
209 N. Eighth Street
Stroudsburg, Pennsylvania 18360

ISBN 978-1-7138-9153-6

9 781713 891536

CURRAN ASSOCIATES INC.
proceedings.com